# The Visual Cultures of Childhood

# The Visual Cultures of Childhood

*Film and Television from The Magic Lantern to Teen Vloggers*

Karen Wells

ROWMAN & LITTLEFIELD
INTERNATIONAL

London • New York

Published by Rowman & Littlefield International, Ltd.
6 Tinworth Street, London SE11 5AL, United Kingdom
www.rowmaninternational.com

Rowman & Littlefield International, Ltd. is an affiliate of
Rowman & Littlefield
4501 Forbes Boulevard, Suite 200, Lanham, Maryland 20706, USA
With additional offices in Boulder, New York, Toronto (Canada), and London (UK)
www.rowman.com

**British Library Cataloguing in Publication Information**
A catalogue record for this book is available from the British Library

ISBN: HB 978-1-78661-103-1 | PBK 978-1-5381-4823-5

**Library of Congress Cataloging-in-Publication Data Is Available**

ISBN 978-1-78661-103-1 (cloth)
ISBN 978-1-5381-4823-5 (pbk)
ISBN 978-1-78661-104-8 (electronic)

For my daughter Devan Carey Wells and my stepson Michael Lennon,
who share a love of film

# Contents

# Acknowledgements

Chapter 4 was originally published as Wells, K. (2013). "The Melodrama of Being a Child: NGO Representations of Poverty." *Visual Communication* 12 (3): 277–93, https://doi.org/10.1177/1470357213483059, and is reproduced here with permission.

# ONE
## Visual Political Culture, Childhood and Youth

*From Object to Subject to Activist*

Some of the most iconic images of the twentieth century are of children: Dorothea Lange's *Migrant Mother*, depicting farm worker Frances Owens Thompson with three of her children; six-year-old Ruby Bridges, flanked by US marshals, walking down the steps of an all-white elementary school she desegregated; Kevin Carter's photograph of a young Sudanese child, later identified as Kong Nyong, crouched over, weak from hunger, his head on the sand; Huỳnh Công Út's photograph of nine-year-old Phan Thi Kim Phuc fleeing a South Vietnamese napalm bombing.

These iconic images with their juxtaposition of the innocent (in the sense of not culpable) figure of the child and the guilty perpetrators of violence (both structural and interpersonal) are 'arresting'. The power of the image of the child to arrest the spectator, to demand a response from her (especially, from 'her') has given the representation of children a central place in the history of visual culture for social reform.

The central task of this book is to unpack that history in relation to its deployment and activation of the power of the image of the figure of the child, and understand its impacts on discourses of social justice. It explores the power of these images as they have been mobilised in film, video and television to tell stories about those whose experiences do not fit with the visual narratives of Hollywood's 'dream factory' and whose lives demonstrate the exclusions of the American Dream. It focuses on how moving images of children and youth have been deployed to visualise social exclusion and how those representations have been affected by

1

**Figure 1.1.   Dorothy Lange's 'Migrant Mother' is one of the most iconic social reform images of the twentieth century.**

changes in technology that have increasingly made the means of visual production available to young people.

The primary sources analysed in this book are almost entirely drawn from the United States. I made this decision to focus on one country because visual representation draws on cultural tropes and cultural histories that are historically and spatially specific. Therefore, to understand and analyse the relationship between cultural politics as it relates to the figure of the child and to visual representation requires a focus on a specific history and region. I also want to provincialise the United States. I am not focusing on the United States because it is a global hegemon, or even because US culture has a global distribution that currently exceeds other global cultural flows. I do not want to argue that what is true of visual cultures of childhood and social reform in the United States is true of visual cultures of childhood and social reform everywhere.

In this chapter, I describe the three broad movements of the intersection between visual political culture and childhood: from children as the object of the camera's gaze, a representation that began in the nineteenth-century social-reform movements and continued into documentary and NGO fundraising campaigns; to children and youth as the central story-line and intended audience for social-problem feature films from the mid-twentieth century; and through to micro-casting of vlogs and other film and video forms by youth activists and micro-celebrities in the twenty-first century. These three modes of representation in what might broadly be called the *social problem* film (Roffman and Purdy 1981; Sloan 1988) address different audiences: the child as a suffering other interpellates the spectator as a witness to 'distant' suffering (Chouliaraki 2006) in order to encourage the audiences to either indirectly (through donations) or directly (through making law and policy) change the conditions of the lives of children and their families. The social-problem feature film is part of commercial circuits—it may want to inform, but it also wants to entertain audiences and attract sufficient viewers to make a profit. It consequently has to speak to a much broader audience than those who share the experiences depicted in the film. While many of the directors and writers of social-problem feature films share at least some of the experiences of those they depict and want to use representation to build a positive, community identity grounded in resistance to oppression, they also need to entertain the audience and not alienate those audiences who do not share these experiences or the director's critique of them. Nonetheless, and despite the limitations and contradictions of inserting critiques of racial capitalism into films that depend for their continued circulation on their commercial success within racial capitalism, the social-problem feature film opens up spaces for communities of praxis to form around directors' and writers' critiques. The third mode, made possible through Web 2.0, extends this process of addressing different audiences by making it possible to directly address a community of spectators who share the identity work and political commitments of the children and youth who produce and upload videos to YouTube and other social media platforms.

The three modes that I have just described are not sequential. It is not that the objectifying/witnessing gaze was replaced by the subjectifying/

identificatory gaze, which has in turn been replaced by the activist gaze. Rather, all three modes continue to circulate. In fact, Web 2.0 has made it possible for feature films and nineteenth-century social-reform photography to circulate anew in digital space. Current NGO digital fundraising interpellates the spectator as a witness to distant suffering in ways that are remarkably similar to those that circulated in the late nineteenth century. Feature films are increasingly generating profits online through digital platforms like Amazon Prime and Netflix, as much as they are from cinema releases. Nonetheless, the low costs of production for making videos and uploading to platforms like YouTube, Facebook, Instagram and Vimeo have expanded the possibilities for addressing a specific, narrow audience. This is a practice that mirrors the development of narrowcasting in television and has implications for how critical publics are made that are engaged in social reform and centre children and youth.

In the first section of this chapter, I trace the emergence of social-reform film in visual cultures of childhood in the late 1800s and early twentieth century in the use of photography in social-reform campaigns depicting the impact of capitalism and urbanisation on working-class children's lives, the recording of 'disappearing worlds' in ethnographic film, and the development of public-health broadcasting in the colonies. These three forms all informed and contributed to the subsequent development of documentary film discussed in chapter 3. In these productions, the child figures prominently as a figure of innocence, and the youth as a figure of futurity, particularly as one who is in the process of crossing over from 'tradition' to 'modernity'. While in these productions, the child and youth are rich signifiers, they are not themselves involved, other than as subjects and actors. In the twentieth century, as film technology developed and professional film schools that brought new social groups into filmmaking were established, young adults themselves began to make films that addressed the social problems that had hitherto been represented by adults and, generally, adults who were not women, working class or from racialized minorities. At the same time, new audiences emerged for what could broadly be called 'social reform' film: audiences whose own lives were represented on screen. In the second section of this chapter, I explore the question of whether or not these films form a coherent genre and what kinds of social-reform messages they carry. In the third section, I consider what the new and emerging technologies of visual digital culture promise for social-reform visual cultures and their relationship to the figure of the child.

## SOCIAL REFORM IN NINETEENTH-CENTURY VISUAL CULTURES
## OF CHILDHOOD

The visual pleasure of looking at children, their generally highly photogenic character, and the increasing acceptance that children should be the target of government welfare policy frequently put children centre frame in the visualisation of social-reform projects. In the nineteenth century, the state became centrally involved with the problem of the poor child. In the urban centres of Europe and North America, that concern manifested itself in campaigns against child homelessness and child labour and for improvements in child hygiene and the expansion of school education. Working children were hardly a novel feature of either political-economy or socio-cultural fields, but their concentrated presence in the city, often apparently without family care or supervision, and the increased hold of the psy-disciplines and their discourses of development potential on the social imagination, made them acutely visible. While Lewis Hine's photographs are the most well-known of the visual record of children working, they were part of a wider visual culture of social reform that centred the suffering child in the late nineteenth century; for example, the discovery of the tubercle bacillus in 1882 revealed that TB was not genetic but, rather, highly contagious. This led to one of the largest public health campaigns in the United States, which continued until 1954. Here too, images of children and youth figured centrally in the campaign (https://www.pbs.org/wgbh/americanexperience/features/plague-gallery/). Similarly, Jacob Riis's photographs of overcrowding and slum housing frequently centred children.

The visual culture of social reform anticipated moving film in its use of the lantern slide show as an educational and entertainment technology. Although it was a technology that predated the photograph, the combination of photographs and a script that was read aloud to the audience could create an intensely affective atmosphere. Lantern slide shows were very popular with nineteenth- and early-twentieth-century audiences, often attracting audiences of thousands. These visual cultures combined the use of photographs of evidence of injury and disease with the affective power of images of children, and the construction of a story about how injury could be remedied and disease healed that continues to be repeated in contemporary NGO films, especially those aimed at fundraising.

Late-nineteenth-century film did not directly contribute to the visual culture of social reform, which continued to use photographs and lantern slide shows into the early twentieth century. However, ethnographic film history is as long as the history of film itself and, while not directly addressing social reform, it certainly has a relationship to the history of the social-problem film. Ethnographic film, or applied visual anthropology, was not concerned with the kinds of witnessing that social-reform

photography wanted to evoke, but it was nonetheless asking the spectator to witness the disappearing of cultural worlds.

Felix-Louis Regnault made the first recorded ethnographic film in
1895. It was a film of a Wolof woman (name unrecorded) making pots
using the Wolof method of making pottery by hand (without a wheel),
shown at the Exposition Ethnographique de l'Afrique Occidentale (Ethnographic Exposition of Western Africa). Regnault wrote up his notes
from the film, which were published in December 1895, the same month
that the Lumière brothers gave 'the first public projection of "cinemato-
graphe" films . . . which launched the motion picture industry" (Brigard
2003:16). While Brigard dismisses claims that Robert Flaherty's *Nanook of
the North* (1922) was an ethnographic film, it has been called 'the first
documentary film, the first ethnographic film, as well as the first art film'
(Rony 1996:300). *Nanook* is a film in the anthropological tradition of visually documenting 'native cultures breaking down and disappearing
under the onslaught of White civilization' (1996:303). Family life and
changing practices of childhood within the family were central features
of what the ethnographic documentary drama wanted to capture in its
endeavour to record putatively disappearing cultures.

In the European colonial territories, the imposition of colonial rule
was legitimated through appeals to the improvement of the health and
education of children. Establishing the colonial project as one that would
improve the lives of children and youth were key strategies for attempting to establish the legitimacy of colonial rule within the norms of democratic liberal governance. Part of that effort involved representing African
and Asian children as in need of rescue by benevolent forces, both missionaries and metropolitan welfare states. Development in general, and
children's health and education in particular, were of central importance
in the late-nineteenth-century justification for imperialism, both for the
power of the figure of the suffering child in mobilising support for colon-
ising projects as a form of liberal imperialism to secure the improvement
of the population and also the metonymic carryover of actual, real children to the tutelage role that the colonial state abrogated to itself for the
colonised population in general. In this reframing of government, control
and extraction of resources as responsibility and development, children
and young adults were significant bearers of tropes about moving towards modernity and away from what was depicted as the backward-
ness of culture in colonised territories.

The colonial educational film, intended for African audiences, began
with public health films made by colonial health administrators in Nigeria and Kenya. William Sellers, a government health official, made a film
in 1929 to combat a plague epidemic in Lagos by showing how rats
spread disease and encouraging a rat-extermination campaign. In 1932
Sellers set up the Health Propaganda Unit in Nigeria that combined 'film
production, mobile film shows, exhibits, school services, and field days to

promote better sanitation, nutrition, childcare, and overall public health' (Smyth 2013:84). Millions of Hausa in northern Nigeria watched these mobile cinema screenings (Larkin p. 89, cited in Smyth 2013:84). In 1939 the Colonial Film Unit (CFU), headed by Sellers, was set up to make war propaganda films for viewing in Britain's African colonies to engage their support for the anti-fascist war (1939–1945), which involved not only forced conscription of colonial men into the British army but also the forced requisition of crops to feed the British public (this continued after the war and caused a famine in Malawi). During the war, Sellers's mandate was extended to include instructional, mass-education films, of the type he had been making previously, but within the new framework of moving towards self-rule as set out in the Colonial Development and Welfare Act of 1940 (and subsequent acts) and the white paper 'Mass Education in African Society' (1944). The Colonial Film Unit was disbanded in 1955. It produced over two hundred short films. After the war, direction of the CFU moved to the Films Division of the Central Office of Information and produced instructional films for African audiences and gradually moved towards African film production, in preparation for the decolonisation of Africa (Rice 2010).

These films share many of the themes of social-reform films in the United States and the United Kingdom and draw on their narrative structures rooted in longer histories of theatre and the bildungsroman novel. This can be seen, for example, in one of the most well-received films in Ghana and the United Kingdom, *Boy Kumasenu* (Sean Graham 1952). This film tells a story with distinctly *Oliver Twist* overtones of the titular character being 'lured by the false stories of his cousin Agboh'.

> Kumasenu leaves his village to seek adventure in the city of Accra. But he soon becomes lonely and hungry and is eventually caught by the police while trying to steal a loaf of bread. A kindly African doctor and his wife take pity on him, find a place for him in their home and help him to find work as a mechanic. Some time later, Agboh learns of his whereabouts and forces the boy to join in a scheme to rob the doctor, but Kumasenu manages to warn the Police in time. They capture the gang and Agboh is also arrested, thanks to the boy, after a fight in which he risks his own life. Kumasenu's story ends with the doctor watching his protégé at work on one of the harbour's new motor boats. (*Monthly Film Bulletin*, March 1957, 28, http://www.colonialfilm.org.uk/node/332)

Other films featuring stories about children include *From Fear to Faith* (James Swackhammer 1946), in which a young Shona adult who was rescued from probable death as a twin and raised in a mission school in Zimbabwe returns to the village of his birth. Initially shunned after he 'heals' a boy with fever (apparently by giving him water) the women in the village accept him; he then teaches new agricultural methods, and all the villagers, with the exception of his living twin brother and the rainmaker, convert to Christianity. His brother, who is initially very hostile to him and plots to kill him, also converts to Christianity. The film, although short, manages to effectively convey the colonial view that children being separated from their parents (in this case through being rescued) will incubate new ideas about health, which they will then be able to persuade others to adopt, because of their superior efficacy. It is aimed at British audiences including prospective white settlers.

*Basuto Boy* (Aubrey Graham 1947), aimed at British children audiences in Rank's cinema clubs, tells the story of a herds boy who is left in the mountains on his first day of work after finishing school (he is about twelve years old) to look after the village's cattle. Four horseman ride over the brow of the hill and steal the cattle. He rides, on his own, back to the village, and the village men ride out and capture the thieves and retrieve the cattle. The villagers do a dance in his honour. The film's moral, repeated several times is 'don't lose your head'. The music, theme and action are in the genre of the Western. The director, Aubre Singer, went on to be the Director General of the BBC.

These kinds of social-reform moving images—from the lantern slide shows of the late-nineteenth and early-twentieth centuries, and from early ethnographic film to the public health films and information children's films of the Colonial Film Unit, up to the middle of the last century—reveal interesting elements of the relationship of photography and film to the representation of reality and the narrative structure of real-life stories that suggest that social-problem feature films and documentaries shared, and continue to share, key features. The standard division, for example, between the fictional feature film and the nonfiction documentary (and its related antecedent) is blurred by the dependence of both on a narrative structure that borrows from narrative modes of storytelling in literature and oral cultures. Furthermore, early documentary film, as I show in more detail in chapter 3, used the reconstruction of events and rarely used the participants' own words, to construct a compelling narrative. In addition, particular kinds of people, especially children but also women, and often whites, were seen as more affective subjects. The idea of the documentary as documenting reality and the feature film as fiction was a much later development in documentary film, not really stabilising until the late twentieth century and continuing to be disrupted and contested right up to the present day. In the representation of children and youth living in difficult conditions, the division between the documentary form and feature film lies more in how the audience is interpellated and for what purposes than in a neat division between the fictional and the real.

## THE GENRE OF THE SOCIAL-PROBLEM TEEN FILM

In this section, I address the question of what shifts occur in representation when onscreen life and the audience's experiences converge, to some extent, in the feature film, which was widely seen as marketed to young and, after about 1950, teenage audiences. My interest is not in the entire landscape of the feature film but specifically with those feature films that want to address social problems and want audiences to confront the effects of racism, homophobia and class deprivation as they are experienced by young people. What I want to suggest is that political activists, especially black and feminist directors, saw the potential and importance of mass culture as a kind of visual public culture. I am suggesting that, in the shift from visual cultures of social reform located around the improvement and management of the body and driven by various government (colonial, urban, international development) agendas to visual public cultures that want to close the gap between director/writer, text, and audience, the space for a more open, radical, visual public culture opens up. Far from being 'mere' entertainment, the cultural politics of the feature film that addresses social problems and more or less explicitly demands some kind of response opens up potentially radical or at least disruptive visual cultures of childhood and youth.

### The Development of Black Film and the African American Coming-of-Age Film

In the United States, film entered into a context of an anti-black and anti-indigenous political economy and its attendant socio-cultural fields. The film industry, from its inception, was racially segregated in all aspects of production and reception (Cripps 1993). That the film that is widely, if erroneously, credited with innovating and establishing the conventions of
feature films, is D. W. Griffith's racist *Birth of a Nation* (Haenni 2015), points to the impossibility of thinking about Hollywood film and the representation of children and youth within it without acknowledging the impossibility of talking about 'film' as a unified field. Manthia Diawara opens the introduction to his edited collection *Black American Cinema* with the comment that the release of *Birth of a Nation* 'defined for the first time the side that Hollywood was to take in the war to represent Black people in America' (1993:3). One outcome of this was the emergence of what were called 'race films', which frequently focused on visualising the possibility of 'racial uplift', essentially a strategy of economic independence coupled with particular forms of bourgeois respectability.

It is one of the contentions of this book that film is so structured by racist histories that all black film has to be seen in some sense as counter-hegemonic, rather than as part of a unified field of US cultural representation. Hence, although many coming-of-age films centring white protagonists could not be considered as social-problem or social-reform films but more as personal journeys of character development, black coming-of-age films in the United States cannot avoid at least some signification as also social-problem films. Furthermore, although 'race films' is a term that originates in and is still mostly used to theorise the development of early black cinema, the theme of 'racial uplift' and its (im)possibilities continues as a key theme in black coming-of-age films by young black directors. Indeed (unlike the bildungsroman structure of what we might gloss as white coming-of-age films), black coming-of-age films (in which the main protagonists often do not survive into adulthood) and the constant threat of a not-always-named but always present violence (an uncanny presence haunts the narrative) suggest that these might be thought of as more a subgenre of horror than of either the bildungsroman or of teen melodrama.

If hood films are a subgenre of horror, another cycle of African American films perhaps fits more closely into the genre of melodrama in their attention to women and children and the violence of men. These films, which seem to be part of racial-uplift films, often involve the recuperation of the South and of white Southerners through framing the South as a unified cultural space characterised by hospitality, Christian charity, and family feeling, and shared by black and white characters.

While it is probably too early to pronounce the emergence of a new genre of black youth film, what might be called 'Afro-optimism' in contrast to Afro-pessimism, the success of the futuristic/sci-fi film *Black Panther* (Ryan Coogler 2018) perhaps points to new directions for future film. In some ways it is a continuation of racial-uplift movies, emphasising the economic independence of that strategy over its attachment to bourgeois demeanour. If Tre's father in *Boyz n the Hood* insists on the necessity of locally owned real estate firms for political power for black people in America, *Black Panther* simply extends that idea by insisting on the necessity of black control of not only land but also technology and energy, linking the absence of control over the means of production directly to the failure of the political organization the Black Panthers, and to the future possibility of reinvigorating black self-political organization in the US city. Its enormous success at the box office ($1.4 billion) and its cross-audience appeal (i.e., to white audiences as well as black audiences) opens up the likelihood of a new cycle of black film, just as the financial success of *Boyz* did in 1991 (Guerrero 1993).

*Kitchen Sink Dramas*

Working-class subjects and the hardships of working-class life were key themes in early silent film; they show the fuzzy boundaries between the documentary and the feature film. Steven Ross, in his widely cited *Working-Class Hollywood: Silent Film and the Shaping of Class in America* (1998), shows that not only depictions of working-class deprivation, but also critiques of capitalism, were major themes in silent film. He lauds D. W. Griffith, who in 1915 made the racist film *Birth of a Nation*, as 'one of the most powerful critics of class injustice that the movie industry every produced' (1998:37). Although Ross agrees with most critics that 'Griffith turned out many films that offered nostalgic and racist visions of the Old South', he also claims that Griffith 'also produced some of the most stark-ly compelling depictions of working-class life ever made by an American filmmaker' and had 'unrestrained sympathy for the working poor' (ibid.). It is not that Ross ignores the influence of Griffith's racism on his work but clearly for him this does not undermine Griffith's ability to represent the working class. He says, '[a]lthough he was hostile to blacks . . . Griffith offered white workers a measure of hope and suc-ceeded in making movies about their problems an integral part of American political culture' (1998:39). These claims reinforce my earlier point that US film is bifurcated by the history of racism in the United States and this extends to the representation and reception of social-re-form films.

A series of British films in the late 1950s that focused on the coming of age of young working-class men and women provides perhaps the first feature films in Britain directly addressing how post-war prosperity was transforming working-class cultures. Jean Welsh (2015) notes that the films addressed a new working class who were being transformed into consumers by post-war prosperity and reconstruction. The thesis of these films, Jean Welsh argues, is shared with Richard Hoggart's *The Uses of Literacy* (1971), which contrasts 'the "good" authentic working-class cul-ture of the past with the "shiny barbarism" of the modern consumer culture he sees as destroying it' (Welsh 2015:475). A statement which itself recalls the desire of ethnographic film, discussed in the previous section, to capture and lament the passing of lost cultural worlds. The independent film company Woodfall was 'a prestigious force in British cinema' (2015:473), and it produced over twenty films, including many that focused on young working-class characters including *Saturday Night and Sunday Morning* (1960), *Look Back in Anger* (1959), *A Taste of Honey* (1961) and *Kes* (1969). While it is difficult to know to what extent these films influenced filmmaking in the United States, it is worth noting the importance of independent cinema in representing the interface between politics and culture. These films also connect to the colonial films dis-cussed above in their theme of young people being the bearers of moder-nity against the weight of tradition.

## Melodrama and Women's Film as Children's Film

Melodrama has been extensively analysed in relation to its representation of gender, and in particular the role of the woman as the suffering innocent and the man as both victim and villain, and the depiction of home as the woman's domain in contrast to the public world of men (Gledhill 1987). Frequently, if insufficiently analysed, the 'woman's film' centres not only a woman but also her children. When this woman-child(ren) pairing is analysed in melodrama, one sees that it has focused on the maternal relationship from the mother's point of view and on what it reveals about the cultural politics of motherhood (Fischer 1996:56–72) and its role in making gender binaries appear both normative and derived from biological sex.

Much less attention has been paid to melodrama's representation of children or, more broadly, the social-problem film as melodrama. Linda Williams's *Playing the Race Card: Melodramas of Black and White from Uncle Tom to O.J. Simpson* (2001) is one of the few texts that extend the analysis of the genre to the representation of race and racism. In doing so, as feminist analysis of melodrama has also done, she establishes the form of the genre and its relationship to the political sphere. Similarly, I want to argue for the utility of thinking about melodrama in relation to children and youth. Like the figure of the woman, the figure of the child is also, in fact more so, an icon of innocence, and her suffering is read as being experienced through no fault of her own (the basic plot device of melodrama). In the social-problem film, it is frequently the parent, especially the mother, who is the one who causes the child's suffering, and the rescuer/hero are other adults who are outside of the child's cultural milieu.

Unsurprisingly, coming-of-age films that centre non-normative representations of gender are most often about coming out as lesbian, gay or bisexual or, less often, as trans. LGBT visibility for young audiences has increased significantly in the 2000s (albeit relative to a very low base of a handful of mostly tragic queer films, e.g., *Killing of Sister George* (1968), *The Children's Hour* (1961), *Heavenly Creatures* (1994).

Timothy Shary (2012) has made the argument for youth film to be considered a genre, one defined by the age of the protagonists and the predominance of particular youth sites (the school, the family home) and adolescent identity conflicts (first love, first sex, conflict with parents). Catherine Driscoll, in her *Teen Film: A Critical Introduction*, proposes four 'necessary conditions' for teen film: the emergence of the modern idea of adolescence; the incorporation of that idea into film regulation and censorship; the active marketing of film to youth; and the 'translation of modern adolescence into institutions for the representation, analysis, and management of adolescence' (2011:13). In this view, the genre features in a teen film make it a subgenre of teen film. Thus, hood films are categorised as subgenres of youth films rather than as subgenres of gangster films. For Roz Kaveney 'contemporary films about teenagers which treat them as a problem to be solved are outside the genre' (6), excluding from the genre coming-out films like *The Incredibly True Adventures of Two Girls in Love* (1995) or *But I'm a Cheerleader* (1999) and films that deal 'primarily with African American teenagers' (7).

This book depends on the idea that there is a connection between different kinds of moving images that feature children and youth, but that this lies more in broader socio-cultural signification of the categories 'child' and 'youth' rather than to generic elements in film. Indeed, many of the films that I analyse in this book have not been included in monographs on teen or youth film and, as I discuss in chapters 5 (on black teen film), 6 (on LGBT film) and 7 (on working-class film), many films that articulate youth with social problems and social reform borrow and develop elements of film genre (Western, melodrama, and horror, especially). Early youth social-reform films in the 1960s could be considered as in the social-realist tradition, and many of the films analysed here merge the social-realist tradition with other genres.

## SOCIAL REFORM AND PERSONAL LIBERATION: CHILDREN AND YOUTH AND WEB 2.0

The film industry has always been interested in attracting young audiences and is always searching for ways to innovate storylines in order to bring in new audiences. The space for black film in the 'hood-cycle' opened up because cinema audiences were deserting the cinema, and the production companies were looking for low-budget, high-impact films. *Boyz* cost $6.5 million and brought in $57.5 million at the box office. The films that followed in its wake were also low-budget films, and therefore low risk—Hollywood was not so much investing in black audiences as testing the market. Cinema was trying to reproduce what television was already doing: narrowcasting, or dividing the audience into market segments and producing outputs for each of these markets. Most of these would be low-budget films. Directors who produced films with crossover appeal would then be able to negotiate a higher budget for their next production. Many of the directors of youth social-problem or social-reform films, including black films, coming-out films, and young working-class films were themselves very young (in their early twenties). So, by the time Web 2.0 changed web-based interaction from viewing to creating content, visual culture already had a well-established history of youth media production and a tendency towards market proliferation, fragmentation and specialisation.

Just as photography got taken up within visual cultures that already knew how to read the image of the child (see chapter 10), user-generated content draws on existing visual cultures, especially of film and television, but also of photography (Instagram looks a lot like a digital lantern slide show). However, the intensification of user-generated content

(UGC) or producer-consumer (prosumer) content changes the relationship between the producer and the audience in complex ways.

Whether Web 2.0 is a meaningful descriptor or simply jargon, it is
certainly the case that user-generated content has proliferated on the web
in the twenty-first century, not least through social media platforms like
Facebook, Instagram, YouTube, Snapchat and Twitter. Teens are active
on social media, and nearly 40 per cent of US teens share self-created
content online, and this is true of all groups regardless of gender, age,
race, ethnicity or socioeconomic status (Lenhart et al. 2010:23), and about
20 per cent remix content online.

The content that users share on social media platforms often centres
the users themselves and their own identities. In *AuthenticTM*, Sarah Banet-Weiser (2012) argues that personal identity has become a brand. A
brand is an identity for a commodity. It is intended to both differentiate
this commodity from all other commodities that are materially more or
less the same (Coca-Cola from Pepsi, Levi's from Wranglers) and to build
brand loyalty so that consumers continue to buy one brand rather than
another, even if the brand they attach to is more expensive than other
brands. Sarah Banet-Weiser and other media-advertising scholars claim
that people, perhaps especially young people, are taking branding practices and applying them to themselves. The implication is that this is
more than learning to think of ourselves as kinds of people (people with a
gender, a race, a class, etc.) but rather to think of identity as individual
rather than social: as the outward expression of an authentic and unique
interior self. Following on from this is the claim that people (at least those
engaging in social media) then project themselves as a brand-commodity.
They do this in order to attract buyers, one of which is other corporate
brands and audiences whom these corporate brands want to build brand
recognition and loyalty with. The social media producer, in other words,
wants to become the 'face' of particular brands, and brands want to connect with micro-celebrities or 'influencers' who embody and signify what
the brand means. The shift in marketing towards engagement and conversation over 'top-down' messaging has complicated the relationship
between social-reform/justice visual culture and commercial circuits.
However, it is important to keep in mind that visual culture under capitalism has always been a commercial enterprise and that political economy is always imbricated in and over-determines socio-cultural fields.

Corporate brand-personal identity merging is clearly a practice that
corporations have long been interested in for obvious reasons. Brand
loyalty makes future financial projections more reliable and enables di-
versification in commodities building on brand loyalty; for example, market scepticism to tablets was overcome by their connection with Apple
and the loyalty of Apple users to the brand. Marketing firms recognise
that it is a practice that was easier to maintain in an era of relatively stable
identity commitments, and it certainly is not only marketing hype to

claim that Gen Z have a different relationship to brand identity (i.e., of actual commodities) than previous generations. Brand loyalty may still be a thing, but it is also evident that it does not always extend to other commodities attached to the same brand (for example, Coca-Cola's foray into water did not go too well) and that consumer boycotts can quickly degrade brand value if companies do not react quickly or effectively (Pepsi's attempt to commercially leverage Black Lives Matter backfired spectacularly) (Victor 2017). Brand commitments, in short are not as stable as they were, and it is unclear if people do think of themselves or their identities as brands. However, the move from broadcasting to narrowcasting combined with the low level of barriers to entry into home video production and uploading is shaping the visual culture of youth social activism.

*Micro-Casting, Micro-Mobile Technology and LGBT Youth Digital Activism*

The shift from narrowcasting to micro-casting describes the shift from thinking of the market as relatively large social categories (nation, gender, ethnicity, class) to thinking of it as divided into multiple small communities based on lifestyle and in which particular political commitments become associated not with activism in the sense of targeting shifts in law or policy, but with authentic, truthful, self-expression which is literally articulated through speech acts and enacted in performance. Hence when *Teen Vogue* markets itself to young social activists, it does so by engaging very superficially with the identity politics of Gen Z. This is entirely about building markets and brand identity by bringing in the followers of micro-celebrity social media producers to those markets and tracking them and the association between particular kinds of politics and specific patterns of consumption. This enables advertisers to build much more granular pictures of whom an outlet (for example, a digital magazine) engages with and therefore what products to advertise through that outlet. In short, when corporations engage with youth social activism, it is probably uncontroversial to say that this is in order to mine Gen Z's data and its money, rather than for the authentic political commitments of the corporate body.

Despite the emergence of Black Twitter and the fact that user rates for African Americans are comparable to, and often exceed in relative terms, the social media activity of other ethnic groups, black activists struggle to achieve the same level of amplification by other media that, for example or perhaps especially, LGBT activists do. Since amplification is as much about brand building and is ultimately tied to building consumer markets, advertiser platforms (which is what digital magazines are) are looking not only for what interests Gen Z but also those sections of Gen Z that have the money to buy the commodities that advertisers are selling.

Nonetheless, mainstream media and magazines do amplify the messages of the social media activists they engage with, many of whom are part of political movements. Social media is widely engaged with by teens, and there are no differences in the degree of engagement by gender, race, ethnicity or even socio-economic class. Furthermore, young(ish) African American adults (18 to 29) are more engaged with social media than other ethnic groups. Mainstream media is being more or less abandoned as a source of news and information by adults under 30 and teens (Millennials and Gen Z, respectively); this opens up space for minority representation. This is not unambiguously positive since it also opens up space for far-right representation. Some scholars and commentators have also expressed concerns about the loss of a national public sphere if micro-casting becomes the norm for both producers and audiences. However, those concerns ignore how partial (in both senses of the word) mainstream media has been and may account for why African Americans have been particularly active on social media.

## CONCLUSION

This chapter has sketched the contours of three forms of visual public culture and its representation of children and youth: the object of visual culture, the subject of coming-of-age fiction films, and the creator of digital content for social justice. The purpose of doing so is to begin to answer the two core questions that this book wants to address: What difference does it make to the message who the producer is, and how has the place of children and youth changed in visual public culture? In the following chapters, I unpack the answers to these questions through the analysis of photography, film and digital media. In the first section (chapters 2, 3 and 4), I show how sentiment or a politics of feeling connected to the relief of suffering animated social reform and placed the figure of the suffering child at its centre from the end of the nineteenth century. The audience or viewer for these productions was always assumed not to share the circumstances of those depicted in photography or on film. I show the continuity in this approach to social reform and the figure of the child from the social-reform photography at the end of Black Reconstruction/ the (so-called) Progressive Era through to contemporary NGO fundraising. In the second section (chapters 5, 6 and 7) I explore in depth the coming-of-age film as it relates to the depiction of black, queer and working-class youth. A critical distinction between these productions and social-reform photography/film is that the audience is assumed to have some connection in experience with life on screen, and these films were and are often made by directors and writers who were themselves raised in similar communities. However, because of the necessity to attract large audiences to meet the significant production costs of film, the audience is necessarily broad. In the third section (chapters 8 and 9), I explore how the low barrier to entry for producing and disseminating content on social media has transformed both production and audience. In the final chapter, I analyse how visual technologies and their platforms, from the invention of the camera to Web 2.0, have shaped how visual public culture speaks to and about children and youth.

# TWO

## The Emergence of a Sentimental Visual Culture

This chapter traces the emergence of a structure of feeling that connected the suffering of innocent subjects to sentimental feeling in order to mobilise demands for political change. In this process, the figure of the child emerged as the quintessentially innocent and vulnerable subject.

Firstly, I argue that representations of the suffering bodies of African Americans during slavery inaugurated the relationship between photography and social reform, and I show the importance of innocence (in the sense of absence of culpability) in connecting these two projects. I then show how African American reformers used photography to project the internal character and sensibility of African American subjects. These two different but connected photographic modes are indicative of a division in how the spectator is interpellated in relation to injustice, which continues through to the contemporary moment. On the one hand, for the suffering of innocents to arouse the sympathy of the spectator they need to see, in order to feel, the injury that suffering causes. On the other hand, and this intensifies through the twentieth century as the interpretation of suffering becomes disconnected from its Christian moorings and attached to tropes of being broken, black Americans increasingly perceived representations of suffering black people to be, in themselves, a site or repetition of injury. In response, as I show in the second section of this chapter, black people involved in social reform increasingly looked for images that projected dignity and wholeness—even of children. Whereas white children were always being, as it were, thrown back into childhood and the dependency that implied, black children were projected forwards into adulthood. African American photographers and scholars produced and commissioned archives of black life that signified the strength of character of black subjects, deploying models of bourgeois portraiture that emphasised how the external portrait, especially of the subject's face, revealed their internal character and their sensitivity. This opened up a divergence between black film and photography and white film and photography in its depiction of suffering, its interpellation of the specta-tor, and its implicit demands for social reform projected in the image that this book traces through other visual mediums, including the feature film and the digital protest video.

## SUFFERING, SENTIMENT AND SLAVERY

The work of evoking and representing feelings about the injustice of slavery, of developing a sentiment that desired social reform and imagined a free future, has carried through various artistic and cultural practices including, music, and painting, since the beginning of the trans-atlantic slave trade. Many of these art forms, especially music, were themselves vernacular or folk art: cultural and artistic practices made by the oppressed to give expression to their suffering and their hope for justice. Clyde Woods, for example, traces the connections between ver-nacular resistance to slavery and music culture in his magisterial work *Development Arrested: The Blues and Plantation Power* (1998). Very often, the hope for justice for Africans in America and African Americans was imagined as only achievable or representable outside of historical time and Cartesian space. This theme continues in contemporary representa-tional strategies of Afro-futurism.

Abolition was the site where photography was first engaged to repre-sent suffering and mobilise social reform. It is here that the story of the relationship between visual culture and social reform in relation to the figure of the child begins; although, as I discuss later in this book (chapter 10), photography develops its representation of the child as a suffering innocent from the emergence of that figure in painting in the late 1700s. In his book *Exposing Slavery*, Matthew Fox-Amato argues that the 1839 invention of the daguerreotype 'would alter the institution of American slavery' (2019:2). While that is certainly too bold a claim, it concurs with the widely held view that to mobilise the campaign for abolition, it was first necessary for free white Americans, who held the political power to force abolition in a racial democracy, to vicariously experience the suffer-ing of enslaved African Americans and that they did so through being confronted by the photographic evidence of that suffering.

Unlike folk music and art that, by definition, give expression to the lives of the oppressed, there was nothing inherently progressive or liber-atory in this technology of photographic representation or its affor-dances. Neither images of suffering nor their absence can be relied upon to carry the truth about a social institution. It could provide the resources as easily for representational strategies in support of conservative forces as for social-reform or progressive agendas. Matthew Fox-Amato, for example, shows how enslavers used the photographic portrait and landscape photography to convey an image of slavery as a stable, paternalistic institution.

Suffering was not a sign of abjection in the nineteenth-century social imaginary in the Anglophone world but, rather, a sign of divinity connected to the central place of Christ's suffering in the Christian mythology of the relationship between God and humans. While suffering ceased to be in itself a sign of divinity or nobility in the nineteenth century, it persisted as a sign that signified the relationship between humans and God. Suffering came to be seen as a desecration or de-sacralization of a Christian God's creation of humans in his image. Representations of suffering African and African American slaves were intended to move the feeling spectator to desire freedom for those depicted and to view slavery as an anti-Christian, even blasphemous, project. It is not so much that slavery (and, of indigenous Americans, genocide) depended on whites denying the humanity of slaves but, rather, that it denied their divinity: their being made in the image of God.

The suffering body of the slave was conveyed in abolitionist imagery, and the suffering subject has continued to be central to mobilising support for projects of social reform since the nineteenth century. This central role of the suffering subject to arouse the feeling of the spectator forms part of a long Christian tradition of the nobility of suffering. While to contemporary audiences, the representation of suffering bodies is often seen as almost pornographic (Lebeau 2008:149–50) in its ability to excite emotions in the spectator while looking at an abject subject, this view of suffering as demeaning the sufferer is a very recent, secular understanding of the meaning of suffering. The central part of suffering in the Christian tradition, encapsulated in the image of Christ crucified on the cross, of martyred saints, and the continued power of images that reference or resonate with the Pietà, the image of Christ's mother holding his dead body, speak to an idea of the suffering subject as noble and Christ-like, as both innocent and divine (Clark 1995:241).

The nobility or divinity of suffering could not in itself produce a desire for social reform; indeed, it could even counter it since removing the causes of suffering could bring the sufferer further from God. Elizabeth Clark argues that the emergence of a new doctrine on suffering propagated by Protestant reformers in the mid- to late nineteenth century shifted the perception of a connection between suffering and divinity. Sympathy for suffering others, also a long part of the Christian tradition but, increasingly in Protestant thought, one found in the world rather than in the scriptures, became a central theme of evangelical and liberal (Unitarian) Protestant thought so that by the 1830s, 'many Americans turned for guidance to the emotions over the intellect, identifying the moral sense more with feeling than with rational thought' (Clark 1995:477).

White middle-class women played a significant part in the emergence of a sympathetic response to suffering and the social-reform movements it generated. Clark argues that the violence that slaves faced was unlikely to resonate directly with the experiences of white men and therefore that these images of suffering interpellated women spectators. However, it seems unlikely that immigrant European men and other working-class non-black men would not have experienced violence from their employers and the state. It is perhaps more to the point that the representations of suffering were addressed to maternal audiences, that is to say, not to women as feminine subjects but to women as maternal subjects (Clark 1995:483). This is the same audience that were so central to work of the child-saving organisations of the nineteenth century and, of course, to the popularity of melodrama in film.

Strikingly, the lone and neglected child, an image that becomes commonplace in late twentieth-century social-reform visual culture is not yet present in these early representations. Certainly, as in W. E. B. Du Bois's portraits of children made for the 1900 Paris Exposition, we find photographs in the public archive of young children on their own, but these are in the tradition of bourgeois portraiture and are generally taken in a studio—a setting that immediately signifies the middle-class status of the subject. The exceptions to this rule are studio portrait photographs of young African American slaves, where, Fox-Amato has shown, the inclusion of the household's slave in the family album was presumably intended to signify one strand of southern white supremacist rhetoric that wanted to project the lie of slavery as a benign and paternalistic institution.

## THE SCHOOL CHILD, THE APPRENTICE AND THE PROMISE OF YOUTH

If the image of the suffering slave was central to the emergence of a visual culture of suffering that mobilised social reform, after the Civil War, and to some extent among free black communities before the Civil War, the image of successful African American youth trained in agricultural science was a recurring trope in response to the implicit question posed by social-reform campaigns: 'what is to be done'. In these images, the projection is of a successful and respectable bourgeois subject-in-training. Here, despite differences of opinion between black community leaders and scholars, most notably between Booker T. Washington and W. E. B. Du Bois, about the most effective way to achieve black liberation, the visual culture of black reform shared an image of black subjects as dignified, bourgeois subjects whose disciplined youth looked towards the future and whose well-mannered children were firmly embedded in the family and the schoolhouse.

The US entry for the African American section of the American studio at the 1900 Paris Exposition is exemplary of these kinds of representations. Frances Benjamin Johnston's photographs of the Hampton Institute students illustrate effectively this particular strand in African American social reform that continues into the visual culture of the late twentieth century (see, for example, chapter 5). The idea of transitions to adulthood being structured not by the passage of time and the changing social relationships one is immersed in (e.g., becoming a parent) but by a particular style of deportment, an attitude towards learning, and above all the possibility of economic independence, are vividly pictured in the visual archive of this period. These kinds of images very clearly show the connection between the enduring significance of innocence for mobilising the spectator for social reform and 'respectability politics' or the projection of a demeanour of thrift, hard work, intelligence and effort.[1]

The photographs taken by the white feminist (and probably lesbian) photographer Frances Benjamin Johnston, commissioned by the Hampton Institute and displayed at the 1900 Paris Exposition, are replete with tropes of social uplift through craft labour and agricultural science that were anticipated to produce an economically independent class of black Americans. Both Booker T. Washington and W. E. B. Du Bois were involved in curating the African American studio of the Paris Exposition, and some authors (e.g., cited in Fisher 2005) have argued that Washington and Du Bois shared a sociological vision. However, Fisher (2005) argues convincingly that Du Bois saw both Hampton's and Tuskegee's projects of economic advancement in the absence of political and social freedom for African Americans as chimeric, at best.

Johnston was an established photojournalist by the time she was commissioned to take the photographs of the Hampton Institute students. There were 159 platinum prints in an album of these photographs, discovered by Lincoln Kirstein in a Washington bookshop sometime in the early 1940s. He subsequently gave them to the New York Museum of Modern Art (MOMA), who selected forty-four of them for a 1966 exhibition curated by Kirsten, who also wrote the introduction to the exhibition catalogue, 'The Hampton Album' (Wexler 2009).

Shawn Michelle Smith (1999), in her book *American Archives: Gender, Race, and Class in Visual Culture*, argues that Johnston's photographs for the Paris Exposition are deeply ambiguous. She interprets the objective gaze of the camera on the subjects as the effect of a 'social distance' made necessary by the terror of Jim Crow and the lynching of black men who had any kind of equal contact, especially romantic or sexual, with white women. She also argues that, in contrast to the photographs that Du Bois curated for the exhibition that 'recuperate a sense of racial autonomy and self-determination', Johnston's photographs 'forward a narrative of assimilation, tenuously erasing racial difference under the signs of a national identity' (1999:177). While that may well be true, it also ignores the fact that Johnston was commissioned to take these photographs by the Hampton Institute and that Booker T. Washington's vision was precisely to accomplish the assimilation of black Americans into America through economic advancement.

Johnston's photographs are extraordinarily accomplished. Most of the photographs are of groups of school students engaged in practicing (and, as in the Hampton pedagogical philosophy, learning through practicing) a craft. They mostly appear to be photographs of students in their late teens. There are also several photographs of kindergarten and primary school students. In most of the photographs, the young men wear military-style uniforms with a stripe down the side of their trousers and an army-style cap. The young women are dressed in Edwardian-style clothes (long skirts, fitted shirts, hats, flat shoes). The environment of the photographic study gives Johnson her cue to represent student endeavour as focused, active, and constructive. One image, *Stairway of Treasurer's Residence Students at Work*, perfectly captures the unity between the Hampton Institute's pedagogical and social philosophy and the photographer's art. While the sharp, precise lines of the image suggest that it was formally staged, the impression is nonetheless of activity, of a group harmoniously working together to literally build a stairway; and of course the conative signification of the stairway as a metonym for progress and uplift (and the treasurer's stairway, no less) is self-evident. Although a black-and-white image, the lighting of the image generates a sense of colour, of light and shade that gives the image a painterly quality that prefigures the use of shadow and light in realist art.

In their arrangement in the album, the photographs begin with comparisons between the social organisation of the 'old-time' and the ways of the 'Hampton graduate'. Although, as in many social reform photographs, the apparent 'before and after' of the pictures implies the passing of historical time (Koven 1997), in fact, it seems, given the composition of the images and the use of light and shade, the 'before' photographs were also taken by Johnston.

A photo entitled *The Old Folks at Home* shows an elderly man and woman sitting at a table eating their dinner in a small room with a large range, a bare floor and a few jugs on the mantelpiece. Its point of comparison is the next photograph in the album, *A Hampton Graduate at Home*. The photograph is of a middle-class house; at the centre of the image is a dining table covered in a white tablecloth (the *Old Folks* table was uncovered). A family sits around the table—three children along one side, a man on the right, a woman on the left. A vacant chair is tucked under the fourth side of the table, as if to invite the spectator to join them. This is an image of cleanliness and plenty, in contrast to the dirt and scarcity of the previous image. There are paintings on the wall of the *Hampton Graduate at Home* of landscapes, the contemplation of the landscape itself being a sign of a particular kind of bourgeois interiority, one which insists on the

**Figure 2.1.   Johnson's photographs for the Hampton Institute index the discourse or racial uplift that animated one strand of the struggle for social reform.**

importance of feeling over science as modes of understanding and responding to the world (Cosgrove 1998:244). To the left of the image, bathed in weak sunlight, is a staircase, repeated here again as a sign of uplift (there is no second floor to the *Old Folks* home). In place of the useful jugs lined up on top of the range, a few ornaments are arranged on top of a piano.

The faces of the people in the photograph are harder to read than the evident contrast between the material plenty of their home and the material lack of the old folks' home. Both the father and mother are staring down, looking towards, but not exactly at, the table. Neither looks happy. The mother looks lost in not particularly pleasant thoughts, while the father appears resigned or sad. Two of the children are looking sideways at their mother, while the third looks, apparently somewhat apprehensively, at his father. In contrast, the old couple in the first image, sitting close together on adjacent sides of the table, seem more at ease. Given Johnston's skill as a photographer, this contrast cannot be accidental: Is some doubt about the satisfaction that uplift will bring being sneaked in here, and if it is, what grounds that doubt?

The next comparisons are between the *Old-Time Cabin* and *A Hampton Graduate's Home* and then between *The Old Well* and *The Improved Well* (three Hampton grandchildren). The old well is being worked by an old man, while a woman and three children, two of them very young, look on, perhaps waiting their turn. The absence of adults at the new well (a young boy, about twelve years old, is pushing the handle, and a girl of about the same age is holding the bucket, while a younger child looks on) perhaps signifies how effortless the improved well is to work. It is worth mentioning that a similar image of white children from this period would almost certainly be a signifier of child labour rather than of progress.

In her analysis of Johnston's Hampton photographs, Laura Wexler identifies how the carefully arranged tableaux within which Johnston photographs each of the classrooms in the school present a kind of still-ness of subjects that holds them in a specific time and place rather than projecting them forwards into the future. This is partly an effect of the incredible stillness of the subjects in the image that, as Wexler says, can-not be entirely explained by the limitations of the camera's technology. Johnston took another set of photographs, of white school children in Washington at more or less the same time she took on the Hampton commission; these photographs, Wexler shows, depict animated subjects in movement even while, necessarily, the film freezes them in a moment in time. Wexler argues that Johnston 'photographed a myth on the eve of its explosion' and that the bucolic, agricultural and small industry that Hampton was teaching its students was already being made redundant by the rapid industrialisation and revolutionary technological develop-ments of the late nineteenth century: the very forces that the Paris Exposi-tion was intended to display. She cites Rebecca West's contemporaneous account of the exposition to point towards the projected redundancy of craft work: 'For the first time the public were shown such new inventions as X-ray photography, wireless telegraphy and automobiles, then about five years old. The entire exhibition was run by electricity and visitors toured the site on an electrically powered moving platform with three tiers, each rolling at a different speed. In contrast, much of the arts on display looked backwards rather than forwards' (Wexler 1988:362). Yet I want to suggest that Johnston's photographs contain more 'excess', to use Wexler's term, than she allows.

What Johnston's pictures display is not only stillness but also the ab-sence of joy or pleasure, and this depiction, some thirty years after the end of slavery and in the middle of the terror of white supremacy that ended and followed black reconstruction, is what is also captured in Johnston's images. Her images won a prize in Paris, and Wexler may well be right that 'this fact should be seen partly as an index to the horror of what the myth [of racial uplift on the Hampton model] repressed. A generation after the Civil War, it was evidently much more attractive for both the Europeans and the Americans to believe that contemporary black life was like life at Hampton than to attend to evidence of catastrophic social disintegration such as the rising incidence of lynching and other racial violence during and after the Reconstruction era' (Wexler 1988:362).

Together with Johnston's photographs of the Hampton Institute, W. E. B. Du Bois curated over five hundred photographs for the African American section of the Paris Exposition.[2] These images convey something of the diversity of African American life at the end of the nineteenth century but overwhelmingly depict young middle-class black Americans—university students at Fisk and Howard—either in groups or as single portraits. There are several portraits of children (mostly girls) and young people (mostly young women). Photographs of groups of workers at a tobacco mill are more ambivalent, conveying something of both the hardship and history of black people's lives in the United States, as are photographs of the Georgia landscape. In the over five hundred images, there are only about twenty photographs of children. Several are of groups of children in kindergarten and day nursery, elementary school children and children with their parents at church, and at the porch of the family house. Du Bois also included several of his diagrams contrasting the conditions of black and white Americans, showing the impacts of racism on black people's lives. The overall effect is a kind of visual argument that shows the disciplined, studious, and moral character of African American youth juxtaposed to the facts about the life chances of black Americans. Although Smith argues that these albums functioned like the snapshot of everyday life, 'a sense of how we looked when we were not "wearing the mask", when we were not attempting to perfect the image for a white supremacist gaze' (Smith 1999:178 citing hooks 1994:50), they were also offered alongside diagrams of African American progress and change and other formal portrait photographs. Given Du Bois's commitment to sociology, the snapshots of everyday life can also be read as a visual ethnography.

Although Smith argues that Du Bois's curated images are quite different to Johnston's commissioned images, here, too, the images seem to be intended to demonstrate a demand for inclusion in the project of bourgeois modernity from which racial capitalism excluded them. Frederick Douglas's portrait is perhaps the most well known of these kinds of portraits, and Douglas himself was the most photographed man in the nineteenth-century US (Gates 2016). While traces of the debates about bourgeois interiority persist through the twentieth century and into the current era in arguments about whether 'respectability politics' progresses or holds back social reform, it is more than a simple projection of a respectable person. Respectability politics also, perhaps even mostly, invokes the importance of innocence to arousing sympathy in the spectator/interlocutor.

Around the same period that Du Bois and Washington were turning to photography to present a new public visual culture of black life, black filmmakers were developing similar projects in 'uplift cinema'. The term 'uplift cinema' was originally used about films that formed part of a wider political project to secure the civil rights and liberties of black adults in the United States. Allyson Nadia Field's (2015) *Uplift Cinema: The Emergence of African American Film and the Possibility of Black Modernity* demonstrates the enduring attraction to filmmakers of using film to correct the negative representations of black people that circulate in white film. As early as 1913, African American newspapers were criticising African American representation on film and commenting on 'the "resentment" that Black moviegoers feel against their egregious misrepresentation "presented everywhere"' (2015:1). Uplift as a political project referred to the praxis of self-help, community service and economic independence that emerged as one response to the failure of Black Reconstruction and the re-incorporation of black people as an unfree class within the US political economy at the end of the nineteenth century. The 'program of racial uplift emphasized individual initiative, mutual assistance, social respectability, interracial cooperation, and economic independence as components of a general strategy for promoting the advancement of African Americans' (Field 2015:2). It is closely associated with Booker T. Washington, the Hampton Institute and the Tuskegee Institute. Vocational education and economic security were the goals of Washington, who was less concerned with securing political rights and economic equality, a position Du Bois labelled the 'Atlanta Compromise' (Field 2015:2). The film projects associated with 'racial uplift' were called 'race films', whose aim was to 'present a humanizing portrayal of African American subjects, "showing them not as fools and servants, but as human beings with the same emotions, desires and weaknesses as other people"' (Field 2015:7). This broad frame did not constrain film in relation to genre or style but only in relation to subject and spectator (that is, they were intended for black audiences). However, although a variety of genres were deployed in 'race film' and uplift film, melodrama figures prominently (Gaines 1987; Williams 2001). Field argues that uplift cinema ended in the 1910s, while recognising that 'the strength of uplift's hold on the social psyche (both Black and white) meant that its influence continued even as its strategies and forms were picked up elsewhere' (Field 2015:245).

THE WHITENESS OF POST-SLAVERY SOCIAL REFORM IMAGERY

If, as the African American section of the Paris Exposition indicates, for black leaders the path to social reform was through representations of the virtuous, disciplined youth and the protected child embedded in the family and the school, the image of the suffering body continued to be deployed by white photographers to press forward the case for social reform of the urban, white and immigrant, poor. If the image of the suffering subject visualised in photography begins with the suffering bodies of enslaved African Americans, subsequent reform photography, while continuing to deploy a sentimental appeal to the emotions of its (putative) middle-class audiences (predominately Anglo), mobilised anti-slavery feeling in defence of white families and specifically their children.

*Lantern Slide Shows*

In their depiction of suffering, the two most well-known social-reform photographers, Jacob Riis and Lewis Hine, wanted to emphasise the pain and hardship endured by their working-class subjects while invoking their shared humanity with their (middle-class) spectator. Their photographs drew on a practice, well established by the end of the nineteenth century, of photographing the innocent and appealing subjects of an otherwise abject spectacle: poverty and homelessness. Thomas Barnardo (1845–1905) had been commissioning photographs of children admitted to his homes for 'Working and Destitute Lads' since around 1870 (Koven 1997). These photographs depicted boys in staged poses of 'before and after' their rescue. Barnardo defended his use of these images, citing Oscar Gustav Rejlander's art photographs of street children in the 1860s and 1870s, especially his *Night in Town* (1860). The tropes deployed in these images were already familiar to viewers, having commonalities with, for example, Henry Mayhew's illustrations in *London Labour and the London Poor* and a photographic tradition developed since the 1850s of documenting the urban poor (Smith, L. 1998:111–32).

Both Riis and Hine showed their photographs in lantern slide shows, the technology of moving film that anticipated the silent movie in its juxtaposition of textual inter-titles and images. The lantern slide show preceded the invention of photography and had been used in some form since the seventeenth century; it had become part of the field of popular entertainment in Europe in the late eighteenth century. In the introduction to their edited collection *Screen Culture and the Social Question 1880–1914*, Ludwig Vogl-Bienek and Richard Crangle comment that 'public performances using the magic or optical lantern became a prominent part of the social fabric of the late nineteenth century in most western cultures' (2014:8). Lantern slide shows were also, by the end of the nineteenth century, a prominent part of colonial cultures, and were used as proselytising forms of entertainment by missionaries in Africa and Asia. This popular form of entertainment and education is now little discussed, and Vogl-Bienek and Crangle want to think about its continuities with subsequent screen cultures including, of course, film. In their search for 'continuities of practice' in spectatorship and in the 'art of projection', they connect lantern and cinematograph media. Secondly they are interested in how what was called, in the late nineteenth and early twentieth centuries, 'the social question' was used to 'spread concerns and promote solutions . . . [and] even be used for practices of social intervention, by instructing the poor' (2014:10). They define the social question as comprising 'complex socio-political questions based on a major contradiction, between liberal claims of civil rights and individual freedom on one hand, and prevalent destitution, pauperism and effective lack of rights on the other' (2014:10). They claim that the use of lantern slides and silent film were extensively used to intervene in the social question and that the other major uses of screen culture, travelogues and Christian discourse overlapped with this theme. Stephen Bottomore, in his chapter on political persuasion and the lantern and cinematography, notes that although many screen media productions did deal with social deprivation, these were not necessarily political films in the sense of trying to mobilise a political response, but rather they were intended, as Colin Gordon has argued, to evoke sympathy (Bottomore 2014:36). He includes in these sympathetic productions, the social documentary slides of Riis and Hine as well as what Kevin Brownlow calls 'social films' which were 'made by various companies especially in America, up to the 1910s' (ibid.). Riley Brothers's *Street Life or People We Meet* is an example of a kind of ethnographic entertainment—in this case of the city—made by the same company that produced and distributed the lantern slides for the campaign against Belgium's King Leopold II's personal rule over the Congo, showing the connections between missionaries, government and colonial as well as domestic visual cultures of social reform.

Children were often the audience for lantern slide shows. Loiperdinger, for example, describes a popular entertaining show ('Man Swallowing Rats'), which was screened for an audience of 1,450 destitute children by the Liberal Club of Fulham, London. The Sunday School Union, which had a membership of nearly six million school pupils 'favoured using lantern slides to make their performances attractive for their target audiences' (2014:20), and the socialist newspaper *The Clarion* organised '"Cinderella Clubs" providing free meals for poor children, entertaining them with music, dancing and the magic lantern. The children were given a bun and an orange upon leaving—and a sample copy of *The Clarion* for their parents' (2014:21).

Jacob Riis delivered his first lantern slide lecture in January 1888 to an audience of the Society of Amateur Photographers of New York. Richard Hoe Lawrence and Dr Henry Granger Piffard took the photographs used in the slide show. He invited members of the press and lectured for two hours showing one hundred slides on the topic 'The Other Half, How It Lives and Dies in New York' (Yochelson 2014:85). In her chapter in *Screen Culture*, Bonnie Yochelson, curator at the New York Museum from 1987 to 1994, outlines his talk. He began delivering his lectures to church groups in the New York area and published a condensed version with twenty-one slides in the 1889 Christmas issue of *Scribner's Magazine*—'a national magazine for upper-middle class readers' (2014:86), and Scribner published his book *How the Other Half Lives* in 1890. In 1892, he published *The Children of the Poor*. Subsequently Riis began to use professional photographers to illustrate news stories he wrote, including buying eight prints from Lewis Hine for 'A Modern St. George, The Growth of Organized Charity in the United States', published in *Scribner's Magazine* in October 1911 and including seven of them in the article (Yochelson 2014:92). In a paper, 'The Camera and the American Social Conscience: The Documentary Photography of Jacob A. Riis', Ferenc Szasz and Ralph Bogardus (1974) claim that Riis's success in mobilising public support and action towards reform of tenements and working-class neighbourhoods was made possible by his photography and the lantern slide shows that disseminated them. They say that Riis was the first person in the United States to use lantern slide shows for purposes other than entertainment and for social reform (acknowledging that both Henry Mayhew [1851] and Adople Smith [1877] had used photographs to illustrate their books on poverty in London). Echoing the melodramatic mode of 'social question' lectures and lantern slides, Szasz and Bogardus tell us:

> The audiences were also deeply moved. Shudders ran through the Boston crowd, and in Indianapolis the people squirmed with discomfort at some of the more graphic images. In a small Wisconsin country town, a man interrupted Riis' lecture by shouting at one of the slides, "Yes! That is right. I was there." In Washington, D.C., a hush fell over the audience when he showed a picture of an abandoned little girl, and they broke into cheers and applause when the next slide showed her in the care of Sister Irene's Home for Children. (1974:431)

They insist that the success of Riis's lantern slide shows rested on his own photographic accomplishments that distinguished what they see as a lack of compassion by other documentary photography of the poor from Riis's flashlight photography. Paradoxically, they seem to invest the power of his images in his *lack* of photographic training, in contrast to the evident skills of professional photographers like Frances Benjamin Johnson. This resonates with a long tradition in photography, one that continues into the era of social media, of protecting the photograph from charges of being staged or inauthentic by making visible a kind of artlessness in its production (a similar artlessness is on display in social media images discussed in chapters 8 and 9). Riis himself was perhaps unconvinced of either his skill or his art as a photographer, and in the first lantern slide show (according to Yochelson) and in later articles he bought prints from professional photographers, including Lewis Hine. What Riis demonstrates in his pictures is not perhaps so much the skill of conveying the subject's personal suffering in order to draw the spectator's sympathy as it is of rendering the subject more iconographic than idiosyncratic. As Boltanski (1999) points out, the social-reform image depends on the possibility for establishing a link between the person in the image and another person somewhere else—it is this unique one that suffers, the image wants to say, but it could be anyone.

Portrait photographers drew on universally shared symbols, a visual language, to convey the individual sensibility of the sitter. The images that Szasz and Bogardus reproduce from Frances B. Johnston and which they feel are devoid of compassion, convey a sense of the detail and specific character of place and person that is lacking in Riis's photographs. A similar suspicion is often attached to powerful imagery of the poor and goes back to the opening point about what suffering conveys about the sufferer. As I mentioned above, to the modern eye, suffering is always suspect and to view some forms of suffering as noble is to incur charges of indulging in 'poverty porn'. Michael Sundell reproduces the text from a gallery label of an exhibition of Hine's photographs at the New York Public Library in 1983. The photographs had been tinted in sepia so as not to distract 'attention from the social content' (1986:168). The curator explains this decision on the gallery label: 'in viewing [the original photographs], one is reminded of Andre Bazin's comment about Lucchino Visconti's film *La Terra Trema* [The Earth Trembles, 1948], to the effect that it is hard to feel pity for oppressed people whose faces suggest the nobility and strength of character of Renaissance Princes' (ibid.). This comment nicely highlights the difference between the African American visual culture discussed above, which, precisely, wanted to depict the nobility of its subjects in contrast to their subjection under slavery, and that of poverty reformers which relied on suffering to invoke compassion and support for reform.

However, the problem of rendering adults as suffering innocents, and the possibility of adding insult to injury through producing abject images of poor adults, was not only the concern of black visual culture. Indeed, it is part of the thesis of this book that the reason the child or youth becomes increasingly visible in social-reform campaigns is because the child in the modern era is quintessentially an innocent subject. So while Hine is probably best known for his photographs of child labourers, his photographs of adult immigrants arriving at Ellis Island attempt to convey precisely the nobility of the person portrayed. This also fits with a widely held view that external appearance is a key to internal character and that the role of portraiture is to capture, through the sensitive depiction of external signs, the interiority of the subject. Hine taught photography at the School for Ethical Culture and encouraged his students to study religious art and apply its composition to photographs. The question of all social-reform images—of the status of this particular individual in relation to all those of his or her 'class'—is also at play in Hine's photographs which convey the particularity of a person or group in time and space, while nonetheless, Sundell claims, generalising their circumstances. In his own lecture on reform photography and 'social uplift' Hine ends with a lengthy quote from George Eliot's 1859 novel *Adam Bede* (like Browning's poem discussed below, pointing to the cross-influence of literary and visual artistic forms) that conveys effectively Hine's commitment to portraying beauty in working class-subjects and settings:

> Paint us an angel, if you can, with floating violet robe, and a face paled by the celestial light; paint us a Madonna turning her mild face upward, and opening her arms to welcome the divine glory, but do not impose on us any esthetic rules which shall banish from the reign of art those old women with work-worn hands scraping carrots, those heavy clowns taking holiday in a dingy pothouse, those rounded backs and weather-beaten faces that have bent over the spade and done the rough work of the world, those homes with their tin pans, their brown pitchers, their rough curs and their clusters of onions [Let us] see beauty in the commonplace things, and delight in showing how kindly the light of heaven falls on them.

*The Cry of the Children* was released in April 1912. *The Cry* illustrates the deployment of white suffering and invokes white solidarity across the class line while depicting the nobility and religiousity of adults and the innocence of children. Child labour exploitation was a 'favorite topic of journalists, photographers, politicians and filmmakers' (Ross 1998:51). Carl Laemmle's company, Universal, produced *The Blood of the Children* (1914) and *The White Terror* (1915) (Ross 1998:51). Directed by George O. Nichols, it took its storyline and title from Elizabeth Barrett Browning's popular and sentimental poem 'The Cry of the Children', first published in 1843. It is noteworthy that Browning contributed a poem, 'The Runaway Slave at Pilgrim's Point', to the abolitionist volume *The Liberty Bell*. Like 'The Cry of the Children', it is a melodramatic narrative in which an innocent mother and child are injured through no fault of their own (by rape in 'Runaway', by work and hunger in 'The Cry', leading to the death of the child and, in 'Runaway', also of the slave).

The inter-titles of this silent film are lines from the poem. The music score of the film is typical of what we would later recognise as melodramatic film. It was produced and distributed by Thanhouser Films. It was widely viewed as 'one of the most important expressions of the pre–World War One reform movement, in particular child labor'. Commentary on the film has largely focused on the subject of child labour, rather than the aesthetic qualities of the film; although Ned Thanhouser, the grandson of the man who started Thanhouser Films, does comment in his note for the Library of Congress on the effective use of mise-en-scène and 'fluid and well-paced editing'. Filmed in a factory setting, it contrasts the struggle and poverty of a white working family of three children and a man and a woman with the opulence of the white mill owners, a childless couple. The mill owner (husband) works in the office of the mill while the mill owner (wife) does no work. The plot is driven by the attempt of the mill owner (the wife) to adopt the youngest child of the working family when she sees her playing in the woods: a picture of angelic innocence and joy. At first, the girl (Alice) seems to be pleading with her parents to let her go with the mill owner, but when she realises that the move would be permanent, she runs to her mother and refuses to go. It is interesting to note that the parents apparently offer their daughter (who is about four years old) the choice of whether to stay with them or go with the mill owner, presumably so that the spectator can see that, although the family love the child deeply and are overjoyed when she decides to stay with them, they are not standing in the way of her desires since this might mean a better life for her. The mill owner leaves, visibly frustrated and annoyed at having her desires left unmet. She later returns with her husband, and another conversation ensues in which the girl is again asked what she wants to do and in response clings to her mother. Her father shrugs his shoulders, and the mill owners leave. In place of the child whom she has not been allowed to adopt, the mill owner is given a small dog by her husband; the substitution of an animal for a human echoes the opening titles that quote the opening lines of Browning's poem: 'The young lambs are bleating in the meadows / The young birds are chirping in the nest / But the young, young children, O my brothers, They are weeping bitterly! / [They are weeping in the playtime of the others—excluded from the inter-titles], *In the country of the free*' (emphasis added).

The mill workers go on strike but are forced back to work by hunger. Alice goes to work in place of her sick mother, but the work makes her weak. She goes to the mill owner's house to ask them to adopt her, but the woman is now repelled by Alice, who is no longer the skipping, joyful child she met in the woods. Soon afterwards, Alice dies while at work in the mill. While the funeral is in progress, the mill owner drives by and sees the funeral group; on being told what has happened she starts to sob. The working family go home and sit around their table, the mother inconsolable. For a brief moment, Alice appears as a vision of an angel smiling down on the family. The next scene shows the mill owner recollecting the funeral of the girl, and the film ends as she sobs and her husband looks on anxiously and hopelessly. This final scene demonstrates the impossibility of a satisfying resolution (at least for a secular audience, although the conversion of Alice to an angel offers a classic melodramatic resolution within a religious worldview of the irresolvable contradictions of the social-reform film). The implication of closing on the weeping mill owner and the lines of the final inter-title is that she will now be moved to reform the mill and end family poverty. The sentimental sympathy of a bourgeois woman (in an era when women's feeling for suffering others was a central dynamism of the social policy reform movement) is implicitly offered up as an alternative resolution to ending the suffering of the poor (the other being Alice's other-worldly future).

Ned Thanhouser, in his notes on the film, comments: 'Although some elements of the story are melodramatic, clichés are to be expected from that era. However, the cinematic skill and social importance certainly contributed to a new social-realism style. The film marked the emerging political power of film, and the potential [of film] for making contributions to society' (https://vimeo.com/18500930). Steven Ross notes that the film was included in an evening of socialist entertainment put on by Bronx socialists in 1912 that included other short 'pictures portraying the class struggle and working-class life'. It was attended by over one thousand adults and children, and the organisers announced their intention to 'avail themselves of this novel means of propaganda' (Ross 1998:107). However, it is relevant to note that the founder of Thanhouser Films, Ned's grandfather Edwin, did not go into the film industry as a social reformer but saw it as a business opportunity (Thanhouser 2011:90). This tension between commercial and political circuits of visual culture continues through feature films and into digital visual culture.

The film incorporates many of the thematic elements discussed in this chapter. Mill workers were the central target of child-labour reform despite the fact that (as with contemporary campaigns against child labour in factories in the Global South) a minority of mill labourers were children, and, conversely, a minority of child labourers were mill workers. It is also salient that the vast majority of mill workers were white. The shift from smallholder agricultural work to industrial labour reproduced the racist division of labour that already characterised the southern workforce and traced the afterlife of slavery in the free labour market. This whiteness of post-abolition social reform is evident in 'The Cry of the Children', in which all the characters are white (including the mill owners' servant, who in fact would most likely have been African American). The film's opening title, 'In the Land of the Free' points out the rhetorical commitment of the United States to freedom but does so through an appeal to 'white solidarity' (Cedric Robinson) across the class line. Spectators would be aware that despite the abolition of slavery, African Americans were far from universally free in the context of the Jim Crow South, the defeat of Black Reconstruction in 1880 in the post–Civil War South, and the expansion of the penal labour system, which disproportionately affected black men and black boys. The inter-title, 'the young, young children, O my brothers, They are weeping bitterly!, In the country of the free' emphasises the entitlement of white children to be free and the double affront of white children being 'slaves' when black children were free.

Mill labour was often done by women whose children accompanied them to work, and children's labour was not one-for-one substitutable by adult labour. While the absence of men was often constructed as idleness, it in fact was a reflection of a gendered division of labour in which yeomen continued to hold onto and work smallholdings, while women went to work in factories. For the labour reformers this gendered division of labour posed a problem to the discourse of labour reform: how to shift the blame for child labour from 'idle' men (as a dominant bourgeois narrative had it) to factory owners. *The Cry* has to struggle with this problem and deals with it through an extending visualisation of the family as more than mere ciphers for the effects of poverty. Affection, care and the interior lives of each of the working-class core characters are conveyed in lighting, music, and the gestures and glances of the actors. The father plays a central role in the film as an active and caring figure: he is the first to get out of bed in the opening scene of the film, he touches his wife's face gently to convey his sympathy for her being cold and tired, and he lifts Alice up and holds her tightly and joyfully when she refuses the mill owner's demand to adopt her. The father's actions are intended to convey his innocence and to demonstrate both that he was a good father and that he had no power to redress the poverty and hunger of his family.

In her discussion of the inter-titles in the film, Sarah Berry considers the role of the poem's adaptation as the insertion of lyrical time into the narrative time of the poem. While inter-titles in silent film were generally intended to carry the narrative through either exposition or dialogue, the adaptation of the poem in this instance serves to disrupt the mimetic or natural properties of the narrative. This practice of using inter-titles, which survives in sound film through the use of non-diegetic music and voiceover, functions as a kind of container for the excess that cannot be resolved within the narrative of the melodrama.

CONCLUSION

In this chapter, I have traced the emergence of a sentimental visual culture that represented in film and photography the development of a politics of feeling in US political culture. A politics of feeling encouraged the representation of suffering as both noble and affective. In visual culture, this connection between suffering and sentiment emerged, firstly, not with children but with the representation of African and African American adults in slavery, whose suffering was mobilised in support of abolition. White children emerge as the quintessential suffering subject of visual political culture after the end of slavery and in relation to the poverty and deprivation experienced by white (mostly European immigrants and yeoman) families. In contrast, African American reformers, in the same period that Hine and Riis were photographing poor white children, had moved away from suffering as the site of their demand for representation and equality towards political and economic uplift. In these representations, the black child is dignified, patriotic and educated.

## NOTES

1. The album is available here: https://www.moma.org/d/c/exhibition_catalogues/W1siZiIsIjMwMDA2MjMwOSJdLFsicCIsImVuY292ZXIiLCJ3d3cubW9tYS5vcmcvY2FsZW5kYXIvZXhoaWJpdGlvbnMvMzQ4MSIsImh0dHBzOi8vd3d3Lm1vbWEub3JnL2NhbGVuZG-FyL2V4aGliaXRpb25zLzM0ODE%2FbG9jYWxlPWVuIiwiaSJdXQ.pdf?sha=10d4510d38e82d04.
2. https://www.loc.gov/pictures/collection/anedub/dubois.html.

# THREE

## 'And Then the Kids Took It Over'

### Documentary Film, Racism and the Civil Rights Movement

This chapter shows how some of the visual tropes that emerged through documentary photography continued into the development of documentary film. It focuses on the period from 1950 and the emergence of youth as a specific group and problem for social reform to the late 1960s and the passing of the 1968 Voting Rights Act. Representations that deployed images of suffering to evoke sentimentality were increasingly absent, whereas the use of images conveying strength of character to establish the legitimacy of demanding political rights expanded in documentary film. Documentary film also developed as a mode of education, particularly around health, in which the narrative depicts a problem and its resolution. Very often, these problems revolved around the health of children, and the story was aimed at their parents.

The purpose of this chapter is to trace the ways that children and youth are represented in social-reform documentary film to understand how the shifting discourses of social reform were carried into the representation of the child and youth. The selection of documentary film that should be analysed in order to understand this dialectic relationship between social reform and the figure of the child poses many problems. Unlike the coming-of-age social-problem feature film, analysed in the next section of this book (chapters 5, 6 and 7), the representation of children and youth in documentary film is scattered through a large archive. This archive is both expanding, as 16-mm film is digitalised and made available online, and contracting, as copies of films are lost or decay. The importance of children in the development of social reform in the Pro-

gressive Era is fairly well established, and the photographic canon of
social-reform photography in that period is also fairly well established,
principally the work of Hine and Riis. In contrast, as documentary film
emerges as a distinct practice and proliferates, it is less easy to identify
what counts as documentary social-reform film. More broadly, while the
canon of documentary film is also well established, it is also problematic,
like most canons, in its inclusions and exclusions (Bruzzi 2000).

To begin my search for a kind of authoritative selection of documentary film on children and youth in social-reform films, I began with the
Library of Congress's National Film Preservation Registry. At the time of
writing, there were nearly 760 films included in the registry (see https://
www.loc.gov/programs/national-film-preservation-board/film-registry/
complete-national-film-registry-listing/). I identified from the current
registry all the documentary films listed (excluding news archive film).
Of the sixty-five documentary films, I then looked in detail at those that
focused on stories about children and youth. These eleven films are: *4
Little Girls* (1997), *All My Babies* (1953), *Into the Arms of Strangers: Stories of
the Kindertransport* (2000), *Crisis: Behind a Presidential Commitment* (1963),
*Felicia* (1965), *Growing Up Female* (1971), *High School* (1969), *Hoop Dreams*
(1994), *The Jungle* (1967), *The March* (1964) and *Paris Is Burning* (1990). It is
noteworthy, given the general under-representation of black lives on
film, that eight of these eleven films deal with black life in the United
States and the impact of racism on black people's lives. Even *All My
Babies*, a film about midwifery in a black community in the South, was a
response to the higher mortality rates of black infants, which were themselves an effect of racial capitalism. The exceptions are *Into the Arms of
Strangers*, *High School* (although there is discussion of racism in this film),
and *Growing Up Female*. Four of the films focus specifically on racism and
desegregation: *4 Little Black Girls*, *Felicia*, *The March*, and *Crisis*. Since
school desegregation was such a critical event in the involvement of
young people in the struggle against racism in the United States, I also
included the Academy-nominated film directed by Charles Guggenheim,
*Nine from Little Rock* (1964) and his earlier film about school desegregation, *A City Decides* (1957), neither of which have yet made it into the
Registry. This chapter analyses in depth seven of these films.[1]

## DOCUMENTARY FILM GENRES

Stella Bruzzi argues that conventional approaches to documentary film
history, which construct a kind of 'family tree' or genealogy of the form,
overstate or simply misrepresent a trajectory of development that moves
from the expository to the performative over time (2000:1). Her argument
is certainly borne out in the analysis of children in social-reform film
where several different genres of documentary film were circulating at

the same time, deploying very varied approaches to narrative structure and the relationship between reality and representation. Robert Flaherty, who is often cited as the founder of documentary filmmaking, continues to be associated with what John Grierson (who coined the term *documentary* and is regarded as the founder of British social realist documentary) approvingly described as the 'creative treatment of actuality'. In this definition, Grierson wanted to distinguish Hollywood feature films from other films that were nonfiction but were not newsreel or archive film and that included some fictional elements. He claimed, 'Documentary, or the creative treatment of actuality, is a new art with no such background in the story and the stage as the studio product so glibly possesses' (Grierson 1933:8). Clearly Grierson wants to put distance between Hollywood film (the 'studio product'), the novel and other textual fiction forms, and theatre (likely, especially melodrama).

This insistence on the distance between documentary and fiction film nonetheless hints at an underlying unity between the two; there is no need to disavow an object that shares no genealogy with the 'pure' object. Documentary film rested on the development of a new technology, but it tells stories that borrow their narrative structures precisely from the 'story and the stage' (Grierson 1933:8). Nor can its attention to social change or social problems put distance between itself and the studio film. As is now widely recognised, melodrama in Hollywood film frequently invokes the broader social structures that shape personal frustrations and failings. As a genre of narrative storytelling, documentary film shares many characteristics of the studio film, particularly when it makes use of melodramatic music and visual metaphors to carry a larger story about oppressive social structures without referring directly to them. The space between documentary and melodrama is therefore not as broad as Grierson would have liked it to be.

Documentary filmmakers also want an audience, and this requires that the documentary film borrow from other modes that audiences are already familiar with. From social-reform photography, documentary film inherits a combination of the evidential quality of the filmic image and the address to a sentimental spectator, who is empathetic to but usually does not share the specific experiences that are depicted in the documentary.

## SCHOOL DESEGREGATION

By the mid-1950s, the child had been the target of several social-reform campaigns and a distinct visualising of particular development pathways necessary for the child and therefore the nation to fulfil its future potential. Nonetheless, it was not until the 1950s that the adolescent or teenager emerges as an object of concern. Previously, most child reform campaigns focused on the vulnerability and dependency of children made to grow up before their time or exposed to hazards not of their own making; it is in the 1950s that the young adult comes into focus as both a social problem and an index of future potential for both the individual and the nation. Documentaries about racism and specifically about school desegregation visualise the comforting but unwarranted idea that young people are more inclined towards equality and less inclined towards discrimination and prejudice than older generations. This of course situates racism as a psychological effect of social and cultural segregation rather than an ideology enforced by economic and political structures.

One of the iconic images in US visual culture in its intersection with social-reform agendas and the figure of the child is the image of Elizabeth Eckford walking through a crowd of threatening white teenagers and adults as she enters Little Rock Central High in 1957. The desegregation of Little Rock High took place three years after the decision in *Brown v. Board of Education* that segregation was unconstitutional. The NAACP, who sponsored the *Brown* case, recognised the power of the child as a symbol of both innocence and the imagined future of the nation.

Despite the still contemporary power and legibility of that image, there has been surprisingly little written about the visual culture of school desegregation. Melinda M. Schwenk, in a paper on USIA documentary films and the 1957 Little Rock integration crisis, cites Branch's observation that 'the prolonged duration and the military drama of the siege made Little Rock the first on-site news extravaganza of the modern television era' (Branch 1988:223 cited in Schwenk 1999:289). The power of this visual spectacle to condense the violence of white supremacy and its continued practice in the United States nearly a century after the end of the Civil War and the abolition of slavery contrasted with USIA's attempts to position the United States as a multi-racial and tolerant country. Schwenk cites the USIA endorsement of photographer Edward Steichen's 'The Family of Man', an exhibit of 503 photographs from 68 countries intended to demonstrate the fundamental unity of human cultures, as part of this strategy of projecting the United States as a diverse and equal society. The Little Rock images ran counter to the US government's foreign policy strategy and the public image it wanted to project on the international stage. In recognition of this tension between how the United States wanted to project itself on the international stage and its continued federal- and state-level racism, both structural and interpersonal, the US government banned the domestic distribution of USIA films intended for foreign audiences. It is noteworthy that *Nine from Little Rock*, despite its Academy Award nomination, has not been included in the National Film Registry. The only films about this defining event in US history are *Crisis*, which emphasises the president's role in desegregation, and a white graduate student's film *Time of Dreams* (1976) about how white residents in Greene County, Alabama, felt about desegregation.

The director of USIA's motion picture service from 1962 was George Stevens Jr., the son of Hollywood film director and producer George Stevens. Stevens commissioned a documentary on the Little Rock Nine from documentary filmmaker Charles Guggenheim who had previously produced *A City Decides* (1957), about school integration of a previously all-white St Louis neighbourhood (Schwenk 1999:293). *Nine from Little Rock* makes no direct critique of the Arkansas state government other than a statement about 'the politician who encouraged the mob', and Schwenk argues that this was because 'a USIA film could only indirectly charge the Arkansas state government with impeding the nation's civil rights progress' (1999:294) (an earlier film on racism in the United States that Stevens commissioned was never released, probably because it endorsed or encouraged civil disobedience by civil rights protestors).

Most of *Nine*'s narrative is carried by voiceovers; while these are attributed to the Little Rock Nine, the narrative was actually dubbed by professional actors in St Louis (Schwenk 1999:295). This was conventional practice in documentary film in the 1950s, which rarely used direct speech from the film's protagonists.

Schwenk also mentions that Pierce told her in an interview that an incidence after filming in which he (who is white) and Elizabeth Eckford were refused service at a restaurant in Xenia, Ohio, influenced his editing and music score choices for the film to downplay 'the nation's progress towards racial equality' (Schwenk 1999:296).

*Nine from Little Rock* opens in the style of a film noir. Dramatic music plays as the camera pans from shadows on the lawn to an imposing, classical building. The film title, in capital letters, appears across the screen as the camera pans up and out. The opening credits appear over a shot of a wire fence in front of grass, signifying perhaps very literally the boundary that separates 'the Nine' from the green grass of a quality education. Yet as the camera pans up, a young black man dressed in a suit and tie, hands in pockets, walks towards the camera across the grass. He is clearly on the inside of the school boundary. This shot prefigures the incoherence of the film's narrative. A head-and-shoulders shot sharply defines him, and the wire fence now appears both larger and also behind him. A voiceover begins to narrate: 'Where do you begin? Where do you look?' The man turns his head to the left looking down, a look that signifies recollection, and the camera cuts to a running track as the narrator continues: 'Like an ancient battlefield the ground is silent although people still move in familiar places'.

The narration is ponderous, voiced by an actor who sounds considerably older than the youth on camera. The reference to 'an ancient battlefield' is a metaphor that aims to place desegregation outside of contemporary time. On the track, three young men or boys are jumping hurdles; a black boy is ahead in the race, two white students behind him. 'Now on this field Negro and white run together, remembering not how it was in

Little Rock, Arkansas in 1957'. The camera cuts back to the suited youth, who is now leaning against a fence, arms crossed. A fade shot, signifying personal memory, has a white runner cross the screen over his face, the image superimposed over the young man's face, and a second later, a black boy runs across the screen wearing white running clothes. 'Perhaps it is best for those today to look where they are going and not where they have been'; the camera follows the black runner as he runs around the track. The narration continues: 'When you're a dark man in a country where the Negro is demanding more and more an equal chance' (camera frames the runner in a half body shot, head up, clearly in movement and looking forward) 'you have the right to look back to discover if you are really moving forward or if the world is just moving beneath your feet' (1:30). This narrative framing, delivered in a ponderous tone that suggests authority and clarity, is ambiguous, at best. It wants to establish the racism it is about to show is in the past ('where they have been') but also seems to question if this is really progress or an appearance of progress as the world moves 'beneath your feet'. It is hard to know exactly what is intended by the second clause: 'if you are really moving forward or if the world is just moving beneath your feet'. As his memory of running the track fades, the camera returns to the present moment and the camera again frames the man in a suit, now looking forward and up while he says, 'I have a special reason for looking back, my name is Jefferson Thomas' and 'I'm one of the nine from Little Rock'. The camera now frames the front of the school. The next few minutes are archive footage of black students entering the school while a crowd of whites, men and women and children, jeer, and the white police push back the crowd with their batons. The crowd of whites surge forward, and as the police push back, the press cameras are visible in the foreground. The pace of the music speeds up; high notes convey the terror of the scene. Despite the size of the white crowd who are either openly hostile or appear to be experiencing this event as a form of entertainment, the narrative voice, supposedly of Jefferson Thomas says: 'There was a minority in our state who found it to their advantage to bring hate to Little Rock in 1957' (2:25). Jefferson says, 'We watched as the white children went to school and we stood outside' (2:39). As he says this, the screen fills with an image of a white boy raising the US flag and Arkansas state flag up the school flagpole. Several scenes then show the US Army marching, and then several show a white family's house, or perhaps a group of young whites on the veranda of a black family's house. A young white woman holds her hands over her face; it is not clear whether she is shielding herself from the camera or she is shocked or crying. Scenes of young white soldiers pointing bayonets in the backs of equally young white men follow. As the actor says the names of the Little Rock Nine the camera shows them all coming out of a building together and getting into a US Army car with a military escort. This section ends with the narrator commenting that people would be watching to see if we would 'live up to our new opportunity', asking 'How would history judge us?' —framing desegregation not as the correction of a historic injustice that merely gives black students their due, but as a 'new opportunity' that they may not be proved worthy of.

Milliejean Brown-Trickey is the first to narrate her story, but the film does not mention her name. She was suspended from Little Rock for dropping a bowl of chilli on two white boys who were harassing her and then expelled after she called a group of girls who threw a bag of combination locks at her 'white trash'. Perhaps the difficulty of incorporating the racism that Milliejean faced from the head teacher of the school is too disruptive to the narrative of progress and gratitude for her to be named, so she is never in fact introduced except that she says 'I was the eldest one'. She is shown at Illinois University; her social milieu as it is depicted in the film is mostly white people, and her only comment about racism is that she has learned things that have helped her to 'come to terms' with herself and that she now understands why 'some Americans act the way they do'. The camera pans down to the ground and the muddy water at the edge of a lake: 'I know now that some Americans have a fear of the Negro, a fear born of a way of life that has been dead in this country since the end of slavery' (7:30); 'that's what the mob in Little Rock was afraid of, that the negro that had done so much with no chance, might do so much more with an equal one'. The image is appropriate, for the script is certainly muddying the waters here. The 'way of life that has been dead . . . since the end of slavery' is presumably not slavery (which would be tautological) but segregation. The fear, that this has spawned, the film implies, is of the unknown other (unknown because segregated). This is a dominant theme in desegregation narratives, entirely ignoring both the fact that white people were around black people all through slavery and that the reversal of Black Reconstruction and the enforcement of segregation through terror and so-called Jim Crow laws continued after slavery and into the period that is reflected on in the film (1957 to 1964, with the Civil Rights Act still four years away). As 'she' says this (again, the script is narrated by an actor), the film cuts to her sitting at a picnic table with three friends. A young black man to her right opens a bottle of Coca-Cola and several other empty Coke bottles are visible on the table. The use of heavy-handed metonyms was also a feature of Guggenheim's earlier film *A City Decides*. Here, Coca-Cola bottles stand in for the American way of life and freedom (Chidester 1996:750). The group of friends are laughing together, and a cut shot shows the other half of the table is also full of laughing students, black and white, women and men. The music score reflects the light-heartedness of this day of cycling in the Illinois countryside.

The film then returns to the school. The school bell rings, and students are leaving classrooms and walking along the corridor. Jefferson stands against a wall as they file past. He looks over their heads towards the camera, making him a ghostly presence in the hallway, apparently unseen by the other students. He introduces Elizabeth by noting that the rest of the Nine went to predominately white colleges, except for her. The film takes up her story as she explains that she attended Central State College, which was founded as an all-black college but is now integrated. News footage shows her walking alone 'that morning', followed by the mob and the press as the National Guard troops look on. This seems to be the morning before President Eisenhower made the state governor stand down the National Guard. Although the events leading up to the US Air Force defending the Nine are not recounted in the film, we know from other sources that Elizabeth Eckford missed the instruction from the NAACP organiser to join the group and enter the school by the back door; consequently, on the first attempt at integration she tried to enter through the main entrance and was alone. The film then focuses on a large circle of predominately black students at her college, their arms around one another, singing what is probably the college anthem ('for God, for Central'). The camera picks out an Asian woman and two white students in the group. In a scene remarkably similar to one in Spike Lee's *School Daze*, a group of college boys with Alpha Phi on their baseball-style jackets sing an R&B song a cappella. As other students join in, the camera focuses frequently on a white woman clapping and singing with the other students. The voiceover, narrating the integration of the college seventeen years ago when it 'opened its doors to whites', comments that although 20 per cent of students and faculty are now white, there are still those who are against integration because 'the Negro is like most Americans possessing no monopoly on tolerance and hoping that the few, who are not informed, will not be confused with the rest of us' (10:44). With this dissembling of the equivalence between the reluctance of some students at a historically black college to integrate and the violent and threatening behaviour of the white crowd at Little Rock, the film returns to Jefferson who is still watching the crowd move through his old school.

As Jefferson moves through the crowd and starts upstairs, he looks over the stair rail, and the narrator says, 'Four years ago a Negro walked these halls in fear. Some of the hate outside had come inside. And there were a few who tried to impose their will on the many' (11:14). In a scene that again dissembles the terror of racism, Jefferson is apparently confronted on the stairs by a white student who says, 'Can I help you?' Jefferson responds: 'I'm looking for Miss Poindexter's room' and the white student replies, 'That's room 214'. While this exchange is presumably supposed to display the anachronistic character of Jefferson's fears, seven years later, it also conveys the terror of walking up the stairs (Elizabeth was thrown down the stairs by white students, a fact not mentioned in the film). Although Jefferson does not look older than the boy who asks the question, the question itself implies that Jefferson does not belong there. The white boy's utterance 'Can I help you?' is also the first direct utterance in the film; when Jefferson starts to reply the camera cuts away from his face to his hand griping the banister of the stairs. The camera returns to his face as he says, 'Thank you very much' and slightly laughs, at his own error in imagining the boy was being threatening or confrontational.

Thelma's story is very short. Her comment that she wants to teach children because they 'accept me for what I am' continues the veiled discourse of the film about racism. She is shown playing with a small white boy, in an early (and historically inaccurate) rendition of the trope of the racial innocence of the white child.

Ernest Green is shown handing out leaflets; he says he wants to graduate college and become a civil rights organiser because 'even in the northern states you find pockets of discrimination, like you do all over the world' (13:59). The film pans a group of young people, who are predominately white. The civil rights song 'We Are Soldiers in the Army'/ 'Freedom Song' plays, but the group are not singing; they are simply looking ahead. A young woman holds a poster that says 'GIVE NAACP FUND DRIVE'. The film cuts to Ernest giving a lecture in a lecture hall of college students; the camera pans the group, mostly white students, and frames a black student who looks annoyed, perhaps bored, or perhaps sceptical. The narrator, speaking in the first person says, 'A white American can never fully understand what motivates the Negroes desire for equality but the white American is becoming more concerned, especially my generation and that makes tomorrow worth dreaming about'. Several scenes show large computers generating reports, a montage intended to signify the possibilities of a science of society to advance racial equality. The film ends as the camera pans across the city to focus on city hall, and the narrator closes with 'It taught all us Americans that problems can make us better, much better' (18:10).

Many of the themes, framing and editing in *Nine from Little Rock* are rehearsed in Guggenheim's earlier film *A City Decides* (1956). *A City* is framed around the story of school integration in St Louis following the Supreme Court's 1954 decision. The dialogue is primarily narrated by a scripted voiceover presented by a local schoolteacher. Its basic storyline is that in the past, white youth were aggressive towards black youth and children because they did not understand them and that this aggression was a consequence of school segregation. This is carried by an image of a white youth pushing over a small black boy who is flying a kite. The words of the Supreme Court on the impacts of segregated education on black children and how it 'affect[s] their minds' is spoken as this white character's face fills the screen, the implication being that it is not only black children who are harmed by segregation. School desegregation is shown as having been carefully prepared for through parent meetings

and the support of religious organisations. On the first day of integrated
school, the press and police keep a low profile, and all goes smoothly.
While at first, black and white students sit in blocks in the same classroom, as the weeks go by, the arrangement of students in the class becomes more integrated. But there has been an incident, and we see the
schoolteacher waiting for a white student, Vince, who refuses to talk and
who has clearly been beaten up. So the violence of desegregation is not
experienced by black children but by a white boy. Unlike *Nine*, which
attempts to achieve narrative coherence through having one black character present the story of the other eight, *A City* centres on one story: a
white schoolteacher's perspective of school integration. This gives the
storyline more narrative flow than *Nine from Little Rock* achieves but also
highlights the failure of *Nine* to present the political organisation of the
NAACP and the nine students as a group rather than a loose collection of
individuals. It strips away the black self-organisation that made integration possible, leaving only, important as that was, personal acts of courage. The presentation of American racism as a story of intolerance for
others who we do not know, and therefore fear of one another, and which
equally affects white and black students, is as dominant a thread in *A
City* as in *Nine*. This is carried more strongly in *A City* because the basic
storyline is that a white student gets beaten up by a group of black students after he accidentally shoots his water pistol at a black girl. The
narrative of *A City* being provided by the white teacher's voiceover and
entirely privileging his perspective on school integration collapses racism
into a psychological error and erases the history of struggle that eventually led to the Supreme Court decision. Furthermore, St Louis is depicted
as a city that was integrated long before the Supreme Court decision
through camera shots and voiceover showing a pre-1954 integrated Cath-
olic school, a teachers' training college, and so on. Consequently, the
teacher's desire for integration is rationalised as important for 'efficiency'
(why have two schools when you only need one) and to correct the
psychological error of perception of others arising from segregation.

   *Felicia* (1965) is a short (13 minute) documentary film made by three
young white filmmakers at UCLA. The film scholars Allyson Nadia Field
and Marsha Gordon nominated *Felicity* for inclusion in the National Film
Registry by film. Field and Gordon also wrote the Registry's extended
essay on the film. While the film is not about desegregation, it does depict
the on-going impacts of racism and segregation on young black people's
lives. It also deploys similar tropes to those used in *Nine from Little Rock*
and *A City Decides* about racism being an effect of fear and ignorance.

   The film depicts a girl, perhaps sixteen years old, ruminating on her
life in Watts and the impacts of racism and economic decline on her
community. It was filmed in 1965 shortly before the Watts rebellion
erupted following a police assault against a pregnant black woman after
a traffic stop. The film opens with shots of a swimming pool, a school and

a park all populated by whites, as Felicia says in a voiceover that 'the city is a pretty good place to live in for most people'. The film then shows a train track with a train coming towards the viewer and the film's title: *Felicia*. The tracks literally divide the city between the wealthy and the poor, which in Watts also means the white and the black neighbourhoods. A shot of a single-storey wooden house is followed by a shot of Felicia drying her face and looking at herself in the mirror. (The mirror and face washing is a frequent trope in social-reform films used, presumably, to gesture towards self-reflection.) A shot of Felicia's siblings sitting at the breakfast table is accompanied by her narration saying, 'Peter's that type that if he can't have all of it, he doesn't want part of it. I guess that's why he quit school . . . but now he's coming to his senses and realises that you just can't do it without an education' (2:18). Most of the film is narrated as a voiceover by Felicia with the exception of one scene where she is talking directly to camera, when she speaks about her previous experience of being in a mostly white school: 'Outside when they got with their friends, and I guess the same on our side, when we got with ours, we sort of ignored each other, but I think it was more on their part' (8:05). She describes how the white students were sure they were going to college, but 'on our side', she says, nobody took this for granted. As she walks home from school, we see shots of the dilapidation of Watts, including a scrap metal/used car yard 'right behind the houses', children playing in yards, broken windows, and men standing around in groups, playing checkers. The film ends with a thirty-five-second shot of Felicia walking along the railway tracks away from the camera. Just prior to this she says, 'Perhaps it's too late for the adults, but its not too late for the young generation like myself' (11.30).

Alan Gorg, one of the filmmakers, has said, 'My CLA filmmaker friends Bob Dickson, Trevor Greenwood, and myself, agreed that white people in Los Angeles, who in those days a half-century ago rarely encountered any black people because of the strict segregation in housing and employment, should learn that black people are people' (LOC). In an interview with Field and Gordon, the filmmakers affirm that the expected audience would be a white audience (Gordon and Field 2016:4). This trope, that segregation causes racism because it means that white people do not encounter black people, ignores the extent to which black people continued to be visible to white people because white middle classes depended in multiple ways on the labour of black people. It also elides the violent history of segregation and its constant and active enforcement by white people and the state. This is also a dominant trope in these films, as if segregation was an unintended outcome and not the systematic practice of discrimination.

Although the film was described on its release as about a black girl, Felicia is of mixed race, and her mother, whom she and her two siblings live with, is Mexican American. It is noticeable in the narrative voiceover that Felicia is only explicit about race once, when she speaks directly to camera about her experience of being at a predominately white school. For the most part she speaks of 'the rest' or 'their side' and 'our side' and 'my people'.

UCLA produced the small group of black filmmakers whose output came to be known as the LA Rebellion or LA School. Field and Gordon connect *Felicia* to those films through its 'subject and aesthetic strategies', although its target as an educational film was school and university students rather than the 'largely art and festival film output of the Black filmmakers who emerged from UCLA in the subsequent decades' (Field and Gordon 2016:4). One aspect of the aesthetic that they connect with the subsequent LA School is its efforts 'to give an account of how objects not ordinarily thought of as beautiful could be, thereby rendering the negative aspects of Felicia's environment more poetic'. This 'cinematic rendering of the beauty of the community of Watts was a preoccupation of a number of LA Rebellion filmmakers in the following decades' (Field and Gordon 2016:21). In this rendering of the beauty of ordinary black life, there is also a connection to the documentary photography of the 1900 Paris Exposition.

James Blue's *The March* (1964) is an account of the civil rights movement's 1963 March on Washington for Jobs and Freedom at which Martin Luther King Jr. made his 'I Have a Dream' speech. The speech is included in the film but is muted because of copyright compliance (3:13 to 29:44). Many of the images focus on young people: for example, an extended scene of about one-and-a-half minutes of young people clapping hands and singing 'Eyes on the Prize'. It is noticeable that, despite the marchers (over 200,000 people) being 80 per cent African Americans, as the camera pans this group, it shows about 50 per cent whites; the camera fixes on a young white man, placing him centre frame for several seconds. In fact, there are very few scenes in the documentary that do not include shots of white people. A large group of whites is juxtaposed with a shot of a black man. He is talking into a walkie-talkie. The voiceover describes how if violence occurs, those with walkie-talkies will be able to summon the help of other volunteers; the group of whites are some of these volunteers. A scene on one of the buses bringing marchers to Washington focuses on interactions between blacks and whites. The scenes of preparation for the march, (making sandwiches, making placards, testing the sound system, erecting the stage) all focus on black and white people or on whites alone. A scene of marchers holding hands and swaying while singing 'We Shall Overcome' focuses on a line of young white boys (9:51). The voiceover says, 'We are not going to fight our white brethren with malice . . . we are going to fight them with love. We're going to absorb their hatred in love'. During this speech, the camera focuses on a young white man, then a young white woman, and then a white boy.

THE TERROR OF WHITE SUPREMACY

The documentaries analysed above were all directed during the civil rights movement and were made by white filmmakers and predominately for white audiences. In contrast to their repetition of the idea that racism is a psychological error caused by separation and ignorance, or that white racists were a minority in the upholding of Jim Crow and segregation, Spike Lee's *4 Little Black Girls* unflinchingly demonstrates the constant violence of anti-black racism and the commitment of a majority of whites to maintaining it.

*4 Little Black Girls*, a film about the four girls who were murdered by a white supremacist who placed a bomb in the basement of the Sixteenth Street Baptist Church in Birmingham, Alabama, opens with archive footage of black children at demonstrations and of the parents of the murdered children at their funeral, intercut with images of four gravestones and photographs of the girls. The soundtrack opens with Joan Baez singing 'Birmingham Sunday' over archive footage of black children being attacked by police dogs: 'And the choir kept singing of freedom'. The song continues to play throughout the film. The introductory sequence lasts for four minutes and ends with a shot of the memorial with the names and photographs of the dead girls and the inscription 'In Memory of Denise McNair, Cynthia Wesley, Addie Mae Collins, Carole Robertson. Their lives were taken by unknown parties on September 15, 1963, when the Sixteenth Street Baptist Church was bombed. "May men learn to replace bitterness and violence with love and understanding"' (4:12).

**Figure 3.1.   A young boy, sitting on an adult's shoulders, looks over the heads of the crowd in James Blue's *The March* (1963).**

The film mostly consists of interviews with the parents, siblings and friends of the murdered girls interspersed with interviews with civil rights organisers and archival footage.

It begins with Denise McNair's father and mother talking about how they met at university and got married and then moved back to Denise's mother's home city, Birmingham. The interviews are filmed in close-up, the image tightly framing the face of the speaker, intercut with film of photographs from family albums. After Denise's parents and aunt speak, at 7:22 we see a train track, the sound of the train horn, and the train moving towards the camera; this brief scene ends with the camera focusing on the railroad crossing. The soundtrack is jazz. Denise's father starts to speak of his impression of Birmingham when he arrived there in the late 1950s and the difficulty with finding white-collar work as a black man in a blue-collar town. This scene is followed by Arthur Hanes Jr., the circuit judge and defence attorney for Chambliss, the white supremacist and KKK member who was eventually charged and found guilty for the murders, talking about Birmingham as a steel town that grew rapidly, earning it the sobriquet 'Magic City'. Hanes's happy recollection of the city's development is followed by shots of photographs of lynched black men, their white murderers surrounding them and looking straight at the camera, and images of water fountains labelled 'colored' and 'whites'. The archive footage cuts to another white interviewee, *New York Times* journalist Howard Haines, talking about the history of violence against workers in the city condoned by the police and US Steel, combined with 'rural racism coming in from the countryside . . . traditional Old South racism'.

This summary of the terror of Jim Crow is followed by a clip from Chambliss's defence attorney commenting: 'With that background [of rapid growth] the 50s were a time of quiet here'. His positive assessment of Birmingham continues and is intercut with archive footage of racist violence: a white girl wearing a KKK hood / 'Wonderful place to live' / the rest of the KKK march the girl is on comes into view / 'and raise a family' / a figure, lynched from telegraph wires and a label pinned across the chest 'THIS N . . . VOTED' (8:27). It seems this figure is a dummy, but the shock and threat of the image is still visceral. This montage ends with Carole's mother, Alpha Robertson saying (8:32), 'Birmingham was just, Birmingham'; her pause between 'just' and 'Birmingham' conveying the unrelenting racism of the city.

Reflecting on the difficulty of having to stop your child from using the 'white' water fountain, Denise's parents recall: 'It was an awful time for young people to grow up in this city'. Their recollection of telling nine-year-old Denise that she could not eat at the lunch counter in the department store was a painful moment for them as parents unable to defend their daughter. This is followed by an extended sequence of people talking about how black neighbourhoods, churches and homes were regularly bombed by white supremacists, recollections that stand in stark contrast to the DA's complacent assessment of Birmingham as a 'wonderful place to live'.

At about thirty-five minutes, the documentary begins to focus more on the organisation of black people, and especially children, against racism and for their civil rights, situating the murders of the four girls in the context of white supremacist terror, segregation and Jim Crow, and also of an act directed at civil rights organisers and the children they had mobilised. In 1957, the evening news carried footage of a black organiser, Fred Shuttleworth, being violently beaten by young white men with chains outside of the high school were he had taken his children to integrate the school. Images from 1961 show the burned-out buses of the freedom riders, and a photograph of a photographer being beaten by a group of young white men. Commissioner of Public Safety Eugene 'Bull' Conner had a white tank that he drove through black neighbourhoods. The footage shows George Wallace, governor of Alabama, a Democrat and white supremacist, making his inaugural speech in January 1963 before a large and cheering crowd of white people, in which he commits to 'segregation now, segregation tomorrow, and segregation forever'. Underscoring the point of the film that his white supremacist rule was enabled not only by his own ideology or by the endorsement of other white leaders, but also by his support from ordinary Birmingham whites.

From about forty minutes, the documentary hones in on the involvement of school children in the civil rights movement. The organiser James Bevel speaks about how he recognised the power of organising youth, including school children. Bevel's point was that if children 'were organised you would have the whole African American community involved'. Another organiser (uncredited but probably Dr Rev Ralph Abernathy) says, 'When young people today ask me when are we going to be able to get together like you all were in the sixties? Nobody was together in the sixties. It was a small group of dedicated people who got it started, and then the kids took it over' (44). The strategy of involving school children in political organising was very controversial. Young children were taken to jail for five days. At a demonstration in Kelly Ingram Park, fire fighters turned their water cannons on the children, and police dogs were filmed viciously attacking them.

From about fifty minutes, the film intersperses interviews with the parents and siblings and friends about the day of the murders and how they came to hear that the children had been killed, with photographs of the dead girls. Walter Cronkite, CBS correspondent, in a repetition of the theme noted earlier that white people did not know the extent of racism in the United States, comments that 'America understood the real nature of the hate that was preventing integration, particularly in the South but also throughout America. This was the awakening' (1:21). Jesse Jackson argues, 'We transformed a crucifixion into a resurrection' (1:22), but

Figure 3.2. 'And then the kids took it over': Children being led to jail after their arrest for protesting racial discrimination near City Hall, Birmingham, Alabama. *Credit*: Bill Hudson/AP/Shutterstock

somewhat undercutting his claim that the girls' deaths caused real political change, news footage of attacks on black churches follows, and Jackson comments that 'they are burning churches again'. Another interviewee, Rev Reggie White, says that twenty-two churches in the South have been burned since 1994.

The film ends with each of the parents talking about how they have managed to survive their child's murder 'and go on and live'. The film ends with Chris McNair talking about his favourite photograph of his daughter. She is in her nightdress, clutching her doll. He took it with her Brownie camera. The final scene is of a party, perhaps a christening party: children holding gifts, adults dancing.

*4 Little Girls* is a tragic documentary. Although it ends with the hopeful words of Mrs Alpha Robertson, 'I have something to be thankful for after all', its unflinching portrayal of racist America, then and now, leaves little room for political optimism. Unlike the other films discussed in this chapter—which seem primarily aimed at reassuring whites that racism is something in the past, a psychological error and a position subscribed to by a minority of whites and, in any case, an attitude that black people were equally susceptible to—*4 Little Girls* speaks to a black audience. It has no need to soften the blow because the audience that the film primarily addresses has already experienced what it depicts. Yet it also does more than witness their pain—in its footage of police attacking black children, of the 'commissioner for public safety' driving through black neighbourhoods in a white tank, of the governor of Alabama committing to 'segregation forever'—it depicts the political and economic structures that are invested in the continuation of racism. The violence that black children and youth have endured carries over into the representation of black life in the United States in fiction film (see chapter 5) and the importance of death and injury to mobilising political support, encapsulated in Jesse Jackson's claim that 'we transformed a crucifixion into a resurrection' and Cronkite's that 'this was the awakening' continues into the representation of political activism by youth on contemporary digital media (see chapters 8 and 9). Finally, and perhaps because Lee's film was made thirty years after the event, Lee avoids the trope that racism will change as a new generation, raised after segregation and therefore not ignorant of one another, comes into adulthood.

## CONCLUSION

This chapter has shown how the representation of children and youth, and the new generation of filmmakers, followed in part on political changes in the real world that documentary film wanted to record. Children and young people, mostly African Americans, were critical to the success of the civil rights movement. Black children were necessarily at the forefront of the demand to integrate schools. Contemporaneous documentary film, made by white filmmakers, while clearly sympathetic to the demands of the civil rights movement, nonetheless dissemble the involvement of whites in upholding white supremacy and racist terror. The similarities among the disciplined, educated youth of the Paris Exposition (discussed in the previous chapter); the presentation of the Little Rock Nine; and the children in *A City Decides*, *Felicia* and *The March* in this chapter are very striking and clear. No less striking is the contrast between Spike Lee's documentary and these earlier documentaries. Lee is not explaining black people as people for white audiences in the way that the other documentarians here do. Nor does he want to obscure the fact that anti-black racism had the support of a majority of the white electorate. But there is also, arguably, a return in Lee's film to a politics of feeling. In 1977, Robert Chambliss was charged with first-degree murder. Howell Raines says that Chris McNair was given the post-mortem photograph of his daughter after she was murdered because 'they wanted the jury to see the loss of a parent' (1:29). Lee's film presents the story of racism, of the organisation of children and youth against racism and for their civil rights, but he also chose as his vehicle to do this the murder of four girls and, in choosing to include Cronkite's assessment, he takes this murder and the feeling it finally evokes in white people as 'the awakening'.

# NOTE

1. I could not include *Crisis* because it is not currently available in the United Kingdom.

# FOUR

# The Melodrama of Being a Child

## NGO Representations of Poverty

The core aim of international nongovernmental organisations (INGOs) is to address the causes of poverty and to ameliorate its effects. In this aim, they are caught between the apparent intractability of poverty in developing countries and the necessity of convincing their donors that the funds they provide will make a difference to the lives of the poor. This chapter explores the mode or genre that INGOs deploy in campaigning to increase awareness of the impacts of poverty on children and to raise funds for their work in alleviating childhood poverty in developing countries. I focus specifically on children because of the central place that the figure of the child continues to play in representations of poverty disseminated by INGOs, notwithstanding a putative shift in the sector from child saving to child rights.

The three INGO campaigns discussed in this chapter were chosen because of the different niches that they occupy in the landscape of humanitarian aid. Save the Children Fund (SCF) is one of the 'big five' INGOs that together account for over 90 per cent of funds mobilised by this sector. Plan International is a smaller child-focused INGO that relies largely on child sponsorship for their income. Plan International differentiates itself from World Vision (who also rely on child-sponsorship funds) and Save the Children (who also focus on children) by its support for a rights-based approach to including children in development. Action Aid, another INGO, differentiates itself through its political engagement and analysis. Despite these differences in what might be called the 'INGO brand', I show in this chapter that each organisation deploys melodramatic modes in constructing the narrative arcs of their campaign films.

I explore the potential of this mode for generating solidarity between the spectator and the suffering subject. In developing this argument, I use the term *mode* rather than *genre* to signify the melodramatic conventions that cross both genre and medium (Anker 2005:23; Williams 2001:16–18). In particular, I argue that the visceral emotional response and moral legibility of the melodramatic mode produces an identification of the spectator with the experiences of the suffering subject. Progressive scholars have critiqued this form of solidarity, one based on identification, for its refusal of difference and its narcissism. This critique rests on the assumption that solidarity based on group identification (narcissism) necessarily sets boundaries to inclusion that leave others excluded and thereby reproduces forms of social injury. In this critique, difference should not be considered as inimical to the formation of solidarity (Young 1990). Furthermore, melodramatic modes and INGO campaigns of the type analysed here have been criticised for simplifying the structural issues and eliding the broader structural context that causes poverty and hunger (Anker 2005; Chouliaraki 2010:107–14; Kakoudaki 2002; Siomopoulos 2006). In contrast, I argue that melodrama directly confronts the emotional and ethical question of what kind of world we want by making visible the injury wrought by social inequality in ways that elicit a visceral response (Butler 2004:128–51). Indeed, melodrama has been one of the most important cultural forms for giving expression to the felt experience of class, racial and gender injury (Siomopoulos 2006:179) and for engaging working-class audiences. It has done so since its inception in early nineteenth-century theatre by simultaneously deploying a Romantic Manichean vision in which good triumphs over evil with realist representations of the privations of working-class life (Holmes 2001:7; Newey 2000:29). My analysis of the following films suggests that the structural powerlessness of the NGO subject, the intractability of their situation, lends itself easily to representation in a melodramatic mode. In these films, which take as their central figure the suffering child, the spectator is invited to identify with the grieving parent who watches their child suffer. The deployment of the melodramatic mode allows a visceral identification with a subject whose life is radically different to that of the putative audience of the film. Despite their differences, the cultural familiarity of the mode in which they are represented, and of the conditioned response to that mode, invite an identification which might otherwise be withheld. Central to the power of the melodramatic mode is its moral legibility; I argue that both the transparent emotional demand made by the figure of the child and the simplicity of the solutions offered to their problems contribute to the moral legibility of these NGO campaign films. Moral legibility is made visible through the actions of the villain who orchestrates the fall from grace of the innocent, undeserving victim. In the NGO films analysed here, I show that the role of the villain is occupied by the unresponsive spectator. The final sequence of a melodrama is the space of return or redemption. This space is occupied by a projection of a different future that will be made possible through the responsive spectator's intervention. In the final section of this chapter, I argue that the criticism of melodrama as a mode or genre that substitutes politics with compassion is misplaced; compassion for distant others may be at least as critical to the formation of solidarity as a politically informed understanding of the structural causes of social injury.

## THE FILMS

I analyse three short NGO films used for campaigning and sponsorship: Save the Children's *A Child Like Asha* from its No Child Born to Die campaign, Plan UK's Sponsor a Child campaign, and Action Aid's *Happy Homes* from its Sponsor a Child campaign. All of the films are available online. These films effectively convey the ubiquity of the melodramatic mode in NGO campaigns and their deployment of familiar tropes of poverty to make an emotional appeal for help with the assurance that 'the solutions are simple'.

The Save the Children film (http://www.youtube.com/watch?v=KvMgtTkVj18) opens with a tableaux scene of a very young child lying almost completely still on a bed. The film is accompanied by plaintive piano music. The camera gradually moves in to focus on the child's face. As it does so, the voiceover says: 'Asha would ask you something if she could. She'd ask you to save her life but she's too exhausted. She's starving. She'd look you in the eye, she'd ask you again. If she thought that someone, somewhere had the heart to help. If Asha could ask you, would you help?' The camera moves closer in and then fades to black. A second later, the voiceover says, 'You can help', and a telephone number appears on a black screen. In the next scene, a naked child is lying on a cloth on a bed, tubes protruding from his nose, a blanket between his legs. The voiceover says, 'You can save children's lives by calling Save the Children today. To help a child survive, will you give just £3s a month?' Scene 3 is a head-and-shoulders shot of a young child wearing a necklace with a cowrie shell. As the infant turns towards the camera, the voiceover says, 'Please give your support today'. The child nods his head, opens his eyes wide and raises his eyebrows as the voiceover says, 'Please/help a child like Asha right now'. The screen fades to black and SCF's phone number appears on screen. In the next scene, a child held in a woman's arms laughs as she feeds her a packet of food. The voiceover says, 'We know what it takes to save a child's life. The solutions are simple'. The scene changes: a boy leans forward to eat from a packet being offered by an unseen adult's hand: 'But we need your help'. Screen fades to black: '£3 can buy the food to keep a child alive'. In the final scene, the first image is shown again. The starving child looks blankly at the camera. The red banner of SCF is shown at the bottom of the screen. 'Asha can't ask you but we can start saving lives. Give £3 a month. Please will you stop children dying? Call 0800 119 4013 and give £3 a month. Thank you'. The music stops, and the child's face stays on screen, completely still for a moment before the screen fades to black.

The Action Aid film (www.actionaid.org.uk) is narrated by the main protagonist, Aklima. She speaks about her transition from a life on the streets to living in 'Happy Homes' supported by Action Aid, and eventually to working in a shop and imagining a future in which she owns an embroidery shop. As she speaks, the film intersperses head-and-shoulder shots of the narrator speaking to the camera with a series of scenes of girls begging, washing pots, living on the pavements in shelters made of polythene. Aklima met her rescuer, who told her about Action Aid. She moved to 'Happy Homes', and the film shows her being taken to a shop in the market and working in a shop. The film ends with the narrator talking to the camera. She is standing in front of shelves of cloth and smiling: 'My name is Aklima Akter Liza. I am Action Aid'. The final scene brightens to white, and the screen fills with text: 'Currently the best option for girls like Aklima is to have a job; otherwise they would be back on the streets of Dhaka'. 'Happy Homes can only offer shelter for girls up to the age of 15. Action Aid wants girls to stay in Happy Homes until they are 18'. The music stops as the Action Aid logo fills the screen.

The Plan UK film (www.youtube.com/watch?v=doYW55UXbYo) opens with a girl sitting on a bench in front of a hut looking through a photo album. The narrator says: 'For too many girls like Adisa, childhood brings few happy memories'. As the narrator continues, a series of images are shown with statistics written over them: a girl carrying water/ 'they don't go to school, instead they fetch water'; a girl wearing a white cardigan and an elaborate necklace/'they get married young'; a young girl holding a baby/'and often die giving birth. Girls like Adisa want someone that believes in them'. The film returns to the girl looking at the photo album in which she is looking at a photograph of the previous scene: 'they want a plan'. The scene switches to a white woman sitting at a table reading a folder. 'Call 0800 130 30 11 now and sponsor a girl with Plan'. The woman starts to complete a direct debit form. 'Your £15 a month will go to supporting grassroots projects in her country' (shot of children in school uniforms running across a field towards a school). 'With your support more children can go to school' (shot of children at desks in school), 'have clean water close to their homes' (image of children at a water pump) 'and enjoy a healthy childhood' (image of a child with medic taking temperature). As a sponsor you can encourage her through letters and photos' (shot of girl sitting at a desk writing a letter). The camera pulls back to show children walking past the girl towards the school as the narrator says: 'giving her the confidence to reach her full potential' (shot of sponsor reading the girl's letter). In the final scene, a large group of school children in uniforms speak directly to camera: 'We are the plan'.

## NARRATIVE EXCESS AND VISCERAL IDENTIFICATION

Melodrama developed out of the legal prohibition of speech in popular theatre in eighteenth-century Europe (Brooks 1995). Because of this prohibition, producers were forced to deploy pantomime, with its dependence on gesture and scenery, to convey character and plot development; music (the 'melo' of melodrama) worked with the other nonverbal signs to the same effect. When the prohibition against speech was lifted after the French Revolution, melodrama became *the* popular mode of theatrical representation. Its acuity in conveying the internal struggles of characters through gesture, music and mise-en-scène was important to the adaptation of European melodramatic theatre by silent film (Elsaesser 1987 [1975]; Williams 2001:87). In the transition to talking film, the melodramatic mode remained important for its economy of sign making (Brewer and Jacobs 1997; Singer 2001). Character in melodrama is not expressed through dialogue but through situations, mise-en-scène, action tableaux and episodic narration (Gledhill 1987:23). Through these signs the spectator is invited to viscerally identify with another's experience, particularly their suffering and the incontrovertible unfairness of their situation. The key to melodrama is its moral legibility (Buckley 2009; Brooks 1995; Gledhill 1987; Kakoudaki 2002; Williams 2001), the clarity with which it identifies and differentiates the victim from the villain. The appeal of melodrama turns on its representation of innocence wronged through no fault of its own. Critical to the effective representation of innocence is the powerlessness of the suffering subject; it is the subject's lack of structural power and capacity that signifies the impossibility of being culpable for her own suffering. It is for this reason that melodrama invariably centres on women and children and, to a lesser extent, racialised minorities.[1]

Film scholars have argued that the dependence on nonverbal signs in melodrama is a function of the inability of the narrative to be resolved through action (Brooks 1995; Mercer and Shingler 2004; Singer 2001). This inability arises because of the constraints on the range of action available to the characters as a consequence of their structural position. So, for example, the poor girl who is threatened by a rapacious landlord has limited scope for challenging him because no power stands behind her. The inability of the narrative to be resolved through action generates an excess that cannot be contained within the script and is displaced onto colour, music, gesture and other nonverbal signs. In melodrama, the action is constrained by the passivity and impotence of the victim in her confrontation with villainy and injustice. The realism of the narrative, the child's exposure to hunger and extreme poverty and the urgency of rescuing the child from starvation and privation cannot be resolved within the narrative: an adult sits next to a child but is powerless to stop the child's suffering. The action is externalised to the audience and to the mise-en-scène and music. It is the audience that gasps, shrieks and is horrified by melodrama while the characters themselves are resigned to their fate. Echoing Spivak's famous declaration (Spivak 1988), in the NGO melodrama, the characters cannot speak.

In this section, I explore, through my analysis of the nonverbal signs deployed in these three films, how the NGO campaign film resolves its narrative excess through nonverbal signs that invite a visceral identification with the suffering subjects of the film.

*Colour*

In each of these films, colour is used to signify shifts in the narrative, although none make use of deep, saturated colours that are generally associated with Hollywood melodrama (specifically with Douglas Sirk's films) (Haralovich 1990). *Happy Homes* is mostly shot in naturalistic colour; however, the tones of the first half of the film are less bright than those of the second half. Once the narrative moves into its second half, after the narrator speaks about meeting the women from Happy Homes, the colours are bolder and brighter. Vivid block colours (red and green) are used in the scenes of the girls learning to sew. In the shop where Alkima goes to work, the shelves are stacked with brightly coloured cloth, and a roll of bright red cloth is being cut on the table as the employer and Alkima's rescuer speak. The room where the narrator is shown using a sewing machine is bathed in light. In the last frame, where Alkima is seen striding confidently along, the scene is again brightly lit. Finally, she is shown laughing, against a background of neatly stacked brightly coloured textiles. The scene is then flooded with light and finally black writing against a white background, in contrast to the white writing against a black background that opened the film, signifying a shift from mourning to celebration. The Plan UK film changes from monochrome to colour when the scene shifts from the girl looking through a photo album to the sponsor looking at a folder: from Africa to Europe. When the camera returns to Africa, after the sponsor's intervention, it is now filmed in colour. In both of these films, then, the space of suffering is conveyed through the use of monochrome and subdued colours and the space of redemption through bright, vibrant colours. The use of colour in *A Child Like Asha* is the most ambiguous. In each of the scenes, the main character(s) are wearing or lying on different-colour textiles: purple, lilac, orange and blue are prominent in the first scene, yellow in the second, green in the third, white in the fourth, soft pink in the fifth. While no clear semiotic schema can be discerned in these colours, changes in colour are used to signify a new episodic moment or tableaux (from dying, to sickness, to healing, to healthy, to developing), and these episodic moments are loosely related to shared cultural readings of colour: purple/death, yellow/sickness, green/newness, white/life (Kress and Van Leeuwen 2002; Van Leeuwen 2008).

## Gesture

Gesture is used in these films to give voice to the film's characters who are otherwise literally speechless. In none of the films do the people who populate the narrative speak. In the Action Aid film, the main character speaks, but as she does so, the film cuts between head-and-shoulders shots of her speaking to camera and scenes of poverty that represent the life she once lived. In the Save the Children film, the suffering (and then recovering) children plead with the spectator through facial gestures: opening their eyes, nodding, even raising an eyebrow in a peculiarly quizzical gesture. In the Action Aid film, gestures indicate the shift in circumstances from begging to industriousness. In the first half of the film, the main gestures are those of a girl begging—clasping her hands in supplication, prodding a woman to get her attention, gesturing to her mouth to signify her hunger. The camera focuses on the begging girl's gesturing hands. In one scene, a girl walks along holding a bottle of water and an orange; she is adequately dressed and neither begging, working or scavenging (as the other children in these episodes are). She walks with a pronounced limp, and it is this disability that explains her inclusion in the narrative. In melodrama 'physical disability, operating as a material "mark or sign" within this system, produces emotional meaning that works to reify the disabled as "necessarily" suffering, and thus deserving of others' compassion' (Moeschen 2006:434 citing Klages 1999:17). In the second part of the film, after Alkima's rescue, the film focuses on the girls' hands as they work—learning to embroider or to use a sewing machine. In melodrama, the body itself becomes a gesture made by 'speaking bodies' (Holmes 2001:6) 'whose very physical presence evokes the extremism and hyperbole of ethical conflict and manichaeistic struggle' (Brooks 1976:57 cited in Holmes 2001:6).

## Music

In Save the Children's film, the accompanying music is mournful. In many NGO campaigns, the music tempo shifts at the point when the donor's gift takes effect on the lives of the poor. In the Save the Children film, for example, the spectator might anticipate that the music accompanying scenes 3, 4 and 5—which show that the nutrition paste that Save the Children uses to treat children with malnutrition is effective—would be more uplifting, even exuberant, than in the earlier scenes. The music does change in scene 3, but it does not have the rousing quality of the shift in tempo of, for example, the Plan UK sponsorship campaign film. Similarly, in the Action Aid film, the music stops when Aklima meets her rescuer from Happy Homes and is told about the shelter. It starts again as she begins to speak of her new life. The tempo of the music changes, and although hardly uplifting or exuberant, it has a lighter quality.

Music is a central element of melodrama; before colour film it was one of the main modes of expression through which shifts in pace of the drama, the entrance of the villain, the fall from grace, the redemption or return of the heroine, were signified. Save the Children retains throughout its film mournful, plaintive piano music. In contrast to the Plan UK and Action Aid films—which both follow the classic melodramatic narrative arc from fall to redemption and signify this through changes in the tempo of the music—the pathos of the Save the Children film rests partly in the pathos of its failure to provide a space of redemption or return to innocence for the child in the opening shot. The film both starts and ends with her dying.

## IDENTIFICATION AND THE ADULT GAZE

Williams locates sympathy for victims at the centre of what she calls 'the melodramatic mode' (Williams 2001:14). For Singer, identification is produced in melodrama through pathos, defined as a 'visceral physical sensation triggered by the perception of moral injustice against an undeserving victim' (Singer 2001:44) with whom the spectator closely identifies. The implication here is that the identification is narcissistic—that the spectator identifies with someone like themselves, of whom they can say, 'There but for the grace of God, go I'. It is important that this sense of identification is not abstract or intellectual but visceral. It is the visceral sensation, the heightened emotion and erasure of calculation that contributes to the easy moral legibility that is the hallmark of the melodramatic narrative. We *feel* the injustice, our desire for the injury to be repaired is intuitive rather than rational. The power of melodrama (and the reasons it is viewed with suspicion) is this appeal to bodily feeling over rational thought.

The Save the Children film is surely the most powerful here: when looking at Asha dying of starvation in the opening and closing scenes of the film, it is surely difficult not to experience an intense unease at watching a child apparently dying in real time; presumably Save the Children intends that this unease will mobilise a desire to stop *this* child from suffering. This desire may be overlaid with the awareness that it is unlikely that Save the Children did not save this particular child. The identification asked of the spectator here is surely not based on similarity. The Western spectator will generally not feel that what is happening to this child could have happened to themselves as a child or that this particular injury could happen to their child. The spectators' identification as an adult is not in fact with the child who suffers but with the (unseen) parent who watches their child suffer (Wells 2012). In the Save the Children film, an adult is watching over the child in all but one scene. In the first two scenes, in which the child is dying (scene 1) or critically ill (scene 2), only the arm of a watching adult is visible, increasing the space for the spectator to insert herself into the narrative of the film as the anxious adult watching over their suffering child. In this respect, the Save the Children film is in a classic melodramatic mode; the suffering of innocent (white) children being watched over by their grieving (white) mothers was a staple of Victorian fiction and melodrama. Linda Williams argues in her brilliant study of race and melodrama (Williams 2001:47–48) that adaptations of the anti-slavery story *Uncle Tom's Cabin* and the many adaptations of this story to theatre and film deployed this identification with the pain of loving (white) mothers and dying (white) children to invoke in white audiences empathy with racially victimized black slaves. In the NGO film, or at least this NGO film, European and North American audiences are asked to draw on a melodramatic imagination to map the history of the suffering of mothers and children from the effects of poverty in their historical narratives onto the contemporary experience of African families.

In the Action Aid film, the main character narrates her life story of suffering, rescue and redemption over scenes of much younger children living the life she lived. As with the Plan UK film, we are presented with a montage of scenes of children suffering the effects of living in poverty before being rescued through the intervention of a kindly adult. The identification of the spectator with the adult who intervenes rather than with the suffering child is most explicit in the Plan UK sponsorship film since it is this spectator that the film is directly addressing ('With your support more children can go to school, have clean water close to their homes'). In the Action Aid film, my contention is that the spectator, as an adult, identifies with the adults in the film: the couples being asked for money, the aid worker explaining Happy Homes to a child, Nahid Apa imploring an employer to hire the once destitute Alkima.

## THE SPACE OF ACTION AND MORAL LEGIBILITY: JUST IN TIME AND TOO LATE

Peter Brooks, in his influential study of melodrama, *The Melodramatic Imagination* (1986) [1976] locates the emergence of theatrical melodrama as a response to modernism and, in particular, the loss of faith in a religious order attendant on modernism. In other words, melodrama provides a moral certainty that had once been provided by religious faith and a political order that legitimated its sovereignty through natural right.

Whether or not we are living in a post-sacred age is debateable; however, moral certitude is widely recognised as one of the defining characteristics of melodrama. Ben Singer, in his study of the relationship of melodrama to modernity, suggests that nineteenth-century melodrama 'filled a psychological need by offering moral certainty through utterly unambiguous designations of virtue and villainy . . . [its] paranoid fixation on the relentless victimization of innocents expressed the inherent anxiety and disarray of the post-feudal, post-sacred world of nascent capitalism' (Singer 2001:11). This moral clarity, or perhaps more accurately the absence of ambiguity, makes melodrama a powerful device for ensuring that the range of possible responses to the image are rather constrained. Even if the spectator does not respond in the way that the melodramatic representation demands, the cultural familiarity of the mode makes it likely that she or he will at the very least know what the expected response is. Linda Williams claims that melodrama is 'a democratic, modern form that believes it is on the side of the weak and oppressed against the power of the strong . . . its key, however is not simplistic "black and white" moral antinomies, but what stands behind them: *the quest to forge a viscerally felt moral legibility in the midst of moral confusion and disarray'* (Williams 2001:300, my emphasis). In her view, melodrama endures, despite criticism both ideological and aesthetic, because it is a 'mode of storytelling crucial to the establishment of moral good' (Williams 2001:12). Similarly, Mercer and Shingler, in their account of the genre, note, among other features, the recurrence of 'obscured (camouflaged) social criticism', and they note that one of the earliest film studies texts on melodrama, Elsaesser in *Tales of Sound and Fury* (1972)[1987] suggested that 'under certain social and production conditions, melodrama could be seen as ideologically subversive' (2004:21). Far from being a degraded form, Gledhill claims that 'melodramas goal of moral legibility asks how to live, who is justified, who are the innocent, where is villainy at work now' (Gledhill 2000:234 cited in Williams 2001:317, fn 25).

These are simple matters to adjudicate on in melodrama, and so it is in the NGO films analysed here: 'We know what it takes to save a child's life. The solutions are simple'. In Save the Children's case, the simple solutions include the provision of nutrition pastes and medicines. In the Plan UK film educating girls is the simple solution to poverty. Is it correct to call these moral solutions; aren't they simply pragmatic or technical solutions to more or less specific (and not morally invested) problems? My argument is that the people in these films are morally invested, and the spectator is interpellated as a moral subject (rather than, say, a political or managerial subject). It is not simply that Plan UK's campaign centres on girls but that girls are represented in development discourse as more ethical and exemplary people than boys are. Happy Homes provides housing for girls; no justification is given for this focus of Action Aid's support. The barely disguised implication is that girls on the street are vulnerable not only to sexual violence but also to prostitution. The innocence of the children—they have done nothing wrong and yet they suffer—is central to establishing the immorality of refusing to help 'girls like Alkima' or 'children like Asha'.

## VILLAINS

Melodrama is not only about wordless gesture and the external signs that convey internal character. The melodramatic mode is concerned with the struggle between right and wrong, good and evil, virtue and villainy. Suffering children unambiguously signifies virtue, but where is the villain in the NGO advert?

Melodrama offers a critique of the worst excesses of economic inequality, but, crucially, it does so in relation to (im)morality rather than (in)justice. In melodrama, the Manichean struggle between good and evil is not so much polarised as twinned. The rapacious landlord is thwarted in his attack on a virtuous woman by the gentlemanly tenant. It is this, I suggest, that offers a clue to who the villain is in the melodramatic narrative of the NGO advert: it is the spectator.

This may seem like a puzzling, even melodramatic, claim. My argument is that the voiceover is addressed to a spectator who, if they refuse the invitation to 'stop children dying' or 'to help a child survive' by giving 'just three pounds a month', will reveal themselves to be heartless, indifferent, and uncaring, substantiating Asha's implied fears that there is not 'someone, somewhere' with 'the heart to help'. The question 'If Asha could ask you, would you help?' is posed not only rhetorically (of course you would help) but also as a moral choice.

The villain in the melodramatic mode is not only the one who refuses to help but also the one who causes the fall from virtue. This begs a further question: Granted that the child is depicted as virtuous, in what sense is her death, which the film anticipates, a fall from grace? Is it that her suffering itself signifies her fall from grace? The suffering child is an ambiguous figure. If, on the one hand, she invites the sympathy of the spectator, Erica Burman has suggested that a kind of rage against the defilement of our psychic investment in and nostalgia for a happy childhood may also be invoked in regarding images of suffering children (Burman 1999). In any event, the implication is that suffering is here a fall from virtue caused by our (the spectators) prior refusal to feed this particular child/children in Africa.

## A SPACE OF REDEMPTION AND RETURN

If suffering and arrested development are the signs of the child's fall from grace, then the home that they return to is signified in the Save the Chil-

dren film by laughter, the presence of a loving mother, and the appropriately developing body. In the Plan UK film the depiction in colour of the
girl's life post-sponsorship signifies the return to a proper childhood, to
education and the anticipation of a future. The space of return represented in these melodramas is the return to our contemporary ideal of childhood. When the advert begins, the child is already distressed; the loss of
innocence has already taken place. We bring to the image of the suffering
child our knowledge of the beginning of their story and anticipate, in the
melodramatic mode, their return to innocence. Yet, in this advert, 'Asha'
is not returned to innocence, and the film ends as it began, with the image
of her suffering body. This is the dialectic that Williams identifies in the
melodramatic mode between 'in the nick of time' and 'too late'; between
pathos and action.

Similarly, in the Action Aid film, an on-going story of other children
who continue to live on the streets, beg, and be hungry is the storyline
that both illustrates and is the excess of Aklima's story. Aklima's space of
return to innocence is signified by the break in the music when Aklima
meets her rescuer. This moment of silence, as if we are holding our breath
while we find out if Aklima will be rescued, is followed by happier music. Aklima says, 'You would not recognise me. I am working now' exactly mirroring the nineteenth-century before-and-after narratives of Dr Bar-
nardos in which organised work for an employer in a trade is the new
start, the making of a respectable child.

## MELODRAMA AND THE EXCLUSION OF POLITICS

Melodrama has been widely criticised for its reduction of politics to eth-
ics or morals. It has been claimed, for example, that the news coverage of
the September 11, 2001, attacks by Al Qaida on the United States deployed a melodramatic mode in which 'designations of right and wrong
became depoliticized because they were codified as universal moral
truths' (Anker 2005:35). It is interesting that the construction of 'universal
moral truths' should be counter-posed to the sphere of politics since it
could equally be argued that universal moral truths are precisely where
the rule of politics can be legitimately grounded (Kelly 2000). If politics is
not about moral decisions about questions of the public good, then what
is it about? Nevertheless, this suspicion of melodrama for its simplifying
of complex causes and its insistence on simple solutions, in short, for its
moral legibility, is a recognised characteristic of critiques of the melodramatic mode.

Clearly melodrama does not offer a deep or thorough analysis of political problems. The economy of the mode in relation to language is what
lends it its emotional power. It works precisely because it does not insist
that for the spectator to really understand what goes on here, she or he

needs to become familiar with a whole history, sociology or political economy of the suffering that confronts her or him in these representations. Melodrama refuses the claim that knowledge is a precondition for action. The epistemology of melodrama is the gut feeling that what the spectator witnesses is wrong. It is this insistence, this privileging of feeling over rationality that has both made of melodrama a discredited cultural form and ensured its central place in popular culture from the soap opera to the disaster film. Given the long history and broad dissemination of the melodramatic mode through different media forms from silent film to the soap opera, it is a fair bet that most spectators will have the genre literacy necessary to understand the form (Kakoudaki 2002:109); it is this which makes melodrama such an obvious mode for NGO communication.

The deployment of the melodramatic mode to discuss political questions has also been criticised for the individual relationship that it sets in place between the spectator and the suffering subject. Here the argument is not so much that melodrama renders the causes and solutions to suffering as legible and simple as much as that the singularity of individual identification is antithetical to the multiplicity of political identification. However, although melodrama's power does rest on its ability to engage the individual spectator in a visceral emotional response with another individual's suffering, both the spectator and the subject are at the same time rendered as one of a multitude of spectators and suffering subjects. The NGO film in melodramatic mode strives to destabilise the solution of public problems through personal recovery by its insistence that the main character in the films is both singular and multitudinous. It is as Boltanski says, that the spectator should be made to feel that 'it is he, but it could be someone else; it is that child there who makes us cry, but any other child could have done the same' (Boltanski 1999:12).

Although many scholars accept that melodrama has generated sympathy 'for disenfranchised political subjects' (Siomopoulos 2006:180), they also doubt the political significance of compassion. Siomopoulos, for example, starkly argues that this sympathy has 'never translated into political progress' (2006:180). Her commentary is on the historical and political context in which the melodrama *Stella Dallas*, about class uplift through marriage by a mill worker, was produced, and she relates its plot to the wider political discourse of the New Deal.[2] She points to the limits of the melodrama for critiquing the underlying structural issues that generate the inequalities and impoverishment of working-class families represented in the film. Furthermore, she argues that sympathy cannot be mobilised for politics because it supports the distribution of public resources on the basis of empathy with suffering rather than entitlement (Siomopoulos 2006:180). She argues that empathy cannot be an effective site from which to base social justice. In support of her argument, she cites Hannah Arendt's commentary in her chapter 'The Social Question' from *On Revolution* (2006 [1963]). However, this is misplaced since what Arendt is arguing in 'The Social Question', is not only that this particular mode (an emotional mode or compassion) of responding to the suffering of poverty is an inappropriate, indeed dangerous, place from which to make political decisions about the distribution of resources, but also that poverty itself is not part of the proper sphere of politics. She claims that nothing 'could be more obsolete than to attempt to liberate mankind from poverty by political means; nothing could be more futile and more dangerous' (2006:104). Arendt's point is not that compassion is less effective than entitlement for resolving the 'social question', that is, the suffering of poverty. Her point, in fact, is that the French revolutionaries insisted that compassion demanded that the poor should have the entitlement of being released from poverty. This fact was so unequivocal for the revolutionaries that it could not countenance discussion and dialogue but should be resolved through violence. Compassion, Arendt says, 'will shun the drawn-out wearisome processes of persuasion, negotiation, and compromise, which are the processes of law and politics, and lend its voice to the suffering itself, which must claim for swift and direct action, that is, for action with the means of violence' (2006:77). For Arendt, revolution should be about freedom and not about necessity. She argues that 'the whole record of past revolutions demonstrates beyond doubt that every attempt to solve the social question with political means leads into terror, and that it is terror which sends revolutions to their doom' (2006:102).

Arendt's argument does not, then, support Siomopoulos's (2006) claim that compassion is no basis for political progress because it refuses the entitlement of the poor or marginal to economic resources. In fact, Arendt is arguing that the poor do not have an entitlement to economic resources. Nonetheless, Siomopoulos's objection to melodrama—that it substitutes empathic identification for entitlement—is widely held. Politics of identification provoke anxieties about how the boundaries of inclusion are drawn (of who the 'we' is that identification rests on). Secondly, emotion as a call for political action is seen as at least potentially reactionary since an emotional response to injury cannot in itself be adjudicated as right or wrong. However, the belief that political claims should be evidence based and rely on rational argument when applied to social injury is also problematic. It assumes that, for example, racism or other forms of exclusion on the basis of (non-)identification arise from a cognitive dissonance and can be corrected through knowledge, information and rational inquiry. However, this simply substitutes information for emotion without addressing the necessity of a dialogue about values, about what kind of world we want (and who the 'we' is that wants this world). Melodrama is at least as capable of forcing us to confront the question of what kind of world we want and whom we stand in solidarity with, as are realist modes that assume this question has already been answered.

## NOTES

1. Although (structural) powerlessness is widely viewed as key to melodramatic victimisation, Linda Williams, in her very influential *Playing the Race Card*, argues that victimhood has become so central to US political subjectivity that subjects who do possess structural power (e.g., white men) have become represented as melodramatic victims. She cites Michael Douglas in *Falling Down* as one example of this and, somewhat controversially, claims that Griffith's racist film *Birth of a Nation* should be read in the melodramatic mode with white men as the suffering subjects.

2. The New Deal refers to a programme of welfare reform and government-sponsored public works in the United States intended to mitigate the effects of the Great Depression of the 1930s and to stimulate economic recovery.

# FIVE

## 'You Need to Be Glad That You Graduated from High School, and That You're Alive at Eighteen'

### Coming-Of-Age in Black Film

The first part of this book (chapters 2, 3, 4) explored the tropes, themes and genres of the visual culture of social reform and its deployment of the figure of the child. Fiction films are directed at different audiences for different purposes. The aim is not (only) to educate but (primarily) to entertain, and the circuits of distribution are commercial rather than public. The subjects depicted on camera and the intended audiences are more or less aligned, and the directors themselves are often young and from the same socio-cultural milieu as the subjects they depict. This chapter and the following two explore what difference these differences make to the tropes, themes and genres that are used to tell the stories of social injustice experienced by young people in the United States.

This chapter is about coming-of-age films by the African American directors who have used this form to dramatize the problem of social, political and/or economic injustice for young African Americans. At the end of chapter 3, I suggested that the contrast between Spike Lee's *4 Little Girls* and the other documentary films dealing with the racist violence that the civil rights movement faced can, at least in part, be accounted for by Spike Lee's political commitments to making films that accurately reflect black American's experiences and that are addressed primarily to a black audience. In this and the next two chapters, I continue to develop the argument that directors and writers who share the experiences they represent on film bring a different sensibility to filmmaking and are addressing audiences that also share the experiences represented on screen.

Of course, I am not arguing that all black (or working-class or queer) filmmakers share the same political commitments. However, I am suggesting that this situated-ness, when invested in films about social injustice and young African Americans, may produce a field that can be called 'black film' or 'black coming-of-age films'.

To develop this argument, I first situate it in the wider debate about whether there is a field of black film and what its parameters might be. I then analyse three genres or themes within black film: racial uplift, Afro-pessimism, and Afro-optimism.

## BLACK FILM

Making fiction film is a costly business. One of the problems with defining black film is what role white studios play in the development, production and distribution of film and to what extent that role compromises the vision of black film directors. While I cannot explore this in depth in this chapter, it is inevitable that, given that the film industry is driven by profit, film directors will find their vision will be constrained to some extent by the need to make a film that will bring in large box-office receipts and, for the most part, that means a film that will attract diverse audiences, including white audiences. While some directors may not want to make large-budget films (although even low-budget films involve significant financial investment), reaching broad national or global audiences usually requires studio support.

**Table 5.1. Select Black Coming-Of-Age Films' Budgets and Box Office Receipts (in millions of dollars)**

| | Release Date | Budget (break-even week) | Opening weekend | Gross (US/Canada) | Gross (world) | Director | Production Company | Distributor |
|---|---|---|---|---|---|---|---|---|
| Precious | Nov. 2009 | 10 (w2) | 1.8 | 47.5 | 63.6 | Lee Daniels | Lionsgate | Lionsgate |
| School Daze | Feb. 1988 | 6.5 (w4) | 1.8 | 14.5 | No data | Spike Lee | Columbia | Columbia |
| Boyz n the Hood | Jul. 1991 | 6.5 (w1) | 10 | 57.5 | No data | John Singleton | Columbia | Columbia |
| Menace II Society | 1993 | 3.5 (w1) | 3.8 | 27.9 | No data | Albert & Allen Hughes | New Line Cinema | New Line Cinema |
| Straight Outta Compton | 2015 | 28 (w1) | 60 | 161 | 201 | F. Gary Gary | Universal | Universal |
| New Jack City | 1991 | 8 | 7 | 47.6 | 47.6 | Mario Van Peeples | Warner Bros. | Warner Bros. |
| Juice | 1992 | 5 | 8 | 20.1 | No data | Ernest R. Dickerson | Island World | Fox Broadcasting |
| If Beale Street Could Talk | Dec. 2018 | 12 (w7) | 0.2 | 14.9 | 20.5 | Barry Jenkins | Annapurna | Annapurna |
| Crooklyn | May 1994 | 14 (no data after w4 – 11.6) | 4.2 | 13.6 | No data | Spike Lee | Universal | Universal |
| Do the Right Thing | Jul. 1989 | 6.5 (w2) | 3.5 | 27.5 | 37.5 | Spike Lee | 40 Acres & a Mule | Universal |
| Fruitvale Station | Jul. 2013 | 0.9 (w2) | 0.4 | 16.1 | 17.3 | Ryan Coogler | Forest Whitaker's | William Morris Endeavor |

| Release Date | Budget (break-even week) | Opening weekend | Gross (US/Canada) | Gross (world) | Director | Production Company | Distributor |
|---|---|---|---|---|---|---|---|
| The Hate U Give | 2018 | 23 (w5) | 0.5 | 29.7 | 34.9 | George Tillman Jr | Significant Productions / Fox 2000 | (WME) Entertainment / Twentieth Century Fox |

Table 5.1 clearly shows how major studio support translates into significantly larger audiences. *Straight Outta Compton*'s box office receipts on its opening weekend were larger than the lifetime earnings of any other film on this list. Its international sales alone at $40 million exceed the lifetime sales of seven of the ten films listed here. *Straight Outta Compton*'s success also points to the importance of the crossover between film and music audiences for generating sales. Casting rap artists and featuring rap soundtracks was a critical factor in the success of the entire body of hood-cycle films (Watkins 1998:188). The drive for this scale of sales is also indicative of the desire of studios to produce and market black film 'not only for black consumption and pleasure but, more important, for white consumption and pleasure' (Watkins 1998:194).

For Watkins, the dependence of studio outputs by black directors on attracting white audiences does not undermine the claim of rap/hood-cycle films to be progressive in their depiction of the struggles of young black people (actually, mostly men) living in violent and poor neighbourhoods. He wants to hold onto the 'labor of ideological struggle' that the films represent and insists on them as 'an important site of youth agency' (1998:195). In contrast, film scholar Jared Sexton has argued that 'to have a black director behind the camera makes no substantive difference to the conventions of Hollywood filmmaking, whether at the level of narrative structure, plot, characterization, or film form' (2009:48). This question of to what extent capitalist appropriation of ideological struggle compromises or invalidates the claims of films or other cultural products to be an expression of resistance has become increasingly significant as public funding for arts continues to contract in the United States (and elsewhere).

If the economic base of black film generates one set of questions about the (im)possibility of an independent critical cultural field, the relationship of representation to reality generates another. As in working-class and queer films, questions (especially in film reviews) about authenticity and reality are routinely posed about 'black film'. It is as if the representation of black life-worlds on film, even on fiction film, is always taken as a quasi-ethnographic practice. As Watkins says about the reception of hood-cycle films, 'In spite of its overwhelming and obvious entertainment function in a vast popular culture marketplace, the ghetto action film is typically viewed by critics, the news media, and filmgoers as an authentic portrayal of ghetto life . . . official transcriptions of the lived experiences of poor black youth' (1998:226). Reviewing *Precious* for the British newspaper *The Observer*, Philip French finishes by saying, '*Precious* ends on an affirmative note. . . . The film does not, however, address itself to any larger social context. We have experienced a story, not read a case history'. While this comment affirms the status of the film as a narrative story, the very fact that it needs to note that it is not 'a case history' paradoxically implies at the same time that, in fact, the spectator might approach it as a case history. The influential film critic Roger Ebert says of Gabourey Sidibe: '[s]he so completely creates the Precious character that you rather wonder if she's very much like her'. Reviewing *The Hate U Give* for the *New Yorker*, Richard Brody says 'its unstinting vigor and empathetic but unsentimental nuance mark it as a distinctive and exceptional political film'. *The Hate* is based on a young-adult novel and centres on the experiences of a teenage girl. Directed by George Tillman Jr (whose previous films include a biopic of Notorious B.I.G.), *The Hate* certainly portrays a contemporary issue of great political significance—the police murders of young black men—but it is not what would usually be called a 'political film', nor can it be situated squarely within a critical or radical tradition of filmmaking since it ends with an endorsement of the police and gives a black character, a police officer and uncle of the main protagonist, a speech defending police killing black people during traffic stops.

The requirement that 'black film' provides a vehicle for representing black people's experiences in a sociological or anthropological way has been central to many scholars' definition of 'black film'. Diawara, for example, notes the importance of realist film in the black filmic tradition (1993:23–25). Wanting to avoid an essentialist definition of black film in which all films by black directors could be incorporated into this genre, scholars have instead focused on particular kinds of representation of black experience as the defining characteristic of black film. In their edited collection on Michael Roemer and Robert Young's *Nothing but a Man* (1964), David Wall and Michael Martin insist on the appropriateness of including this film, directed by two white directors, in the canon of black film. Their reasoning is that it is a sensitive portrayal of black family life in the conditions of racial capitalism. In a similar vein, David Green's *George Washington* (2000) and Quentin Tarantino's *Django Unchained* (2012) have both been cited as black films despite being directed by white men. The former fits into a genre of 'coming-of-age' films with young black protagonists at the centre of the narrative and therefore serves as a comparison with Roemer's *Nothing but a Man*, which could be considered as part of a group of films that depict the impacts on black family life of living under racial capitalism. This could also include (LA School director) Charles Burnett's *Killer of Sheep* (1978) (although it is perhaps a little ironic that *Nothing* is one of the few 'black films' to form the subject of an edited collection). On the other hand, *Django Unchained* is more akin to a Western and revels in its depiction of violence against black people, albeit with a resolution in which the subjugated protagonist, Django, exacts some revenge on the white family who enslaved his wife. Ironically, to the extent that Tarantino manages to pass *Django* off as a black film, it is, I would suggest, because of previous films that were effectively homages to Blaxploitation films, which are often cited as part of the canon of black film because they centred black protagonists although—with the important exception of van Peeples's *Sweet Sweetback's Baadasssss Song* (1971), Gordon Park's *Shaft* (1971) and Gordon Park Jr's *Superfly* (1972)—they were mostly directed and produced by white men (Guerrero 1993:159).

The inclusion of Blaxploitation films in the canon of black cinema implies that 'black film' has more to do with mise-en-scène and plot than with the authorship of the film. In his *Framing Blackness*, Ed Guerrero argues that the Blaxploitation genre was 'made possible by the rising political and social consciousness of black people . . . which translated into a large black audience thirsting to see their full humanity depicted on the commercial cinema screen'. This 'surge in African American identity politics also led to an outspoken, critical dissatisfaction with Hollywood's persistent degradation of African Americans in films' (1993:70). Paula Massood (1996, 2003) points out that the city itself is an important character in black film and is relevant to this centring of mise-en-scène, as is the music of the film (both diegetic and non-diegetic) and the style of the main characters. This works especially well in the context of the United States, where the history of racism and the racial segregation of space in the city creates a site for the staging of African American life in the specific space of urban neighbourhoods. The so-called hood, or ghetto, movies of the 1990s are emblematic of the central role of place, specifically the de-industrialised city, to a subgenre of black film.

## BLACK TEEN FILM

While the majority of the hood-cycle films centre teenage characters, they have a peripheral place, at best, in the main accounts of teen film; indeed, Roz Kaveney specifically excludes them from the genre. The preoccupations of those films, what we might call 'white coming-of-age films', are organised primarily around the school, identify formation and transitions to adulthood. The former is a site that is broadly communitarian, and the latter is circumscribed by a clear trajectory—going to college before getting a job, a house, and a family. Identity formation is represented in these films as something like the development of character ('what kind of person am I?') rather than the defining of social identity. Indeed, the conflict between, essentially, becoming a bad person or a good person drives much of the storyline in teen dramas.

These themes and sites do not cross over easily into black film because of the conditions of life for the majority of black people in the United States. In this sense, the connections between off-screen and onscreen life are impossible to avoid. While the desire for verisimilitude, mimesis, or authentic representation may be both impossible and undesirable, only in post-race films (admittedly a Hollywood staple) can the school be represented as a site of comfort, community, or support for black students in the United States, given the reality of the 'school to prison' pipeline and the role of the school as a prison-like container of black and working-class children. Similarly, transitions to adulthood in the United States are far from assured for young black people, either in the sense of going to college and attaining satisfying work (or any work) or even actually living into adulthood without experiencing or witnessing social, and often personal, trauma (as Ronnie says in *Menace II Society*, 'You need to be glad that you graduated from high school, and that you're alive at eighteen'). Indeed, the impossibility of staying in the neighbourhood while transitioning to a successful adulthood is a key theme in black coming-of-age films. While black coming-of-age films also centre the question of character formation (of what kind of person you are going to be), this is a much more over-determined question for black characters on film because blackness in a racist society more or less aligns with a presumption of being bad, and the good character in black teen film, conversely, displays a heroic or extraordinary kind of goodness.

Teen films are primarily subsets of broader genres, particularly action and romance. Romance is a rare quality in black-teen film. As, more broadly, in the depiction of black sexuality on screen, heterosexual relationships are mostly depicted as coercive and brutal. Mills (2018) talks about the absence of black love on screen, and that critique resonates very strongly in the depictions of black love in teen film: both romantic or sexual relationships and also family relationships.

The close connection between film and music is also a significant feature of black-teen film. This is not only because several directors started out directing music films and then transferred to feature film or even because of the obvious pull of music to teenage audiences (important though both these elements are). It is also, I suggest, because the music, particularly hip-hop, carries the excess of the film's narrative that the story itself cannot carry. It has a similar function to another persistent feature of teen black film, the narrative voiceover.

One scholar has suggested that the voiceover is an aesthetic feature of black film, one that references the oral tradition of early African American communities. While this may be true, the voiceover also enables the director to treat the film as a hybrid form of the epistolary and the dialogic. The voiceover—often taking the form of the reading aloud of a diegetic text (a diary, a letter, even a homework assignment)—carries considerable narrative excess. In many black teen films, very little of the film's narrative conflict is established or resolved through diegetic dialogue; rather, music and voiceover carry the meaning of the main action and its resolution. In *The Hate U Give* the main character sets out, in an extra-diegetic but direct address to the spectator, the problems that she has with reconciling the expectations of her predominately (entirely, apart from her and her brother) white private school and school friends with those of her neighbourhood friends. This conflict cannot be carried through diegetic dialogue and action for the first half of the film because

the conceit of the film is that, from the point of view of the white characters, this conflict is invisible because they don't see race. Therefore, they
do not make explicit demands on her to behave in 'white' ways or understand the costs that would fall on her if she behaved in school in the
'black' ways that her white school friends act out in their performances of
black talk, gesture, demeanour and song. In contrast, when she is with
her cousin at a party in her own neighbourhood, her cousin and her
friends openly (and diegetically) criticise her for acting white through her
dress, style and speech.

## Racial Uplift in Black Teen Film

Spike Lee's *School Daze* (1988), set in a fictional historically black college
in the United States, which has the slogan 'Uplift the race', both centres
and critiques the so-called race man or racial uplift film. The main fault
line between the groups of characters in the film is between respectability
and revolt. The fraternity men, dressed in a quasi-military uniform are in
conflict with the revolutionary men, and this conflict is played out between men over their access to women as well as between women. Re-
formist racial uplift is aligned in the film with light-skinned, middle-class
women who have straightened hair and wear light-coloured contact
lenses, and women who are dark skinned, working class, and have natural hair. In one of the most powerful and disturbing moments in the film,
Spike Lee's character, who wants to join the fraternity, is told by the
fraternity leader, Julian, that he has to have sex with his (the leader's)
girlfriend, Jane. When the camera takes us into the bedroom where Lee's
character and Jane are sitting on the bed, he says, 'You don't have to', and
she says 'Shut up and undress', an exchange that to some extent removes
the charge of rape but retains the sense that women are objects of exchange in the men's 'uplift' politics. Similarly, the girlfriend of the revolutionary character Dap challenges him, asking if he only wants to date
her because it fits with his revolutionary black politics.

In Lubiano's critique of Lee's *Do the Right Thing*, she argues that the
film is 'imbued with the Protestant work ethic' and is arguing that 'these
problems could be averted' if African Americans have jobs and own
property. She finds *Do the Right Thing* 'relentlessly formulaic in its mascu-
linist representations and its conventional Calvinist realism' (1991:266).
While there is no obvious contender in the film for the figure of the 'race
man' of the racial uplift film, the importance of economic security to
political power is as clear in Lee's films as it is in Singleton's *Boyz*, in
which the father, Furious Styles, an estate agent, embodies and expresses
the trope that economic independence, the ownership of land, property
and businesses, is a prerequisite for political power or even just dignity
and security.

## AFRO-PESSIMISM AND POLICE VIOLENCE

In his important text, *Red, White and Black*, Frank Wilderson III coins the phrase *Afro-pessimism* to group together several African American scholars, mostly humanities scholars, who, he says, critique the impossibility of blackness being aligned with subjects rather than with objects. His argument is that since the transatlantic slave trade inaugurated modernity, the attachment of blackness to enslavement cannot be undone within the same order that produced it. The scholars he groups within Afro-pessimism include the film scholars Kara Keeling and Jared Sexton (2010:59). He argues that film theory in relation to black American cinema from 1967 onwards is 'underwritten by a sense of urgency regarding the tragic history and bleak future of a group of people marked by slavery in the Western Hemisphere; this, they would all agree, is the constitutive element of the word *Black*' (2010:59). Black film theory for Wilderson is therefore concerned with 'how cinematic representation hastens that bleak future or intervenes against it' and 'hinges on these questions: What does cinema teach Blacks about Blacks? What does cinema teach Whites (and others) about Blacks? Are those lessons dialogic with Black liberation or with our further, and rapidly repetitive, demise?' (2010:59).

Afro-pessimist political philosophy insists on acknowledging the 'after-life of slavery' in the continued onslaught of the violence of the state in its alliance with capital against black people. Closely connected to this is the failure of contemporary state institutions to protect black people and instead, in fact, to expose them to violence, especially in relation to the police and the judiciary. In film, this theme plays out most obviously in the depiction of police violence.

In *Boyz n the Hood*, the first night that Tre goes to live with his father, their house is broken into. Furious Styles, Tre's father, shoots the intruder, who escapes, leaving behind, like some hood Cinderella, a single trainer. The police are called and two cops—one white, one black—arrive over an hour after the intruder left. The white cop gets out of the car, approaches Furious and asks what happened. Styles says in response that he called 'over an hour ago', the black cop shouts at him 'we didn't ask you that' and comes forward. The white cop steps back from his partner and stands next to the police car looking slightly uncomfortable and even apologetic for his partner's outburst. The black cop tells Styles, 'It's too bad you didn't get [kill] him' and then turns to Tre (age nine) and asks, 'How you doing little man?' Styles sends his son inside the house. 'Something the matter?', asks the cop, 'something the matter?' Responds Styles, 'Yes something's the matter; it's a pity you don't know what it is, brother'.

The fact that in black-white police partnerships, it is the black cop who is unreasonable and violent and the white cop who is a restrained and calm is a repeated trope in Hollywood film. Jared Sexton, in his analysis of Denzel Washington's character in *Training Day*, argues that this kind of depiction is enabled by a 'racial coding of state violence as black' (2009:56) that allows for 'a reorientation of criticism away from the racial state' and toward 'more comfortable and familiar topics' as 'the supposed black propensity toward violence and vice' (2009:56).

In the second half of *Boyz*, which jumps from Tre at nine to Tre at sixteen, Tre and his best friend, Ricky, are driving away from a 'drive-in' meet-up at which—after challenging someone for pushing him into Ricky's brother—Doughboy jumps out to defend him and for a moment Doughboy seems to have won the day; however, shortly afterwards, the gangsta who started the argument shoots into the crowd with a semi-automatic. Everyone scatters, including Ricky and Tre in Tre's father's VW Beetle convertible (itself a symbol of Furious's political commitments). Shortly after that, they get pulled over by the police. The cops are the same pair who responded to the call to the police when their house was burgled seven years earlier. Here again, the black cop is menacing, pushing his gun beneath Tre's chin and threatening to shoot. His white partner stands to the side looking uncomfortable. A call comes in over the radio, and the white cop suggests they should leave. The violence of the cop's demeanour, producing the sense that one wrong move could get Styles (first father, then son) arrested or worse, and the contrast between his behaviour and his white partner's is echoed in other films in this same genre.

The police are in several scenes in *The Hate U Give*, whose central narrative act is the murder by the police of the childhood best friend of the main character, Starr. Here, there is also a scene in which the white cop is less murderous and threatening than the black cop. The scene takes place outside a fast-food restaurant in a mall. The family are celebrating Starr's appearance on a TV show to talk about the police murder of Khalil. They have just said grace, and then the father, Maverick Carter, sees that the gang leader King is in the car park. King has been threatening Maverick and his family since Starr's friend got killed because he fears that Starr's testimony to the police could 'expose' King's drug dealing. King has tried to prevent Starr from going public about the murder and threatened retribution if she did. Maverick goes outside to confront King, but before the conflict escalates further, the police arrive. King and his gang drive off, and Maverick is questioned by two officers; once again, one of the partners is white and the other black. The black cop puts Maverick into a chokehold. He releases him only when the white cop recognises Starr as the witness to the police murder. Here again, it is the white cop who restrains the violence of the black cop.

Starr's uncle Carlos is also a police officer. It is his intervention in the police station, after Starr is taken in for questioning following Khalil's murder, that gets Starr released. Starr and her mother are being aggressively interrogated by two officers about the murder when Carlos comes into the interview room and says, 'Let's go'. The police, clearly surprised, say, 'You know her?' In subsequent scenes, Carlos puts the police point of view to Starr, arguing that the police will inevitably be anxious and act proactively when they pull over a black man, and insists that it is unreasonable to be critical of the police for this 'defensive' reaction.

Indeed, despite the use of Tupac's music and the title itself (a reference to Tupac's 'Thug Life') and the narrative turning on the murder, by a policeman, of the central character's best friend, a young black man, the film is resolutely pro-police and places the blame for the extent of violence and disorder in black neighbourhoods on drugs and the gangs that organise their distribution. At the end of the film, Starr, in a voiceover, says, 'The hate you give? The hate WE give' and then proceeds to make a speech about the community itself being the source of children's exposure to violence. As the camera pans out to a scene of children playing in the street (not unlike the opening scenes of Spike Lee's *Crooklyn*), the voiceover rapidly resolves the contradictions in the plot and sets up a 'happily ever after' conclusion to the film. Central to this resolution is that once the drug lord, King, is arrested and jailed, the community is released from the grip of his violence; they and the police are no longer afraid, and children can play in the street again.

Cultural critic Todd Boyd claims that a new generational shift has occurred in black popular culture 'governed by a hard-core ghetto sensibility that represents a radical break' (Watkins 1998:66, Boyd 1997) from both the 'race man', or racial-uplift films, or what he terms the 'new black aesthetic' of black American bourgeois nationalism. While hip-hop does give expression to black working-class culture, it may be stretching a point to argue that hip-hop cinema is both working class and progressive because, if not in 1997 then certainly by 2018, hip-hop film and music identify the accumulation of private property by individual black people (for the most part, men) as the resolution to the problem of lack of meaningful political power. While the hip-hop films are more or less unapologetic in advocating the accumulation of private property for the sake of wielding political power (within an unreformed political structure) and gaining access to cultural resources (including women), the presumption of the first wave of new black cinema that private property enables black people to have access to economic power that in turn will reform racial capitalism is another kind of black nationalism that may jettison respectability but is otherwise familiar from nineteenth-century discourse about the relationship between economic sovereignty and political power.

## THE COMPANY YOU KEEP

'At some point in your life you're going to have to decide who you's going to be. Ain't nobody else going to do that for you.' Juan speaks this line from *Moonlight* to Little; it is preceded by the line 'there's black people everywhere'. Both statements address Juan's awareness of Little's same-sex desire and try to open up a space for Little to anticipate his desire being acceptable to black people somewhere. The line 'you got to decide who you are going to be' is in many ways emblematic of the coming-of-age film as a genre: it is the core problem that the film sets out to engage and resolve. For characters/film that centre upper-middle-class white lives, this problem is generally engaged in a classic melodramatic mode: the main character falls into bad company, rejects their family, does some (more or less mildly) reprehensible things, and returns by the end of the film to a new recognition of the importance of their family and the love their family has for them. In contrast, in the majority of black films, this structure is almost reversed: the main character 'falls into' good company/habits, rejects their family and/or neighbourhood, and by the end of the film, establishes a new life away from the abject family/ space.

In *Precious*, for example, the eponymous main character lives with her violent mother, who sanctions her boyfriend's (Precious's father) constant rape of her daughter (a rape that we find out at the end of the film has been going on since Precious was three years old). Precious is very good at math, although illiterate. The school expels her when she gets pregnant (it is not at all clear why, given that this is her second child by her rapist father). Because she is good at math, the head teacher gets her a place in an alternative school, 'each one, teach one'. The class is a small group of black and Latinx girls who are trying to get their GED so that they can go to college, having failed at school for various reasons. The teacher's main strategy is to encourage them to believe in themselves, and to write—stories, poems, and so on. This group of girls become Precious's friendship group, visiting her in hospital when she has her baby and throwing a party for her when she comes back. More important though than this group is the teacher who brings them together. The teacher lets Precious stay in her house for a few days after Precious has a fight with her mother that culminates in her mother throwing the television down the stairs, almost killing Precious and her baby. It slowly dawns on Precious that her teacher is a lesbian and this, and the conversation between Miss Rain and her girlfriend the first night Precious stays in the house, is what establishes the difference between her own mother, house and neighbourhood and this one. Precious says in a voiceover: 'Mama say homos is bad peoples. But homos not who rape me, homos not who let me sit up in school sixteen years and learn nuffin and homos not sell crack to peoples in Harlem.' The film ends shortly after that so it is not entirely clear if Precious' future will involve her leaving Harlem, but it is clear that her intelligence, and going to college, is held out as what will enable her to escape the awful violence that she has been continually subjected to.

*The Hate U Give* sets up from the beginning the impossibility of being good and staying in the neighbourhood—either the neighbourhood or the people in it have to be transformed. Here, despite establishing Starr's natal family as an almost model family, her brother's mother is the girlfriend of the drug lord, King. Her uncle is a cop and lives in a very large house in a (presumably) predominately white neighbourhood. Starr's mother wants to leave the African American neighbourhood they live in but in the meantime ensures that her children should at least not go to school there. So Starr goes to a private school, which is entirely white except for her and her brother. In contrast to *Boyz*, though, the transformation of the neighbourhood makes it possible for a good future to be imagined without having to leave. This transformation is enabled simply through the arrest of King.

Paula Massood, in her account of the place of the city in new black cinema, notes that a series of films released in the 1990s and directed by African American film-school-trained directors 'detail the hardships of coming of age for their young protagonists' (1996:85) within the 'specific boundaries of the hood' (ibid.), meaning South Central LA, Watts, Brooklyn and Harlem. This interest in life in poor, predominately black neighbourhoods connects African American film to narratives that are 'deeply planted in the tradition of African American writing dating from the turn of the [twentieth] century' (ibid.), in which the city is simultaneously a utopian and a dystopian space.

In his account of hip-hop in black film, S. Craig Watkins argues, citing Boyd, that 'a new black popular culture sensibility—the new black aesthetic—supplanted the race man ideology sometime during the middle to late 1980s' (1998:567). *Race man ideology* refers to the racial-uplift film where the 'race man' means that the achievements of a black man, typically in education and petty-bourgeois capitalism, come to stand in metonymically for the potential of all black men that is denied through racial capitalism but that can be overcome through a particular projection of respectability. But, at least in Watkins's account, it is not entirely clear how the new aesthetic, which he connects to a black nationalism that flourishes in its access to new cultural resources because of access to higher education, is different to the old aesthetic. It is a third turn that he (and Boyd) connect with 'a hard core ghetto sensibility that establishes a radical break' and the incorporation into black film of a working-class aesthetic.

Coming-of-age stories by African American directors generally share a concern to represent the difficulty of simply transitioning to adulthood for many black youth. Frank Wilderson (2015), in a paper on *12 Years a Slave*, argues that black life in America escapes narrative form because the arc of the story depends on possible resolutions that are not available to black people in the Americas. While this is clearly empirically wrong to some extent, given the growth of a small but often very rich black upper class, it is nonetheless interesting to stay with Wilderson's theoretical frame, Afro-pessimism, to consider what filmmakers and writers do with the impossibility of transition either to adulthood itself or to the adulthood that aligns with the figure of the hero that is central to so much narrative cinema. Ryan Coogler's *Fruitvale Station*, for example, has been criticised for its presumed inability to craft a narrative out of the twenty-four hours prior to Oscar Grant's murder by a BART police officer. Similarly, Barry Jenkins's adaptation of James Baldwin's *If Beale Street Could Talk* (2019) is told as a series of vignettes in the lives of the two central characters, Tish and Fonny. If this episodic form is a consequence of the impossibility of narrative resolution, then it is also possible to consider both *Beale Street* and *Fruitvale*, both of which otherwise have racial-uplift elements, as aligned to a radical staging of black politics within the frame of Afro-pessimism.

In *Fruitvale*, the audience knows from the outset that the main character will be shot on the BART Fruitvale platform in the early hours of New Year's Day. That the film is not only based on a true story but is also the fictionalised representation of the twenty-four hours before the murder of Oscar Grant makes it inevitable that this will be the ending of the film. The fact that it is also the beginning implies, precisely as Wilderson argues, that black life in America is impossible while premature death and violence are non-contingent and unavoidable. The film was released as the trial of a Latino man for the murder of a black boy, Trayvon Martin, was coming to a close—an alignment that also suggests the impossibility of a black-directed film about black life escaping a direct and real-life referent. This impossibility is one of the reasons why black film is invariably held to account for its veracity and authenticity in a way that films by white directors about white lives are not.

*Fruitvale* is a film and not a documentary, yet Ryan Coogler, some reviewers claimed, made Oscar Grant unreasonably saintly in his interpersonal interactions with his mother, girlfriend, daughter, family and even passing strangers. Coogler has said that he wanted to create a representation of Grant that was neither saint nor villain and that these two extremes, both aligned with the question of whether or not he should have been shot, were how Grant was depicted in the press in the months leading up to the trial of the policeman who murdered him. Indeed, while Grant is portrayed as a charming, even charismatic, character, were he a white character, his desire to please his mother, convince his girlfriend to forgive him for his infidelity, play with his daughter, reflect on his time in jail, and in response throw his stash away, would barely be registered and is highly unlikely to be read as an excessive or unbelievable representation of goodness. This charge perhaps also confirms the veracity of the claims of Afro-pessimism that there is no scope within white narrative genres for the lives of black people.

So impossible is black life in a white narrative that even when whites appear in black film, they frequently place black subjects in danger. In the middle of the day, Oscar goes to his old workplace to try and persuade the manager or owner to give him his job back after he was fired for being late. He is also there to buy crabs for his mum's party later that evening. While chatting to his brother, who works behind the fish counter, he starts talking to a young white woman who wants to know how to fry fish for a meal she wants to make for her boyfriend. In reference to this request, Oscar asks, 'Is he black?' She says, 'No, but I guess he knows a lot of black people'. Oscar then phones his grandmother and puts her on the phone with the woman so she can give her a recipe. The exchange seems a little odd or improbable perhaps, while at the same time seeming very plausible in relation to the social norms of low-income neighbourhoods, on the one hand, and the free pass that friendly whites often get in predominately black neighbourhoods. Only much later in the film are the complicated consequences of this exchange fully realised. The woman is on the same train as Oscar and his girlfriend and friends when they return from San Francisco on the BART in the early hours of New Year's Day. When Oscar passes her as she walks through the carriage, she shouts his name several times; he turns and as he does so, another man, whom we have seen earlier in the film in a flashback to a prison fight between him and Oscar, says 'Oscar . . .' and attacks Oscar. It is this altercation that causes the train to be held at Fruitvale while the BART police pull people off the train, and some minutes later leads to Oscar being held down by the police and shot.

White extras in black-orientated films tend to carry narrative significance. In *The Hate U Give*, for example, following a police-instigated riot after a protest against the officer charged with Starr's friend's murder being found innocent, Starr and her brother are picked up by a black man driving a truck. He drives past them as they are running from the police and recognises them as 'Mav's kids'. As they climb into the back of the truck, two random white men, ask 'Can we get in?' and are helped up by Maverick's friend. The only purpose of the scene seems to be to reassure white spectators that they are not being presumed to be racist for being white, or to offer a message: no, not all white people. It can also be viewed as a reassurance to white spectators that the black character they are being asked to identify/sympathise with does not view them as part of a racist structure or racial antagonism. While this might be expected in a film that fits more clearly within a racial-uplift narrative than *Fruitvale* does, there are several scenes in *Fruitvale* that seem to offer this same message; for example, in addition to the white 'fried-fish' woman, on the way into San Francisco, Oscar asks a white man if he has a watch, and Oscar and this man then count down to midnight with the man's watch. This is preceded by a multi-racial crowd having an impromptu party on the train. In another scene in San Francisco, Oscar persuades a white restaurant owner to let his girlfriend and another friend use the toilet and then he also asks the owner to allow a stranger, a white pregnant woman, to use the restroom, too. While they are waiting for the women to return, the white partner of the pregnant woman and Oscar talk about marriage and money, and the white man offers that he did not have any money when he got married and that he stole his wife's engagement ring because he could not afford to buy one—a storyline that is unbelievable and serves only to allow the spectator to unsettle or disavow any framing of Oscar's subsequent murder as part of a racist social-structural antagonism.

In *Beale Street*, there are three white characters at episodic moments in the film: a Jewish landlord who shows Fonny and Tish a loft to rent (he is a cipher for a speech about the redemptive power of love, how being 'my mother's son' means that I don't care if someone is 'black, white, yellow, purple'); a white shop owner who prevents a cop from arresting Fonny when he throws a man sexually harassing Tish out of the shop (she seemingly accomplishes this only by refusing to allow it as if the combination of her property-owning class and her whiteness enables her to set the terms within which law will function); and a white lawyer who has agreed to take on their case but only for sufficient funds (and he fails to secure Fonny's release, who has to take a plea). Each of these characters represents the economic and political power that is aligned with whiteness but deploy it in support of, rather than against, Fonny and Tish. Yet, like the white fried-fish woman in *Fruitvale*, the encounter of a black man with a white woman, even one who is being friendly, exposes him to violence at the hands of the law. In *Beale Street*, the policeman, whose arrest of Tish and Fonny is thwarted by the intervention of the shopkeeper, is the man who then frames Fonny for the rape of a Puerto Rican woman. In *Fruitvale*, the fried-fish woman's interpellation of Oscar is the cause of his altercation on the train that then leads to him being killed by a policeman.

## GLIMPSES OF AFRO-FUTURISM

A dominant impulse in black film is the representation of the means through which black people can force the structures of liberal democracy to accommodate them, not so much by expanding those structures as by either creating parallels to them or succeeding within the terms they offer (both of which depend on the accumulation of private property). A second impulse is to demonstrate the impossibility of being incorporated into these structures because of the weight of anti-blackness that inaugurated them and continues to animate them in the 'after-life' or 'wake' of slavery. Both of these forms of representation play out in coming-of-age black film through a validation of education as the route to respectability

and private property, on the one hand, and a foreclosure of these possibilities through either incarceration or death, on the other. Frequently,
both the racial uplift of the first strategy and the Afro-pessimism of the
second oscillate in the same film. The excess of each strategy (that is to
say, the Afro-pessimism that is left out of moments of racial uplift, or the
racial uplift that is left out of Afro-pessimism) is carried through mise-en-
scène, colour, music and voiceover. In addition, as I suggested above, the
episodic direction deployed by some black filmmakers may be accounted
for through the Afro-pessimistic lens of the impossibility of a convention-
ally satisfying (read *white*) narrative form. In the remainder of this chapter, I want to explore the utopic moments that exist outside of both of
these forms and imagine a different future/past, a different relationship
between blackness and time/space.

In *Precious*, there are several scenes in which Precious fantasises about
an alternate reality. In one scene, when she looks into the mirror, she sees
a white girl with long hair. In another scene, when a boy trips her on the
street in an act of sexual harassment and bullying, she is knocked unconscious, but in her unconscious dream/fantasy, she is in the centre of a
round auditorium surrounded by a cheering audience and being kissed
by the boy who just knocked her out. She awakes to find that the sensation of being kissed is in fact a dog licking her. In such a relentlessly
miserable film as *Precious*, it is perhaps odd to suggest that there are
glimpses of Afro-futurism, and it might be more to the point that they
show the power and necessity of a fantasy life that offers an alternative
reality.

A more sustained Afro-futurism is at play in Ryan Coogler's *Black
Panther* (2018). *Black Panther* is set in a fictional African country, Wakanda, in 2018. Wakanda has been built on a fictional mineral, vibranium,
which has enabled it to develop advanced technology in communica-

**Figure 5.1.    Afro-futurism and the continuation of the discourse of racial uplift
through economic independence in Ryan Coogler's *Black Panther*, 2018.**

tions, health and military defence. To protect the country from being colonised and its wealth appropriated, Wakandans have hidden the astonishing development of their country from view, behind a kind of visibility shield that covers the entire nation. The film opens in 1992 in Oakland, California, home to the real-life black liberation movement, the Black Panthers. A young boy, perhaps eight years old, is playing basketball in the yard of an apartment block. Inside the apartment, his father, Prince N'Jobu, is being confronted by a Wakandan, King T'Chaka who has travelled to Oakland to find out how vibranium has been stolen and smuggled to the outside world. In the struggle that follows, N'Jobu is killed, and the boy is left behind to fend for himself. In the present day, a gang, led by a white South African, is stealing vibranium on display in the British Museum; also in the gang is an African American, who we later discover is Eric Killmonger, the boy left behind in Oakland, now in his mid-thirties (played by thirty-two-year-old Michael B. Jordan). Most of *Black Panther* is an action movie involving high-speed car chases, large-scale battle scenes, and improbable technology. However, the narrative is that of a coming-of-age movie in which Killmonger challenges King T'Chaka's son T'Challa to the throne and wins. On assuming the throne, Killmonger instructs his officers to instigate a worldwide black revolution supporting all the diaspora and the continent. Eventually a coup launched by T'Challa and supported by the women's army of Wakanda overthrow Killmonger. T'Challa offers to heal Killmonger who has been fatally wounded in the fight, but he refuses saying, 'Why? So you can just lock me up? Nah. Just bury me in the ocean, with my ancestors that jumped from the ships 'cause they knew death was better than bondage'. With this, Killmonger pulls the knife from the wound in his chest and dies instantly. The final scene takes us back to the same basketball court in Oakland, where T'Challa tells his sister Shuri that he has bought the buildings to start the first 'Wakandan International Outreach Center' in which 'Nakia [his girlfriend] will oversee the social outreach. . . . And you will spearhead the science and information exchange'. He then reveals the Wakandan space ship, and the boys in the basketball court see it and (as the script puts it) 'collectively lose their shit'. Finally another young black boy approaches T'Challa and says, 'Hey yo! Is this yours? Who . . . are you?' T'Challa 'thinks on this and smiles', and the credits role.

*Black Panther* was very well received as a fable of black liberation; although the contradictions of its storyline (including a white CIA officer as the defender of Wakanda's independence) and its pastiche of 'Africa' did not go unnoticed, it was still celebrated as a turning point in Hollywood's representation of black people. Nonetheless, it still ends with a young black man dying, and it puts its faith vaguely in technology, as if the deep poverty of black communities in the United States and the violence faced by African Americans were simply the result of being denied access to technology and education. In this, it is nothing new. As I

**Figure 5.2.   'Who . . . are you?' Ryan Coogler, 2018. *Black Panther*. Marvel Studios.**

showed in chapters 2 and 3, the importance of education to changing the futures of black youth, and therefore of black people in America, has been central to a dominant strand of the struggle for black civil liberties and political inclusion. Afro-futurism is about imagining futures in which black people flourish and, if Afro-pessimists are correct, then that imagined future cannot simply continue from the past but must involve a revolutionary break with it. *Black Panther* cannot quite imagine the revolutionary break, which is unsurprising and probably too much to ask from the Marvel Comics universe! Nonetheless, it does probe at questions of racism, colonialism and global inequality that are surprising fodder for a superhero comic book story.

## CONCLUSION

This chapter has shown how African American coming-of-age films cannot sit well with the canon of teen coming-of-age films because they cannot be read as a story of one character and what kind of person they may become, but always signify larger questions about the relationship of the black community to the state and to capital. (In this respect, the ending of *Black Panther*, in which T'Challa is asked 'Who are you?', is a kind of revelatory question for a black character in teen film). Using Wilderson's frame of Afro-pessimism, I have suggested that black teen film invariably runs up against the impossibility of an ordinary black life in the United States. This shapes, I have argued, not only the storyline but also the mise-en-scène, the excess that is carried in music and voiceover, and the frequent recourse to an episodic rather than narrative mode of storytelling. The directors who make black coming-of-age films are themselves often from the milieu they are making films about, even if they are now firmly situated in the black middle class, and all of the films analysed in this chapter grapple with the question of 'What is to be done?' Frequently, the answer to this question returns to the racial-uplift strategy that has shaped not only US black political culture but also its visual culture right across the history of film and photography. Occasionally, scenes of fantasy imagine alternative futures unmoored from the real history of the past and wishing alternative realities into existence.

# SIX

## 'We've Got a Bright Place in the Sun'

### LGBTQ Coming Out and Teen Melodrama

.

The ur-text of lesbian teen film must surely be the German-language *Mädchen in Uniform*, which I recall seeing at an independent cinema in East London in about 1980 and finding both illegible and disappointing. As a young queer looking for textual representation, it was no doubt its all too 'sub-textual' (Beirne 2012) content that disappointed me. *Mädchen in Uniform* was released in 1931, and it might be expected that contemporary queer films would provide more explicit textual representation of queer desire. Certainly, in an age of ubiquitous pink-washing, Lamar's lyrics, heard in *Moonlight* and quoted in the title to this chapter, seem to indicate that the work of securing liberation is over. Compulsory heterosexuality and doomed same-sex relationships are no longer the dominant trope of the queer (teen) movie. Young queers on film are now depicted struggling to know who they are. This idea of the truth about oneself as being connected to sex is now absolutely central to contemporary discourses of sexuality and, increasingly, gender identity and provides much of the narrative tension in these and other films on queer sexuality and gender identity aimed at teens: the imperative to live the truth about oneself through the affirmation of an individualised expression of sexual identity. In this chapter, I show how these storylines unfold within a melodramatic genre.

While the forms of identification that melodrama encourages are often seen by cultural critics as a repudiation or even betrayal of necessary political commitments, a small body of critical theory recognises the popular-cultural appeal of these narrative forms and at the same time argues for them as a kind of political vernacular. This impulse informed the rescue of the melodrama from its assessment as a debased cultural form in the work of, for example, Peter Brooks (1995), Christine Gledhill (1987) and Linda Williams (2001). Thomas Elsaesser (1987) in his highly influential 'Tales of Sound and Fury', notes that, on the one hand, a refusal in popular culture to 'understand social change in other than private contexts and emotional terms' can be framed as a 'healthy distrust of intellectualization and abstract social theory—insisting that other structures of experience (those of suffering, for instance) are more in keeping with reality', but at the same time, the ignorance of the broader political (and I would add, economic) causes of social change have 'encouraged increasingly escapist forms of mass entertainment' (Elsaesser 1987:437).

The displacement of the structural onto the personal, of political struggle onto sentimental identification, and the encouragement of identification of the spectator with the (necessarily) innocent victim and/or the rescuer-hero are the hallmarks of melodrama. The melodramatic form accomplishes both this displacement and the forms of spectator identification through the failure or refusal to confront the structural bases of gendered, raced and classed exclusions/identifications directly and to instead displace this textual excess of the unsaid onto other modes than speech. In particular the 'melo', or music, in melodrama highlights the displacement of textual excess onto music, but it is also accomplished through the film's mise-en-scène and its use of colour, as well as other semiotic modes.

## THE FILMS

In this chapter, I take the key components of the melodrama genre and discuss how they are carried, and with what effects, in a series of contemporary queer teen films. In deciding what to include in the category of queer teen film, I chose films that centre their narrative around a teenage lesbian, gay, bisexual or trans protagonist. I focus on five films: *Boys Don't Cry*, *Blue Is the Warmest Color*, *Moonlight*, *The Miseducation of Cameron Post*, and *Pariah* because they are all LGB written and/or directed.

Barry Jenkins's film *Moonlight* (2016) tells the story of a black gay man growing up in Miami. The film's structure, which Jenkins has said is influenced by the structure of Taiwanese director Hou Hsiao-Hsien's *Three Times* (2004), is a romantic triptych in which the main character, Chiron, appears as a boy, a teenager, and a man. The film is based on a semi-autobiographical play, *Black Boys Look Blue in Moonlight*, written by Tarell McCraney, who also co-wrote the screenplay with Jenkins. Both Jenkins and McCraney grew up in a poor, majority-black neighbourhood in Miami where the film is shot. Yet the film eschews a documentary realist style in favour of a melodramatic narrative in which colour and music carry the film's semiosis. One critic comments in an interview with Jenkins, 'The significance of utilizing this style with *these* characters, to engage more deeply with the humanity, sensitivity, and consciousness of a queer, black, male adolescent cannot be overstated; it is practically an act of protest' (https://www.filmcomment.com/article/moonlight-barry-jenkins-interview/). That semiosis is concerned with, as Jenkins commented in an interview with *Film Comment* magazine, an 'understanding of how societal norms play a large role in the performance and presentation of love'. In curating the cinema inspirations of *Moonlight* for the Film Society of Lincoln Center, Jenkins notes, in addition to the influence of *Three Times*, the visual homage to Wong Kar-wai's *Happy Together* (https://www.filmcomment.com/blog/shedding-some-light/).

*Blue Is the Warmest Color* (2013) is adapted from the graphic novel of the same name, written by a lesbian. Adele, who is in her final year at school, meets and falls in love with Emma, who is an art student at university. After Adele leaves school, she gets a job as a primary school teacher and moves into Emma's flat. They gradually become estranged from one another, and each becomes more involved with her work. Adele feels pushed away by Emma and one night gets drunk and has sex with a colleague. When she confesses this to Emma, Emma throws her out of their flat. Emma meets another woman, who is pregnant, and they have the child together. The film ends when they meet again at Emma's show, but it is clear that Emma has moved on, although Adele is still in love with her. *Warmest Color* is directed by a heterosexual man and attracted a lot of controversy about whether the film was voyeuristic because of this.

*The Miseducation of Cameron Post* (2018) was adapted from a novel of the same name by bisexual Iranian American director Desiree Akhavan. The titular character is caught having sex with another girl in the car park on prom night. Her aunt sends her away to a conversion therapy centre. After some attempts to fit in with the camp's ideology, a crisis leads to her running away.

Dee Rees's *Pariah* (2011) tells the story of a young black lesbian and her friendships and family relationships. The conflict between her and her mother, who is homophobic, leads eventually to Alike leaving Brooklyn.

*Boys Don't Cry* (1999), directed by Kimberley Peirce, is based on the true story of a trans man, Brandon Lewis, who was murdered in Nebraska by his girlfriend's friends.

## INNOCENCE OR VIRTUE BETRAYED

Absolutely central to the melodramatic genre is the innocence of the main protagonist. In women's film, this innocence is almost always signified in relation to sex, as is the 'fall' that drives the narrative forward. In queer teen film, innocence cannot entirely be constructed through an absence of

knowledge of sex since it is through the sexual desire of the main protagonist that the spectator recognises the film as a queer film. Instead, their
innocence is innocence about the transgressive character of same-sex desire or trans gender identity and/or innocence of a wider community of
queers. The trope of 'I'm not gay, gay', a refusal or innocence, in other
words, of LGB identity, is mostly how innocence is maintained. The exception here might be *Boys Don't Cry*.

In *Moonlight*, innocence is conveyed by the few words that the very
taciturn, indeed near-silent boy Chiron, named Little (and more on shifting names in queer film later), speaks in the film. In one of the few scenes
where he speaks, the last scene of act 1, Little asks Juan, 'What's a faggot?' and 'Am I one?' This naivety about his desire, coupled with his
recognition of the danger of that desire and the hostility towards it of
others, establishes his innocence and, in doing so, foretells his fall. In
*Pariah*, the scene that might echo Chiron's question in *Moonlight* could be
the moment when Alike asks her friend Laura to buy her a strap-on by
making a gesture that Laura quickly and accurately interprets. But like
Chiron, Alike is also taciturn until a sudden outburst of anger (the fall)
undoes her and remakes her.

*Cameron Post* begins when Cameron is at the end-of-year high school
dance. Her boyfriend, Jimmy, discovers Cameron and another girl,
Coley, making out in his car. The scandal this generates is what leads her
religious aunt (her parents are dead, which may be another important
signifier of innocence in childhood films) to send her for conversion therapy. Although she begins the film as the guilty party (although, not
entirely—it is Coley who initiates sex in the car, and she is fucking Cameron), her innocence is restored after Coley accuses her of taking advantage of their friendship. Cameron apparently takes this seriously and
starts doing religious workout classes with her pious roommate, prays
with conviction and stops hanging out with the two, less religiously com-
pliant, friends that she has been more or less solid friends with since
joining the camp. It is another scandal, the attempted mutilation of his
own penis by a boy at the camp, which brings Cameron to her senses and
leads to her and her two friends literally walking away.

*Cameron Post* perhaps defies the convention of innocence, and yet all
the queer teens in these films are in some sense innocent because none of
them straightforwardly accept their queer sexuality. Of course, this refusal or failure to embrace queerness is also necessary to lend the film some
kind of struggle or narrative tension. In a heterosexual film, that might be
achieved through a girl-meets-boy, girl-loses-boy, girl-gets-boy-back narrative structure that is more or less ubiquitous in romance films. Indeed,
Elsaesser claims that the unobtainable object of desire is a recurring
theme of melodrama. In queer films, that same structure might be sum-
marised as girl/boy realises she is queer, girl/boy repudiates queerness,
girl/boy gets queerness back. A key difference is that, in general, the

point at which the main character returns to queerness (or queerness returns to them) is rarely embodied in a person as an object of desire. It is as if through returning to queerness, the protagonist returns to their own true self. This fits well with a current trope that being LGBT is about being your true self/true to your self, and the contemporary preoccupation with sex and sexuality being the foundation of subjectivity.

The identification of the viewer with the main protagonist in the melodrama depends on the innocence of this figure, as discussed above. But equally important to the narrative structure is the threatening of innocence by villainy or corruption. The classic representation of this in 'women's film' is through rape or other forms of sexual violence but also with misunderstanding and manipulation as, for example, when the woman believes she is making love with the man who will become her husband—a belief which allows her to be both virginal and sexual—but the man (and the spectator) know that he will not continue the relationship once they have sex. In *Moonlight*, virtue betrayed is signified by the sex between Kevin and Chiron on the beach. While Chiron clearly feels that this is the beginning of a relationship, Kevin is initially more ambiguous and subsequently violently repudiates any connection with Chiron when he brutally beats him at school to avoid being identified as gay by others and ostracised. Cameron believes that she and Coley are in love, but Coley's subsequent rejection of Cameron is also felt as both a betrayal and, in Coley's claim that Cameron manipulated her, the search by Cameron to restore her virtue by engaging fully in the conversion therapy at the Christian camp. *Warmest Color* is more complicated. In the graphic novel on which it is based, the fallen woman is the young lesbian (Adele in the film) who, feeling lonely in the relationship with Emma, has sex with a colleague at work, a man. When Emma discovers this, she throws Adele out of their shared home, a rejection Adele never recovers from in the film, while in the book she has sex one more time with Emma and then dies of a heart attack—it really doesn't get much more melodramatic than that! For Alike in *Pariah*, virtue is betrayed when Bina, after they have spent the night together, dismisses Alike's desire by saying, 'I'm not gay, gay'.

Frequently the fall from grace in melodrama is the cue for the protagonist's entry into a world of vice (prostitution, crime, etc.). In the queer melodrama, the community of queers is itself this world of vice and, in the case of *Moonlight* (and more generally in what we might call 'racial uplift movies'), the black community and its neighbourhood stand in for vice. Racial uplift in *Moonlight* (signified by Chiron's bookishness and his criticism of the drug dealing by the otherwise exemplary Juan) is interrupted by the sexual harassment from the homophobic thugs in his school that precedes his first sexual encounter with Kevin that, in turn, precedes Chiron's public beating by Kevin. That series of events is the setup for Chiron's unprecedented violence towards his abuser, Tyrell, which gets Chiron sent to juvenile detention. It is in detention that he learns how to become a drug dealer and builds himself, as he later says to Kevin, 'from the ground up, hard'. The opening scene of the film is echoed in the opening scene of part 3, in which Chiron, now called Black, is cruising the same streets and collecting money from his dealers that Blue was cruising in the same way when he first met Chiron as a little boy. In contrast to this, in *Pariah*, the fall is the estrangement of Alike from her mother and her move to her friend Laura's, but the film ends with her going on a bus journey to take up her writing scholarship at Berkeley, hardly a world of vice. I guess. Although there is an implication here that Berkeley will enable Alike to fully express herself, creatively and sexually, and that this is what terrifies her mother and is therefore, if not a world of vice, one of transgression. Indeed, in *Pariah*'s case, we could take the entry of Alike into the queer world that opens the film as the site of the fall, which would make Alike's being queer in itself, before she had acted upon it, the betrayal of virtue.

## HOME IS WHERE THE HEART IS

The title of Christine Gledhill's book on film melodrama, *Home Is Where the Heart Is*, indicates the importance of the family home to the women protagonists of women's film. In women's film, home is a woman's domain, however oppressive and circumscribed that domain may be. It is melodrama's attention to the home and therefore its opening-up of a supposedly private world that gives melodrama much of its political significance. What then does it signify that for queer children, the straight home is, generally, intensely unhomely?

In none of the films discussed here does the family home signify the sanctuary or domain of the main, queer protagonist. In *Pariah*, Alike is not allowed to leave the door to her bedroom closed. Her mother demands the right of constant surveillance over her daughter, whom she suspects of something queer—whether in relation to sexuality or gender or both. Although Bina seduces Alike in her bedroom, Bina's subsequent rejection of Alike re-stabilises the home as a space that is unhomely for queer youth. Most of *Cameron Post* is shot in a boarding school/camp, showing the literal incommensurability between home and queer children. One of the turning points in the film is when a boy has a breakdown and then cuts his penis and pours bleach into the wound because his father refuses to allow him to come home, writing to him, 'I am denying your request to return home at the end of the semester. You are still very effeminate and this is a weakness I cannot have in my home'. In *Warmest Color*, although Adele and Emma do have sex in Adele's family home, this is only in fact possible because the parents assume that Emma is a 'friend'; it never occurs to them that they are having sex. Chiron in

*Moonlight* runs out of his family home when his mother screams 'faggot' at him silently. It is after this that he asks Blue what a faggot is.

The unhomeliness of a family home for queer youth is underlined in *Pariah* in the final scene, in which Alike and her mother are together. Alike sits in front of a poster that the audience (and Alike's mother) can see and which says 'safe'. Havlin and Rivera-Velázquez (2015) comment that *Pariah* figures the rupture of the heteropatriarchal family as a necessary precondition of queer futures; particularly, they say, 'The survival of gender-nonconforming youth of color . . . the conflicts between queer youth and parents committed to heteropatriarchy are only resolved through the expulsion of either the queer youth or the parent enforcing heteropatriarchy' (2015:122). This is also borne out by the character of Alike's best friend, Laura, who is estranged from her mother and has been thrown out of her family home.

In *Boys*, it is the fact that Brandon is having sex with a straight cis woman that guarantees that he is read as a cis man, but once his girlfriend's family realise that he is a trans man, his girlfriend's home, where he has been staying, becomes intensely unsafe for him. The two men, her friends, who go on to rape and murder Brandon first ransack his bedroom looking for evidence. At first Lara's mother defends Brandon's privacy, but as it becomes clear that Brandon is a trans man, she stops protesting. These actions make visible that the 'right' to privacy is dependent on compliance with the norm.

The unhomeliness of home and of private space does not mean that public space, into which the queer youth is thrown, is safe, or at least not always so. Hanging out in the street, that ubiquitous third space (after home and school) of adolescence has an aura of barely suppressed threat hanging over it. (Indeed, this is also mostly true of public space in many of the black-director teen films that I discussed in the previous chapter.) In *Pariah* the street, specifically the Christopher Street Piers, is a rare depiction of non-commercial (and therefore working-class and young) queer public space and community depicted in these films. In *Moonlight*, both Chiron as a boy and Chiron as a teenager are at risk on the street from homophobic violence. It is only when he hardens himself and becomes a dealer that he is safe on the street—his queerness no longer visible to others. *Boys* opens with Brandon running away from his attackers and throwing himself into his gay cousin's trailer.

In *Cameron Post*, Cameron's roommate surprises her one night by waking her up from a dream and then masturbating her. Despite the fact that the door is open and the rooms are regularly under surveillance throughout the night to prevent the girls having sex, they do not get caught. It is probably Erin's piousness that makes it possible for them to have sex without being caught. A similar trope of hiding in plain sight, 'gals and their pals', is in *Pariah*, in which Alike's mother suspects that Laura, who is a lesbian, is the cause of her daughter's queerness and more or less forces Alike to go out with Bina because she is a nice (feminine, church-going) girl. It is Bina who seduces Akele. In *Blue Is the Warmest Color*, the teenage Adele lives with her parents and is able to have sex at home with Emma because it does not occur to her parents that their daughter might be attracted to Emma (or that Emma is a lesbian). Teenage Chiron in *Moonlight* has sex with Kevin on the beach (in the film Kevin seduces Chiron; in the script, the scene is written in a more mutual way). The next day, at school, Kevin beats Chiron up on the insistence of a homophobic and violent student, Tyrell. Kevin's violence against Chiron keeps his sex with Chiron secret.

When Barry Jenkins says that this is also a film about home, he seems to mean *neighbourhood*. While Jenkins sees *Moonlight* as primarily an art-house movie (although its success at the Academy Awards led to a much wider distribution than art-house movies would normally get), he also says, 'You know, *Moonlight* is an "art-house" film and all that other shit, but it's also a film that's just about home' (www.filmcomment.com/article/moonlight-barry-jenkins-interview).

In the absence of a family home and a safe public space, the protagonists in these films find other homely spaces. In *Pariah*, Alike's best friend, Laura, is living with her adult sister and is also working and paying rent. Little regularly sleeps at Black's house and, after Black's death, has his own room there. Cameron and her friends make a space in the forest to hang out and smoke weed.

## LIMINAL AND UTOPIC SPACES IN QUEER TEEN FILMS

The ubiquity in these films of road trips and cars is one way in which the unhomeliness of private space and the threats of public space are managed by their queer protagonists. Cunningham (2011) wants to connect the road trip itself to the structure of queerness, arguing that 'the persistence of the road motif demonstrates how these queer characters are restless identities that can not be anchored in any one place' (2011:171). The road is an antidote to the closet.

The ubiquity of the road trip in queer movies may also be present in non-queer teen movies, but it also speaks to a central problem for young queers on film as frequently as in life: the unhomeliness of home. In the queer teen film, the institutional spaces that form the action in hetero films—mainly, girls' bedrooms (less often, the kitchen and dining room)—and the school do not signify in the same way for queer youth as they do for straight youth. Friendship groups in schools may be centred around cliques, but, at least in their representation on film, there is no queer clique. Even in *Glee*, the television series that was acclaimed for giving queer youth representation in school places: the queer child is in non-queer friendship groups, often as the gay best friend and involving a similar exceptionalism with drag queens in mainstream (non-teen) dramas.

The car and the road trip signify the elsewhere-ness but also the nowhereness of liberation. The car and the road trip can be read as liminal or suspended sites and spaces utopic in both the sense of nowhere and in the sense of an imagination of perfection or freedom. Blue/Juan in *Moonlight* is from Cuba. He tells Little that there are black people everywhere, 'don't you forget that'. This assertion can be read as a claim that Little can have community anywhere, with other black people, but also that black people in other places have other ways of doing black masculinity. While *Moonlight* cannot be considered a road movie, the car as a homely site for Blue/Juan and later for Black/Chiron is signified from the outset as Blue drives through the streets in the opening scenes of the film, and the film ends with a road trip when Black drives back to Miami to meet with Kevin in the film's last scenes.

Alike goes to Berkeley, famed place of liberation and queer theory. Cameron, Jane and Forrest leave not only the camp but also their connection to their family to take a road trip—'We'll be in Canada by morning'. Brandon dreams of an elsewhere but also a utopic nowhere; he is only vaguely aware of how its geography maps onto territory. He tells Jon and Tom when he first meets them that he's going to be 'travellin' all around: Memphis, Graceland, Tennessee'. When they laugh at him and respond 'You dick. Graceland is in Memphis and Memphis is in Tennessee', he looks confused and then brushes it off: 'I know'.

**Figure 6.1.    The Suspended Utopic in Queer Film: 'We'll be in Canada by morning'. *The Miseducation of Cameron Post*, Desiree Akhavan, 2018. Beachside Films.**

There is an absence of queer community in the sense of a group/place of belonging and safety for the main character. Although in *Warmest Color*, Adele meets Emma at a lesbian bar, she finds the setting threatening rather than homely. For her, it is not that she is a lesbian but that she desires Emma. Indeed, Adele's alienation from the community that Emma is part of, and which Adele experiences as both too white and too bourgeois, is precisely the reason for the impossibility of their relationship.

## IMPOSSIBLE (BUT UNENDING) DESIRE

A key trope of melodrama is that the love object is always out of reach. Queer teen film also plays out this trope, which aligns with a heterosexual fantasy (oddly since they are all scripted by lesbian or gay directors) that an invitation to sex by a straight person is always welcomed by queers and that the straight characters', almost inevitable, subsequent rejection of the queer character (and repudiation or refusal of the meaningfulness of their actions) will lead the queer character to be not only heartbroken but to nurture an impossible love for the straight character. *Moonlight* is structured by Chiron's impossible desire for Kevin after Kevin kisses him and then masturbates him after Kevin 'randomly' meets Chiron on the beach. In the final scenes, when Chiron is an adult and a successful drug dealer, Kevin phones him on a whim one day when a customer plays a song that reminds him of Chiron. In response, Chiron drives ten hours to Miami to see Kevin, whom he has not spoken to since Kevin beat him up at high school. Alike's final confrontation with her mother, which leads to her leaving home and then leaving the city, is precipitated by her distress that the girl who seduces her then repudiates her desire, but it is clear that the extreme reaction of Alike to this rejection is because of her fantasy that she and Bina could be together. In *Cameron Post*, Cameron's eagerly awaited letter from Coley tells Cameron that she can't be with her and insists that Cameron manipulated her into having sex. While her friend Jane's response is to shred the letter, in the film, Cameron takes seriously Coley's claim that she (Cameron) had taken advantage of her and becomes immersed in the religious rituals of the camp.

The exception to these tropes of impossible (because repudiated and never reciprocated) yet unending love for a straight other is in *Boys Don't Cry*. Brandon's desire for Lara is almost immediately reciprocated and is sustained. However, despite the reciprocity of their attraction and love for one another, their desire is nonetheless impossible and ends with Brandon's death. After Lara and Brandon have sex (for the second time on screen), which is after Brandon has been violently outed as a trans man by his and Lara's friends (so the first scene in which the audience know that Lara knows what they know, that Brandon is not a cis man), Lara then goes back to her own home to pack a bag, the plan being that Lara and Brandon will leave that night and drive to Lincoln (where Brandon is from). When Brandon, impatient to see Lara again, risks his safety by going to Lara's home and climbing through the window, it is clear that Lara has changed her mind about leaving; the implication is that, had Brandon not gone back to Lara's house, he would not have been trapped by Tom and Jon and could have escaped death.

At first pass, *Warmest Color* breaks with this trope of impossible queer love. Adele desires Emma from the first moment she sees her (they pass each other crossing a road) and then actively seeks her out. However, prior to this active seeking-out, when Adele is still trying to understand/frame her desire for Emma, another girl, a friend at school, tells her she is cute and kisses her. That evening, Adele looks both distracted and terrified. When she goes back to school the next day, she is wearing an orange-red jumper—the first time she has not worn blue or brown. Her waist is a flash of bright orange. She finds the girl in the bathroom and kisses her; the girl doesn't respond. She says she's sorry. 'I didn't think that you'd get so hooked. What happened yesterday, was just. . . . Understand. Nothing will change between us. I won't tell anyone'. Like Bina in *Pariah*, she repels her. Furthermore, as I mentioned above, in the book (although thankfully not in the film), Adele dies at the end of the story; her death was literally caused by having sex with Emma.

## MUSIC AND SILENCE

Teen characters, especially girls in teen film, are usually very talkative. In contrast, in these films, the main queer character is all but silent. Dawson (2015) in a paper on passing in *Boys Don't Cry* and *Unveiled/Fremde Haut*, cites Michelle Cliff's claim that 'passing demands quiet. And from that quiet—silence' (2015:210 citing Cliff 1985:22). While these characters are not exactly passing, their discomfort with queerness, with what it means and how to express it, is carried by their silences.

In *Moonlight*, when Chiron drives to the diner where Kevin works (he has driven for ten hours to get there on the mere suggestion from Kevin that he should come by sometime), he is as silent as he has been in each of the film's three acts. Kevin says, 'There go that damn noddin', you ain't changed a bit, still can't say more than three words at a time, huh?' Alike, in *Pariah*, barely speaks for most of the film, and, tellingly, her longest speech is when she shouts at her mother after Bina rejects her. Brandon is talkative in general, but not when he is with Lana. Cameron barely speaks, and although this is partly because the religious camp compels its residents to speak only to berate themselves, she is also an onlooker with her friends.

All of this silence can be read as the excess that the melodrama cannot directly represent and displaces onto the film's music score. One of the few exuberant scenes in *Cameron Post* is when Cameron, Jane and Forrest are in the kitchen of the camp peeling potatoes. The radio is on. Cameron starts to sing and then jumps onto the table, Jane hands her a potato peeler to use as a microphone, and she belts out 4 Non-Blondes' 'What's Up?', which includes the lines

> And I try, oh my God do I try
> I try all the time
> In this institution
> And I pray, oh my God do I pray
> I pray every single day
> For a revolution

The director of the camp walks in on them, turns the radio off and tells Cameron to come with her. She then gives Cameron a letter from Coley, which the Director has read (the lack of privacy extending to not only space but also communication), in which Coley tells Cameron how disgusted she is with her. Cameron's brief flirtation with sound is abruptly ended, and she takes on the full religious discourse of the camp.

'We've got a bright place in the sun / Where there's love for everyone' (are the lines from Boris Gardiner's track on Kendrick Lamar's album *To Pimp a Butterfly* that opens *Moonlight*. Jenkins has spoken of how the music carries some of the threat and fear of masculinity for Little. On the one hand, Juan teaches him to swim/baptises him and, on the other, the music (Little's theme) has an edge of fear to it—there's a storm coming. While the music displaces some of the textual excess, it also, of course, underscores the dominant mood of the film. In the case of *Moonlight*, for example, Jenkins, discussing the film's score, says 'When you slow things down there's this emotion, this yearning. I think in some ways, in *Moonlight*, we're doing the same thing'. Is Jenkins wanting to use the slowing-down to see the yearning of gay life? When you slow down the music, Jenkins comments, 'you actually reveal even more this sensitivity, and this yearning. . . . I think the lyrics in that song [Jidenna's 'Classic Man'], when you can actually take your time with them, it's some sensitive shit, you know? It's extremely vulnerable' (Pitchfork.com). 'Like Chiron's life, the music always seems on the brink of lapsing into tragedy', says Calum Marsh in his score review (https://pitchfork.com/reviews/albums/nicho-las-britell-moonlight-original-motion-picture-soundtrack/). 'You have this character who is sort of receding inside himself. And the music within the film tells us what he can't. In the beginning it starts out very, very small. Once you get to that third story, the music [the actual soundtrack] starts to get a lot more expressive and sensual' (https://www.filmcomment.com/article/moonlight-barry-jenkins-interview/).

The club is the heart of LGBT culture, the place where we get to be away from the heterosexual gaze; yet most teen movies do not have clubs in them. Like the car radio, it provides a setting for diegetic music in the film's score. *Pariah* opens in a club, and Alike returns to it hoping she will meet a girl, but in Alike's eyes, the club is not a space of safety and community; she clearly feels alienated from it and leaves early. Nonetheless, the music in this scene, which the film opens with, is exuberant and explicit. *Moonlight, Cameron Post* and *Boys*, do not have club scenes. *Warmest Color* does, given that all the music in the film is diegetic, this is also one of the few scenes with music. Adele gets her gay best friend to take her to one the afternoon that the girl she kisses in the bathroom tells her it wasn't meaningful.

## PERFORMATIVITY: NAMES AND STUFF

The significance of naming is also highlighted in these films. The three acts of *Moonlight* are subtitled by the changing names of the central character (from Little, to Chiron, to Black). When Kevin and Chiron have sex on the beach, Chiron's comment about Kevin's nickname for him, 'What kind of dude goes around giving other dudes nicknames?', stands in for Chiron asking/confirming that this naming is a signifier of desire. That Chiron takes the name Black as his own nickname as an adult is an unspoken homage to Kevin's desire for him. It literally brings him into (queer) existence. When Teresa asks him what his name is, and he says 'Chiron, people call me Little', Juan (whose own nickname is Blue) says 'I'll call you Little' but Teresa responds 'I'll call you by your name'. When Tyrell calls Chiron Little in class, Chiron retorts, 'Don't call me that'. Cameron tells the Director of the religious centre that she can call her Cam and she responds '"Cameron" is already a masculine name. To abbreviate as something even less feminine only exacerbates your gender confusion'. Her friend is called Jane Fonda, which, in the book, is related to the fact that she has two fathers (both were her mother's lovers), and they both named her. In *Pariah* Akele is called Lee by her best friend (Laura) but not by her mother, who sees it as part of her transgressive sexuality and, in her mother's belief, her transgressive gender identity.

Melodrama at its best is arrestingly beautiful, and some of that beauty rests in its loving attention to how performance of social identity or the exteriorising of interiority is accomplished. All teen films, indeed all melodramas, revel in the surface. This is the case whether the surface is 'all' there is or is a sign of what has already been interiorised or, especially in contemporary queer film, the surface sign of an interior and presocial 'I'. In teen films in general, dress, makeup, hair, deportment, gesture define gender and (hetero)sexuality, and although in doing so, they are insisting somehow on the naturalness of sexuality and gender, the elaborate use of 'stuff' queers that naturalness. (It is in this sense, I think, that Goldberg wants to claim that all melodrama is queer or queers. As Dawson notes (2015:211), Brandon's dressing scene in *Boys* 'has many similarities to that of a cis man, highlighting that the cultural construction of masculinity does not require maleness and that all gender performativity requires preparation, "tools", and props in order to perform it correctly' (Butler [1990] 1999:185 cited in Dawson 2015: 212). In queer teen film, the stuff is central to the performance of an LGBT identity/subjectivity.

In *Pariah*, too, fashion, clothes and style are central to the presentation of the self in ways that make sexuality legible to others. In the DVD of the film, a bonus short, *Trying Out Identity: Pariah's Wardrobe* (cited in Pritchard 136) underscores this point.

Perhaps surprisingly, genitals and their phallic lack are the 'problem' that both films about trans men and lesbian/bi women visualise. The films want to underscore the scandal of a man without a penis and the impossibility of sex without a phallus. In *Boys Don't Cry*, Brandon starts his period when at Candace's house and leaks on his jeans. He washes his jeans in her bathroom and drives to the petrol station where he steals tampons so as to avoid having to buy them. When he gets back to Candace, he puts the tampon in his vagina and then hides the applicator under the mattress. The purpose of this concealment, in terms of driving the plot forward, is that Candace, searching Brandon's room after she realises he has been stealing and cashing cheques from her, finds the used applicator. The other reason for this scene is that it puts Brandon in the petrol station at the same time as Lana, whom he is already in love with/intensely desires. This is such a peculiar and unnecessary scene in both respects. When the men who rape and kill Brandon also search his room in a later scene, looking for evidence that Brandon is, as they put it, 'a liar', they find a pamphlet that looks like something from a nineteenth-century sexology clinic and his strap-on.

Although Dawson wants to locate the significance of this scene with the problem of the bathroom for trans subjects, this works more for her analysis of *Unveiled* than it does for *Boys Don't Cry*. True, there is a later scene in which, after Brandon is raped, Tom and John drive him to their house and tell him to 'get cleaned up' in the bathroom. In fact, this is how Brandon escapes, in a scene that is a nod to a classic film noir device—the suspect asking to use the toilet and then escaping through the bathroom window.

## VULNERABILITY AND VIOLENCE

In her book *Reel Vulnerability*, Sarah Hagelin (2013) shows that US popular culture and scholarship 'remains stubbornly invested in the myth of the helplessness of the female body' (book description). In her chapter on *Boys Don't Cry* and the *Laramie Project*, she argues, 'The queer body poses a stark challenge to the politics of vulnerability . . . since it disrupts the heterosexist assumptions about the special vulnerability of the female body (2013:104). Despite its rather idiosyncratic reading in which she argues that 'the protracted, unsettling focus on Swank's naked body during scenes of his exposure and rape uses the viewer's sudden, explicit awareness of that body's *femaleness* to heighten audience investment in the character, whom Peirce had previously resisted gendering' (2013:105). This is entirely untrue since the cinematography until that point has centred on precisely the problem of Brandon's masculinity being compromised by his absent penis. As Hagelin herself notes in the next paragraph, Peirce's camera, while showing us the act of binding breasts and stuffing underwear that constitutes the production of Brandon's masculinity, never shows us "Teena Brandon," only Brandon Teena' (2013:105). Despite a very acute analysis of the film and its investment in (white) working-class masculinity, Hagelin seems to use 'gendering' in relation to Brandon/trans men, as rendering female. She says, 'Gendering Brandon during the rape is a kind of cultural short-hand for the vulnerability Peirce needs to establish for Brandon in order for the narrative to work as melodrama' (2013:110); only women bleed, perhaps. But in any case, her point works. Peirce intercuts Brandon's rape with him reporting it at the police station to a trans-phobic policeman who forces Brandon to say that he has a vagina. In a third scene, in which Lana and Brandon have sex and Lana says, 'I don't know if I know what to do', implying that she is going to touch Brandon's genitals. This scene has been subject to multiple critical analyses that argue that Peirce projects Brandon as a woman in this scene, not least because Lana asks, 'What were you like as a girl?' Brandon responds, 'I was a girl girl, then a girl boy, then a jerk', recalling his look in the mirror earlier in the film when he says, 'You're an asshole'. This scene has been the focus of much analysis of *Boys* for its seeming acceptance that male violence makes femaleness (Hird 2001).

In *Moonlight*, homophobic violence structures the narrative of both of the first two acts. Little's story opens with him being chased into an abandoned building by three slightly bigger boys whose shouts grab Juan's attention. When the plywood board is torn off of the window, it reveals, not Little's attackers but Juan. In a subsequent scene in the same act, Juan pulls Little's mother out of a car where she is smoking crack that her boyfriend has just bought from one of Juan's sellers. Initially contrite, she quickly turns on Juan asking, 'So you gon' raise him?' and 'You gon' tell him why the other boys kick his ass all the time? Huh?' Little's friendship with Kevin begins when Kevin instructs him that he can't look soft to the other boys and then wrestles with him, itself signalling to the audience a homoerotic potential in this friendship. The vulnerability of the queer body to violence is not only because, or not even because, it is 'soft' but because its transgression is always in danger of being policed and violently re-orientated by cis straight men. Little escapes being beaten because of Juan, himself the image of tough masculinity but softened by his loving attitude towards Little and towards his girlfriend. There is also a suggestion that Juan himself is gay or bisexual. Is this the point of his being Cuban? In act 2, when Chiron the teenager is brutally beaten by Kevin at Tyrell's insistence and then kicked by Tyrell when he is on the ground, it ends Chiron's softness. He walks to school determined and focused, marches into the classroom, picks up a chair and breaks it over Tyrell's head, knocking him onto the floor and then, when Tyrell moves, bringing it down again. Act 2 ends with him being taken out of the school in cuffs. When we meet Chiron again, he is now 'Black', a trapper, and a hard man; though when challenged by Kevin, who remains soft and genial throughout the film who asks, 'You hard now', he says, 'I ain't saying that'.

In *Pariah*, the threat of violence against queer youth in school and at home is a constant underlying fear carried in music and colour. When leaving the club, Laura wants to stay on the bus with Alike to see she gets home safely. The threat finally explodes when Alike's mother fights with her father and then, when she confronts Alike directly and says, 'Say it, you're a lesbian', pushes her against the wall and then hits her. These actions directly lead to Alike leaving her parents' home and staying with Laura from where she goes to Berkeley.

## CONCLUSION

When teen film, or indeed Hollywood film in general, does not depict LGBT characters as 'beautiful but doomed', it instead resolves the agonism in the narrative through the trope of *we are all the same*. In other words, it disavows the reality of homo and trans phobia, of the queerness of queer life and of, for many queers, the attachment to and desire for a non-normative praxis. As Jack/Judith Halberstam writes of the transgender gaze in *Boys Don't Cry*, 'the filmmaker sacrifices the hard facts of racial hatred and transphobia to a streamlined humanist romance' (2001:298). A small number of films addressing or aimed at teen audiences and centring queer protagonists over the last twenty years suggest that something has changed in the representation of LGBTQ+ youth. Same-sex desire is not the scandal it once was, but I want to end by suggesting that what is absent from these accounts is the sense of sexuality and gender non-conformity as generating solidarity and community. These films privilege a self-knowledge of sex as the truth about oneself over the inter-subjectivity of queer desire.

# SEVEN

## 'I'd Be Lost without the Weight of You Two on My Back'

### Working-Class Teens and the Western

One of the problems with writing about working-class film is the difficulty of identifying what is understood or 'read' in the United States as *working-class*. While the character Juno in one of the films discussed in this chapter would appear, in a British context, to be working-class (blue-collar father, nail technician mother), one reviewer compares 'middle-class' Juno to 'working-class' Precious. Many of the black teen films discussed in chapter 5 are set in mixed-class, black neighbourhoods, and the character who escapes from the violence of the neighbourhood is most likely to be the middle-class character. However, this is not made explicit because being middle-class is subsumed into discourses of respectability, discipline, and even black political consciousness. That, for example, Tre Styles is middle class (estate agent father, lawyer mother), Starr Carter is middle class (father owns a local store), or that Precious's teacher is middle-class is not made explicit in the film's narrative. Rather, the ability of these characters to transcend the circumstances of their neighbourhood, and of the majority of black people in the film, is implicitly or explicitly attributed to their education, their discipline and their family, especially, their father's guidance.

It is also difficult to delineate teen working-class film because, unlike black and queer teens, white working-class teenagers have been present in US film, often at the centre of the narrative, since the inception of the Hollywood system. The most famous US teen rebel, James Dean, and the characters he played in *East of Eden* (1955), *Rebel Without a Cause* (1955) and *Giant* (1956) were neither teenagers nor working class and yet the

111

image of the nihilistic, cigarette-smoking, leather-jacket-wearing white teen boy persisted in visual culture as a powerful trope of class antipathy to bourgeois values or, more generally, to 'decency' or 'respectability'. Recall, for example, how the commentator in *Nine from Little Rock* (see chapter 2) tries to draw a line between ordinary white Americans and the violent whites who resisted school desegregation. This figure of the rebellious teenager itself drew from a long tradition in US film of the Western hero, and that figure has carried over into contemporary film about working-class youth. In the second section of this chapter, I explore the continuing appeal of the Western as a genre for depicting youth coming of age within material scarcity and personal trauma through an analysis of *Winter's Bone, Leave No Trace, American Honey*, and *Lean on Pete*. In this first section, I explore the more popular depictions of working-class teens in the classic teen movie.

## TEEN MOVIES

Probably the most, or possibly the only, famous auteur of teen movies is John Hughes. Not only was his output prodigious, but it also influenced many directors and writers who have made films that are now considered to be classics of the teen film genre (Driscoll 2011:45–56, Kaveney 2006:11–48). Many of his films, most famously *Pretty in Pink*, depict the differences in work, home and school for working-class and middle-class white Americans by focusing on the public school, which is one of the few sites where they come into contact as formal equals. Connecting these two formally equal but socially distant groups is the work of the romantic relationship that drives the narrative. This centres the teen girl (for most of Hughes's films, played by Molly Ringwald, 'the one figure across the films who attempts to navigate the class differences of her social milieu' (Bleach 2010:26). Jon Lewis claims that the central girl protagonist and 'her democratic benevolence, coordinates a victory of romance over cynicism' (Lewis 2013:139); in doing so, she/the narrative elides social conflict in favour of 'the triumph of individuality' (2013:138).

*Pretty in Pink* (which Hughes wrote) is unambiguously a film about class, and inspired the overall storyline of Greta Gerwig's *Lady Bird* (2017). But whereas *Pretty* resolves the problem of how a working-class girl is going to step outside of her class through her romantic involvement with an upper-class boy, *Lady Bird* attaches her desires to high culture and university education. The film opens with a shot of railway tracks echoing a line in *Lady Bird* when the nice middle-class boy (who comes to collect her to go to his grandparents house for Thanksgiving) comments to her parents that she literally 'lives on the wrong side of the tracks', a statement he thought she was using as a metaphor. Her mother cites this as one of the instances that demonstrate Lady Bird's shame of her working-class home. In *Pretty*, the working-class boy who has loved Andie all through secondary school has a similar relationship with her to that of the working-class best friend in *Lady*, and the upper-class boy, Blane ('that's not a name it's an appliance'), is substituted in *Lady* by the upper-class girl who, Julie comments, 'is a moron'. However, although her working-class home embarrasses Andie, she does not desire the upper-class life that Lady Bird seems to aspire to. That said, this might partly be because of the gender and relationship switch: if Andie appears avaricious about the lifestyle of the boy she has a crush on, this invites accusations of being a gold-digger, whereas to envy or desire the lifestyle of a rich girl does not carry the same connotations of inauthenticity or manipulation. While the film attempts to suggest that there is an equivalence between Blane's friends' attitude towards him dating a working-class girl ('If you got a hard-on for trash, don't take care of it around us, pal, all right?' 'Blane. If you want your little piece of low-grade ass, fine, take it. But if you do, you're not gonna have a friend') and her friends' (which is actually only her one friend) attitude to her dating a 'richie' ('If I hate him because he's got money, that's the same thing as them hating us because we don't. Understand?'). What this particular exchange does not capture is the constant harassment, threatening behaviour and actual violence that the working-class children in the school have to deal with and which is shown consistently in the rest of the film. The film does show that the class hatred of the rich students towards the working-class students is consistent and unrelenting.

It is also worth reflecting that this theme of inequality being an expression of interpersonal animosity based on ignorance of the other runs through the visual political culture of the United States. Indeed, one of the reasons that children and young people are deployed in social-reform visual culture is to hold out the promise that they are untainted by interpersonal prejudice because they are not yet fully socialised into irrational hatred of the other and that they are more likely to be exposed to people of other classes and ethnicities than their own, especially at public school. This conceit confuses intolerance of dissimilar others in general, as a psychological attitude with racism and class discrimination. This leads to the presentation of discrimination as something that 'both sides' are equally prone to.

*Lady Bird* is a coming-of-age story in which the working-class teen protagonist yearns for 'culture', for 'something to happen', and to get out of Sacramento. The film opens in a hotel room where Lady Bird and her mother have spent the night following a college interview. From the opening scene, in which they squabble about whether the hotel bed should be made or not, the film quickly establishes the constant friction and misunderstanding between these two characters, which is punctuated by occasional moments of love. Lady Bird is the only daughter of a white, working-class couple who also have an adopted Latino son, Miguel, who has already graduated college (Berkeley) but still lives with his parents and has a job packing groceries. Lady Bird wants to have sex (but once she does, she realises she prefers 'dry humping'); she applies to college on the East Coast (Sarah Lawrence), passes her driving test, buys cigarettes, a lotto card and a *Playboy* magazine on her eighteenth birthday ('because I can'), finds out that she has got into Sarah Lawrence, graduates high school, goes to New York. The film ends with her calling her mum to say she loves her, that she is using her birth name again (Christine), and that she loves Sacramento. This last statement is spoken over scenes that interchange her and her mother driving through Sacramento.

There is a deeply affecting scene in the film in which her mother has stopped speaking to, or even acknowledging, Lady Bird because she has got into an East Coast college. It is not clear why her mother is so angry with her about applying to, and perhaps more so about succeeding in getting into, Sarah Lawrence, but the suggestion is that her mother fears that once Lady Bird is gone, she won't come back or, perhaps, that when she comes back, she will be even more of a snob. It's pretty clear that her mother does not like her (in one scene Lady Bird tries to get her mother to say she likes her as she is; the best her mother can offer is that 'she wants her to be the best person she can be') and resents her daughter's class prejudice ('wrong side of the tracks', 'you're such a snob', 'making your father drop you off around the block', 'that's for rich people, we're not rich people'). But her mother also tries to express how much she does love her in a series of half-completed letters that her father rescues from the trash and puts in Lady Bird's suitcase when she leaves for the airport and that Lady Bird reads in her college room.

This is all deeply convincing. While the portrait of Lady Bird could not exactly be said to be loving, it is attentive, and it is surely no accident that a teacher-nun says to Lady Bird, 'Don't you think maybe they are the same thing? Love and attention?' This is a story about a teenager developing into a young adult and finding her own character, rather than being made to carry a larger story (e.g., about class envy or the difficulty of raising children while barely making ends meet and working double shifts, although these aspects of working-class life also feature in the film). In contrast with black and queer films, which tend to explore a broader moral or ethical idea so that the film is a vehicle to articulate those ideas, *Lady Bird* and similar films are explorations of what it is like to come of age in a specific working-class milieu. The world barely impinges on Lady Bird, and the one false note in the film is the use of TV news of the Iraq war to underline how intensely self-absorbed she is. Even the potential tragedy in the opening scenes when Lady Bird throws herself out of the car her mother is driving to end their bickering—about college, and about Lady Bird's snobbery, and about whether or not she is clever or works hard enough—ends with no more than a broken arm and a pink plaster cast.

One reviewer described the film as a 'steady trot of clipped vignettes [that] comes to seem monotonous and somewhat evasive, a way to move along before anything too hard and hurtful happens' (www.bfi.org.uk/news-opinion/sight-sound-magazine/reviews-recommendations/lady-bird-greta-gerwig-sketches-awkward-adolescence). I find it difficult to agree with this assessment, although a series of scenes that show the school's drama group preparing for their performance comes very close to a pastiche of *Glee* or *Fame*. It seems unlikely that this is unintentional. The rest of the film, in contrast, shows a coherent narrative in which the main character is shown rejecting her family and best friend to embrace the middle-class life of a new best friend, and a new (and very pretentious) boyfriend. After she has sex with the boyfriend, she realises that he is not that interesting, after all, and ditches him for her old friend, who she goes to the prom with. The scenes at the prom of the two girls dancing with one another and having their picture taken together are truly lovely and recall something like the melodrama of *Brief Encounter* in its closing scene ('you've been a long way away, thank you for coming back').

*Juno* is about a working-class, sixteen-year-old girl who gets pregnant the first time she has sex, considers abortion and then decides to keep the pregnancy and have the baby adopted by an upper-class, heterosexual couple she finds through an advert in a daily sales paper. Reviewers and some scholars have debated about *Juno* as a pregnancy movie, and therefore a film about being pro- or anti-choice. However, the writer (Diablo Cody) has refuted this interpretation and has said that the pregnancy/adoption storyline was a device to get the story of a working-class teen girl to connect with the lives of an upper-class mid-thirties couple (Vanessa and Mark). It is this connection that most of the story is constructed around, and it allows us to see the contrast between the constraints of working-class life and the opportunities of upper-class life in white America.

When Juno first visits Vanessa and Mark's house, she and her father drive out of their neighbourhood across town and into the would-be adoptive parents' gated neighbourhood. The houses are large, detached, spacious and set in their own grounds. The camera cuts between the view from the car and the interior of the house where Vanessa is carefully orchestrating the impression she wants to give: arranging photographs and magazines, polishing the banisters (an unlikely activity, given that they almost certainly have a maid). Their house has two bathrooms. The downstairs one is being decorated, so when Juno wants to pee, she goes upstairs, giving us a glimpse of the spaciousness of the rooms. Mark comes up to find her, perhaps to check on her, and on their way down, she notices a guitar in a room on the mezzanine. 'Oh. That's, uh, my room', says Mark. 'Vanessa lets me have a room for all my old stuff'. 'Wow, you get a whole room in your own house?' Juno responds. 'She's got you on a long leash there, Mark'. The film continues in this way, contrasting the lack of variety in food and drink and the absence of spaciousness and order in Juno's family home with the plenty of Vanessa and Mark's.

The role of the outsider in black teen film is to open up the world to alternatives that the teen is eager to enjoy and which they must immerse themselves in if they are not to be destroyed by the world they come from (e.g. *Precious*, *Boyz*). In contemporary film, the role of the middle-class rescuer (black or white) of the poor young character occurs mostly in film about black teens coming of age, but it is a recognisable trope from the much older tradition of child-saving literature and film (*Oliver Twist*, *Great Expectations* being paradigmatic examples). In *Juno*, this trope is substituted by another trope: that the rich are miserable despite, or maybe even because of, their wealth. Conversely, unlike in black films, where black sociality is almost always presented as complicated if not impossible, white working-class sociality is offered in *Lady Bird* and *Juno* as a positive, even enviable characteristic that is almost made possible because of (rather than despite) their financial hardship. While many commentators focused on the imagined pro-choice/anti-abortion politics of the film, and the success of the film, some commentated on the significance of a teen girl who is self-possessed, smart, funny, and seemingly unconcerned with clothes, makeup and boys' attention.

While the pregnancy cannot be ignored since it is the event around which the narrative pivots, this is essentially a coming-of-age story in which *Juno* loses her childhood innocence but is about relationships (family, adult-child, romantic, friendship) rather than about sex. Juno's mother left her and her father when Juno was very young and now sends her a cactus every year on her birthday; the impact of this crushing rejection on Juno is not directly explored, except perhaps in her consistent and usually sardonic refusal to take anything too seriously. However, although it is only attended to in a one-minute voiceover with a screen shot of the cacti in Juno's bedroom, the impact of this rejection on Juno's faith in adult relationships and her inability to romantically commit to her 'friend' (the first/only boy she has sex with) is what drives the narrative. Juno's decision to give her child to Mark and Vanessa rests on her belief that they are a stable, committed and loving couple. This fantasy about her child's future life is shattered when Mark (whom she has been spending time with as she becomes increasingly estranged from her peers by the growing distance between her needs and desires and theirs) tells her he is leaving Vanessa to pursue his fantasy life (which is to be a rock star). It is also hinted at that Mark thinks he and Juno have been flirting. Juno is appalled and runs downstairs, crying, just as Vanessa arrives home. Through Mark's paedophilic act, Juno, who had been seduced (not by Mark but by the comfort and plenty of their home), returns to her own family.

## TEEN WESTERNS

In their review of *Winter's Bone*, Michael Moon and Colin Talley consider the film (and the book from which it is adapted) as an account of 'life in a shatter zone'. They take this phrase from James C. Scott's work on communities who construct lives away from the surveillance of the state and develop a local culture of music, food and social relations that is often deeply embedded or connected to animals, weather, and land. González (2015) places *Winter's Bone* in the genre of the (post-)Western—concerned with borders, frontiers and the search for moral certainty/certitude in a legally ungoverned but highly controlled (by the rules of the kinship group) space.

*Winter's Bone* tells the story of a seventeen-year-old girl, Ree Dolly, who lives with her mother (who has an unspecified mental illness, which means she does not speak and spends long hours staring into space and barely moving), her twelve-year-old brother and seven-year-old sister (in the book from which the film is adapted, the two younger children are both boys). Her father was arrested on a charge of cooking meth, has skipped bail and is now missing. If he does not turn up (literally dead or alive) within a week, the family will lose their house and be 'out like dogs'. The narrative is driven by Ree's search for her father. This search brings her into conflict with her extended family who, we glean fairly early on, have murdered him for snitching to the police and have since hidden the body. The suspense is more focused on the issue of whether Ree and her siblings will get to keep the house, and if she will get killed trying, rather than on who killed her father.

The film's dialogue is very sparse. Meaning is conveyed through gestures, scenery, music and observational camerawork (González 2015) more than through speech. It is dominated by green and brown colours and dark interiors until the point after Ree delivers the severed hands of her dead father to the police, thereby proving that he is dead and releasing him from the bail-bond. After this scene, the lifting of the threat of homelessness is conveyed through the shift in the film's colour palette from green and brown to pale colours and orange tones. The camera, until this point closely framed on head-and-shoulder shots in enclosed spaces (the barn, the car, the room, the cattle pen), opens out to a broader view.

As with *American Honey*, which I discuss below, the viewer is struck by the contrast between how lawlessness and code operates in this rural white landscape, in contrast to its functioning in the hood films, from *Boyz n the Hood* through to *The Hate U Give*. In *Winter's Bone*, defiance of the law and refusal to engage with the law is axiomatic of belonging to the community. Indeed, it is the transgressing of this code that leads to Ree's father being murdered. Contrast, for example, a scene that is a staple of the hood film—a police car pulls up behind the protagonist's car, flashing blue lights. The protagonist stops, and the policeman gets out, torch in hand at shoulder level. He demands that the driver put their hands where he can see them and then orders them out of the car. When the protagonist is African American, this scene would convey fear and terror, and the audience would expect that it will end with the death or injury of the driver. This scene occurs in *Boyz* when the arresting officer threatens Tre by sticking a gun under his chin, only stepping down when a crime is radioed in and his partner suggests they go. It happens in *The Hate* when Starr's best friend is pulled over, steps out of the car, reaches in for his hairbrush and is shot by the policeman. Of course, it also happens in real life; in 2019 alone, the murders of Willie McCoy (20 years old), Antwon Rose II (17 years old), Anthony Jose "Chulo" Vega Cruz (18 years old) all occurred during a traffic stop by a policeman who then shot the driver. In contrast, when the local policeman pulls Teardrop (Ree's uncle) and Ree over when they are driving at night looking for her father's body, Teardrop not only refuses to get out of the car but pulls a rifle onto his lap and takes off the safety, an action that is visible to the policeman who watches it in the wing mirror. 'Is this our time?', asks Teardrop, and the officer backs down, and they both drive off. Subsequently, when Ree takes her dead father's severed hands to the police station to prove that he is dead, the officer says 'I stepped down because you were there, he didn't make me step down'. 'Looked that way to me', she replies and walks out. It would be impossible within a realist narrative structure for a black character to contest police authority in this way without getting arrested, at best. Indeed, such a contestation ending well for a black character is likely to signal that we are watching a superhero film.

Poverty here is not an obstacle to coming of age and coming of age does not depend on being able to leave, in the way that it routinely signifies in black teen film. The film ends on that very matter, when her little brother asks if, having not only secured the house but been given the cash that someone added to the bond (taken to be the person who got her father released so that he could be killed), she will now leave them. 'Why would I do that?', she asks. He explains that he had heard her talking about joining the army (a future she had contemplated in order to get the $40,000 the recruiting posters offered so that she could pay the bond debt). 'I'd be lost without the weight of you two on my back. I'm not going anywhere'. In contrast to the narratives of black coming-of-age films, where the weight of family ties is more like a millstone than an anchor, here growing up does not mean growing out.

What these films have in common with black and queer social-reform films is the importance of moral certitude in navigating a path to adulthood in conditions of poverty, drug abuse and violence. This can be construed as melodrama more than Western. The innocent, blameless figure of Ree is exposed to violence through no fault of her own and

**Figure 7.1.** '**I'd be lost without the weight of you two on my back'. Debra Granik, 2010.** *Winter's Bone.* **Anonymous Content.**

rescued just in the nick of time by the moral action of another. Although Gonzales (2015) is correct to argue that the moral figure, who has to retain their own moral compass despite the lawlessness that surrounds them, is a central trope of Westerns, this figure is also central to the melodramatic mode. The downfall of the central character, usually produced through rape or drugs, is understood in the melodrama to be primarily externally driven, so that the rescue (which can even be through death) restores the central character to their earlier good character. However, although it clearly has melodramatic elements (and arguably, the Western is also a melodramatic form), the constant threat of violence, the loyalty to a family code, and the beauty and (material and emotional) harshness of the setting also mean that *Winter's Bone* can more easily be read as a Western. Indeed, and surely this is the point of genre theory, several other films reveal themselves as being based on similar themes and tropes once they are thought of as Westerns. Whiteness, and the freedom it affords white-coded individuals under racial capitalism is also an important part of this definition. These themes are all present in *American Honey, Lean on Pete,* and *Leave No Trace.*

While the life of the central character in *American Honey* is clearly over-determined by poverty, her white-coded character (played by a mixed-race actor) is free to navigate both geographical and social space. Indeed, what brings Star (the central character) to abandon her younger siblings and go off on the road is her flirtation with Jake, and what keeps her on the road is that relationship: in other words, her longing for personal growth and connection. The film ends with a none-too-subtle symbolism of Star as a turtle coming out of her shell and immersing herself in her natural environment.

*American Honey* was very well received, although, at least for me, it is difficult to understand why. (Richard Brody's reviews in the *New Yorker* [Brody 2016] and *Black Media Review Collective* [Black Media Collective 2016] were rare dissenters.) Appreciation for the lyricism of the scenery, the slightly off-real cinematography of the group dancing and drinking, and a trip through the southern states (starting in Kansas—including an early shot of ruby-red slippers) just before Trump got elected unites most of the reviews in their positive evaluation of the film.

*American Honey* clearly wants to make some kind of commentary on the material deprivation of working-class life. To do so, the director, who is British, connects the work of magazine-subscription (mag) sellers to slavery. This is done through metaphors that align the workers with slaves and the mag boss as a Confederate slave owner. Take, for example, a scene in which Star and Jake sit in front of a fire in the middle of the night, and Jake shows Star the hoard of jewellery and money he has kept from their mag-crew manager. The reason he does this is that, earlier in the evening, lying in the forest after having sex, Star had asked Jake the question a middle-aged trucker asked her earlier that day: What is your dream? Jake says he will show her later what his dream is. When Jake shows her his stash, she says, 'It's like treasure'. 'It is treasure', he replies. 'But how is it your dream?', she asks. 'It's not the treasure, it's what it will buy. You know "40 acres and a mule"'. This is an extraordinary statement from a white man in a contemporary US film, especially one in which their boss, the young white woman who runs the mag-crew, is shown in one scene wearing a Confederate flag bikini. '40 Acres and a Mule' is the name of Spike Lee's production company, and it therefore seems highly unlikely that Andrea Arnold, an independent film maker, albeit from the United Kingdom, could not know that it has something to do with the black experience in the United States. It was the demand of the freed people at the end of the Civil War. The yeoman independent white free-holders whose own struggle to resist being turned into either an agricultural or an industrial waged labourer rested on the demand for control of enough land and means of production to be self-sufficient paralleled with the demand of free African Americans at the end of the Civil War for land and 'machinery' (40 acres and a mule), but this specific phrase belongs to the history of the black experience in the United States and cannot be simply transferred to whites.

Indeed, the whiteness of *American Honey* is necessary to the film's road-movie narrative structure, which itself is a device to be able to show the contrasts of wealth and poverty in the United States. Although Sasha Lane, who is biracial, plays the central character, two scenes in the film suggest that the character is coded as white. When Star first meets Krystal, the mag-crew boss, she comments that Jake had told her about a new 'redneck'; she then asks Star where she is from. Star answers, 'Texas', to which Krystal responds: 'A real American Honey, just like me'. Krystal is white, so these comments have to be read as either addressed to a white-coded character, or as highly charged and confrontational. A third possibility, which is also plausible, is that the director wants to suggest that race is no longer connected with unfreedom and that therefore the United States is now post-racial but still highly unequal.

Another example is the scene in which Krystal warns Star that she is not making enough sales, when Krystal lies on the bed wearing a Confederate flag bikini and then calls Jake into the room and stands up while he creams fake-tan lotion onto her legs. Fake tan is always code for poor whites, and the Confederate flag has similar class associations (in addition to its obvious racist symbolism), but the significance of the highly charged phrase 'redneck', of the Confederate flag or of drinking bourbon ('American honey') is not explored in the movie as a conflict for Star's character, suggesting that she is supposed to be read as racially white. What these symbols establish or assert instead is the connections in the United States between white poverty and ideologies of white supremacy. This is also established in the opening scenes of the film in which the house that Star lives in has a Confederate flag for a curtain.

*American Honey* wants to show the US South in all its beauty (the landscape), variety (from oil fields to wheat fields), and contrasts of poverty and wealth. Krystal's morning talks in which she describes the neighbourhood they are about to go to and sell in is a device for the audience to consider the contrasts of the United States, but the only culture or art in the entire movie is music, most of which is hip-hop. The protagonists have complete freedom to roam through this landscape, a freedom that is simply not possible for the equally poor black and LGBT characters discussed in the other two chapters in this section. Their right to be in public space, to make noise, to dance, to light fires, to get fucked up: none of this results in any attention either from security firms or the police. The nearest that any of them get to security forces is at the start of the film when a cashier calls security on Jake because he is dancing on the tills (to Rhianna's 'We Found Love'). In another scene, Jake pulls a gun on three wealthy white men, whom Star took a ride with to make some real money out of selling magazines. They have taken her back to their house, and the sense of impending rape seems palpable to everyone except Star. To be clear, it is not so much that Star is so inured to abuse that she does not care if she gets raped, it is that it has not occurred to her that this is a likely outcome. In another equally implausible scene, an oil rig worker offers Star $1,000 to 'hang out with him'—*hanging out* means driving to the middle of an oil field to watch the oil burning and then giving him a hand job for a few moments before he gets bored with her obvious lack of interest and does it himself while looking at her naked genitals. This is as unconvincing as it is baffling. Is it a counterpoint to Lars van Trier's thoroughly misogynist *Breaking the Waves*, in which the main character hitches a ride on an oil boat and is raped multiple times before being thrown back on land and dying of her injuries: not all oil crew?

Another interpretation of both Krystal's Confederate flag bikini and Jake's '40 acres and a mule' comment is that Krystal's role as the organiser of the mag-crew—who organises their work, drops them off and picks them up, feeds them and houses them but does not do any work herself—is being rendered as comparable with that of a slave master to Jake's slave. America in this film is white, except for the music and one scene in which the mag-crew exchange a few words and handshakes with a group of young black men who are staying at the same motel. This scene and the music—most of which is hip-hop—seem to want to signify the 'We don't see color' stance of the (other than Lane) all-white cast/characters. If Krystal is the Confederate slave owner and the crew are slaves, then both this scene and the music can be read through the same symbolism. The easy camaraderie between the mag-crew and the black men staying at the motel, signifying their social similarity, and the hip-hop music—most of which is diegetic, being played in the van in which the crew travel (Krystal travels in a car)—is intended to bring this white group into the cultural history of black disenfranchisement in the United States. This offers a surprising connection to chapter 2, in which I discussed how social reform against child labour in the late nineteenth century presented the problem of child labour as one of white children being enslaved while black children were free. Therefore, another way of reading both this film and the child-labour-reform campaign is that both buy into the fantasy that the Civil War ended racial inequality and that the United States is subsequently post-racial leaving only working-class unfreedom to be resolved.

*Lean on Pete* is a low-budget ($8 million) film directed by Andrew Haigh. While critically well received, it has not done well in the United States, taking in only $1.1 million in US and Canadian receipts and $1.3 million in international receipts excluding North America. Despite its minor status compared to the other films discussed in this chapter and the previous two chapters, I include it here as a stripped-down example of the youth Western. The main character, Charley, is a sixteen-year-old boy who lives with his father in a trailer park in Portland, Oregon, and has recently found work as a stable boy for a race-horse owner, Del, played by Steve Buscemi. Lean on Pete is one of Del's horses. Early on in the film, Charley's father is killed by his girlfriend's jealous ex-husband. Shortly after Charley steals Del's van, trailer and horse (Lean on Pete) to prevent Del from selling Pete to the knacker's yard. Charley drives from Portland to Wyoming, where he hopes to find his mother's sister whom he has not seen since she and his father had an argument when he was young. On the way, he gets a job with a Mexican painting and decorating crew; gets beaten up for his wages by a homeless man who had befriended him; nearly gets arrested for running off from a diner without paying the bill; loses control of Pete, who runs into the path of an oncoming car and is killed; and catches a train for the last leg of the journey to find his aunt. The film ends shortly after he is reunited with his aunt. There is very little dialogue in the film, and most of the script is Charley talking to the horse as they trek across the United States.

*Leave No Trace* (2018), directed by Debra Granik, who also directed *Winter's Bone*, took in $6 million at the United States and Canadian box offices and a further $1.6 in international receipts. It was produced by BRON studios and distributed by Bleecker Street Media. The two main characters in the film are a veteran with PTSD and his daughter, Tom. They live in the woods near Portland, Oregon. They forage and hunt for food and occasionally make the trek to Portland to buy stuff they cannot find or make. On the way, they pass camps of homeless veterans. Will teaches Tom to hunt and forage, to make shelters and to understand the signs of the land. She has also learned to read and write. One day Tom makes a mistake, or possibly deliberately slips up, and reveals their location to a hiker. They are tracked down by social services, who assesses them both and interrogate Tom about whether she has been abused by her father. The social workers accept that they can live together and that Will has been a good father to Tom, but they insist that they live in a house, that Will gets work, and that they integrate into a community. This goes fairly well for Tom, who meets a boy and joins the local 4H club. One day they leave, abruptly and against Tom's will. Will leaves Tom in a vacant cabin in a wood while he goes to find food, but he does not return. The next day, Tom finds him, injured and nearly dead. She gets help from a nearby campsite, and they stay there while Will is healing. Once he is better, he wants to leave, but she wants to stay. She has found some kind of community in this clearing populated by people with their own traumas and held together by a loving woman who is motherly towards Tom.

*Lean on Pete* and *Leave No Trace*, like *Winter's Bone* and *American Honey*, use the wandering of the main protagonists to show the viewer the deep poverty of the contemporary, rural, working-class US. This landscape barely features any black or Latinx people, and there are no central black or Latinx characters. The affect is to create an almost ethnographic account of white rural working-class life and sociality devoid of any of the lines of connection or border crossings that one would anticipate in a country as diverse and large as the United States. It contrasts to the depiction of white people in films about black life and sociality in which, while white characters do not feature prominently, they are invariably present as a device to demonstrate the lack of racial animosity of black people towards white people. The exclusion of black people from these narratives also reproduces the racism black people experience in them: for example, the removal of Philip Devine, a young black man from Brandon

Teena's story, although he was also murdered by Brandon's friends at the same time.

A second theme is the violent, hard character of rural and small-town America. The harshness of social interaction, especially between men and especially towards the weak, is a constant theme. While instances of physical violence are few, the constant threat of violence, especially sexual violence and the unpredictability of men, hangs over the films. Connected to this is a brusque, unsentimental mode of speech that is intended to convey a rough affection. And, like the Western, the ability of young people to be inured to and withstand this physical violence and brusque social interaction is depicted as something akin to strength of character and necessary for survival. Ree is brutally assaulted by the women who wanted her to stop investigating her father's disappearance. The women who beat Ree up then come to her house, having decided to rescue her by leading her to her father's bones (which will provide the evidence of his death and release his bail-bond on their house). Charley is beaten by the homeless man who befriends him because he wants his money. Charley responds by breaking into a car, stealing a wrench and beating the man with it until he gets his money back—suggesting that it is not the first time he has defended himself by beating someone. Will and Tom barely speak in *Leave No Trace*, and his love for her is carried in brief touches, and doing things together.

While the teen movie that follows the classic family conflict/school romance established by Hughes's oeuvre and the youth Western diverge in their accounts of working-class life, they do share two features: absent parents, and the importance of making as an expression of care.

## MISSING MOTHERS AND ATTENTIVE FATHERS

In *Juno* and *Lady Bird* and even in *Winter's Bone*, the father is understanding and loving to his daughter, in contrast to the harshness or misunderstanding, or simply the absence, of mothers. *Pretty in Pink* has a loving father who is depressed because his daughter's mother walked out on Andie (the daughter) and him three years earlier. Juno's mother left her and her father when she was very young—and never returned. Lady Bird's father and mother are both present, but her father is much more sympathetic and intuitive than her mother. Tom's mother in *Leave No Trace* is dead. Charley's mother abandoned him when he was a little child. In *American Honey*, Star's mother is alive but effectively abandoned her daughter and younger siblings and left them all with an abusive father.

The absent mother is a longstanding trope of fiction writing, and in recent popular culture, she is replaced, not by absence (against which the child grows up), but by the presence of a dad who does all the things mothers are generally tasked with (emotional and physical support and nurturing) as well as some of the 'dad' things (Boxer 2014). Juno's father is noticeably always fixing something. While the dad in *Pretty* is not competent in 'dad things' and has a habit of sitting around in his underpants and dressing gown in front of his teenage daughter, he is very loving and tries to offer the right advice when she is upset by being dumped from prom by the rich boy. He then apologises for not being her mother ('Sometimes I feel a little sorry that I'm the one you have to talk to about these things') to which she replies: 'I'm not. She couldn't have said it any better than you—I mean it'.

Another persistent theme in films on working teen life is the ability of teens or their mothers to shift, to make-do, to mend and re-create. The 'famous' dress in *Pretty* is made by Andy, who designs it on paper, cuts the pattern out from a dress her father bought her and one her boss/older friend at work gave her, and sews it on her own sewing machine. The stepmother in *Juno* extends Juno's jeans to make them into pregnancy trousers. *Winter's Bone* is full of scenes of Ree making and mending. She teaches her younger siblings how to skin rabbits. She chops wood. She hunts. Tom, in *Leave No Trace*, knows how to track, hunt, build shelters, and find water.

While this making is partly about making do, about having to get by with few resources, to be able to thrift, it is also a substitute for verbal expressions of love, of which there are very few in these films.

## CONCLUSION

The classic teen film centres the story of a girl and her transition to adulthood as she negotiates romantic and sexual relationships with boys and her new place in her own family. To the extent that films like these belong in this book, with its focus on the place of children and youth in social-reform visual culture, they do so only when they foreground narratives of class conflict and working-class life. The Western teen movie, also about working-class teens, is a clearer example of how film takes up or represents class inequality. However, whereas both black and queer films propose some solution to the problems that their young protagonists face, whether through asserting the truth of their sexuality and their authentic selves or through racial uplift, the Western youth film is more likely to assert the importance of family, 'the weight of you on my back', and tradition, 'I'm not going anywhere', over individualism and striking out.

# EIGHT

## On 'Being the Representation'

Increasingly, television features LGBT characters, often in ensemble casts in relatively central roles. GLAAD'S *Where We Are on TV* 2018–2019 report found that 8.8 per cent of characters who were series regulars on broadcast primetime scripted programming were LGBTQ, with equal representation for women and men, and more characters who are people of colour than white characters. This increase in queer representation is not unconnected to the perception that LGBT people have more disposable income than straight people and, more broadly, that what television scholar Ron Becker has dubbed 'socially liberal, urban-minded professionals' or 'slumpies' (Becker 2004:391) are a valuable niche audience. An easy way to appeal to this audience, Jonathan Cohn argues, was to increase the programming of queer characters. LGBT representation, in this view, brings in both straight bourgeois viewers who want to square their liberal values with their materialism and lesbian (and especially) gay viewers who want to see more representation. Cohn argues that '[i]n the process, they helped shape which homosexual and queer identities could be made legible' (Cohn 2016:684) in distinctly classed ways. This close connection between capturing high-value markets and LGBT representation is also evident in how young LGBT digital activists establish themselves through vlogging by monetarising and leveraging their content.

RAINBOW CAPITALISM AND THE AUTHENTIC SELF: 'BEING THE REPRESENTATION'

This chapter analyses the content of YouTube videos produced by people who are LGBT+ micro-celebrities or influencers. The specific issue that LGBT YouTube videos address is how to 'be you' in a broad social context where same-sex desire and gender non-conformity are difficult to give expression to, publically and safely, perhaps especially for young people. YouTube quickly emerged as a platform for the formation of digital publics, and many young LGBT people used that platform to both come out online and to document their transitions. Indeed, it was the ubiquity of coming-out and transitioning videos on YouTube produced by young people themselves that prompted me to formulate the research question that this book addresses: To what extent does having control over the means of visual production and distribution when making film about social justice issues generate new forms of representation?

Given the volume of LGBT videos on YouTube, this chapter focuses on those YouTubers who could clearly be identified as activists, not only from their YouTube content but also from their presence on other social media and mainstream media. YouTube is only one of the social media platforms that LGBT digital activists upload to. All have a presence on multiple platforms including Twitter and Instagram, as well as personal websites. Many online activists also make content for TedX. But the most interesting aspect of convergence across different platforms is in the ways that producer content gets picked up by youth mainstream media (MSM) like *Teen Vogue* and *Seventeen*, who profile 'teen activists' in order to both amplify the platforms of young activists and brand *Teen Vogue* and similar productions as engaged with social reform. This is interesting for at least two reasons. Firstly, it raises questions about the relationship between content and product placement. Secondly, several magazines, most notably *Teen Vogue*, have re-orientated themselves towards the youth social justice market, prompting the question: What does it mean for political critique to be advocated by and connected with a lifestyle brand?

The crossover between an individual's social media presence and corporate media enables YouTubers to monetarise their content by expanding their followers and enables corporate media to promote itself to a rapidly growing market of young people interested in issues that have come to be framed within the increasingly empty signifier of 'social justice'. This crossover also calls into question the extent to which YouTube LGBT digital activism is creating new modes of representation or whether, given its address to consumer capitalism, it is simply pulling potential activists into the domain of the market. In short, is most LGBT digital 'activism' a form of advertising that expands 'rainbow capitalism' through creating the 'branded political activist' (Banet-Weiser 2012:140–43), or is it something more challenging? To address these questions I analysed the content of micro-celebrity LGBT activists Jazz Jennings, Ryan Jacob Flores and Jessie Paege.

Jazz is a trans girl. She first appeared online in around 2006 when she was five years old, and her parents approached ABC to make and broadcast an interview with her. She started her own YouTube channel in 2014 and posts content regularly. She has 650,000 followers and 45 video uploads with views ranging from 59,000 to 3,000,000. She is often cited by other LGBT youth as a role model. Prior to setting up her own YouTube channel, she published on her mother's channel. She also has a reality TV show produced and broadcast on TLC. Jazz's core message is simple and consistent across all of these platforms: be authentic.

Ryan Jacobs Flores first posted on YouTube on August 25, 2014. The post is ten minutes long (10.24) and consists of Ryan talking to the webcam in a room that has a mirror on one wall and a small information poster on another and is otherwise bare. The room is painted light green and has the aesthetic of an office. Ryan talks about his desire to transition, his girlfriend, his upcoming birthday, and his interests (Harry Potter, piano, music) and that he has learned some sign language—he spells his name out in sign language. He says he's 'not white' but Mexican, 'just putting that out there' and that while he is out as trans at school, and people there use he/his pronouns and his name, at home he is not out and uses she/her pronouns and his old name. He has a YouTube channel with 95,995 subscribers. On the channel home page, he has a 'trailer' to his life as a trans man, which he posted in 2016, and which has just over 70,000 views. It mostly documents the impact of T on his changing voice. Most of his posts have between 3,000 and 10,000 views. The titles of the posts with higher views suggest that viewers are watching to understand more about specific elements of transitioning, that is, his most popular post, *Pre-T to one Year on Testosterone Comparison // FtM Transgender*, has 3.2 million views, whereas his least popular are his videos that are playing around with genres and techniques rather than specifically talking about his experiences as a trans man. His pre-T to one year on T comparison post is essentially a montage of him speaking to camera at monthly intervals of being on T—to document and demonstrate the drop in the pitch of his voice, and the change in his body fat and muscle composition. He assures the viewer that 'making these videos was not me trying to impress you with some dramatic transformation' (7:04/7:26); 'it was for me', 'this journey was for me and my happiness'.

Jessie Paege is a bisexual young (twenty-year-old) woman YouTuber. Her channel is mostly content on fashion and makeup. She made a coming-out video in 2018, which she released on YouTube. In 2018 she was a finalist in the Shorty Awards LGBTQ+ Account. The Shorty Awards announced her nomination with a statement that her 'viral testimonials received over 1M+ views, inspiring fans to pursue their own authentic truth. Now with 1.5M+ YouTube subscribers, 1M+ Twitter and Instagram followers, 2018 *Think Beyond Pink* book release, Hot Topic merch line and ladies-only compilation album "Empowerment," Jessie is bolstering her dominating platforms with LGBTQ+ advocacy, philanthropy and education'.[1] About a year after coming out as bisexual, she launched a brand partnership with Tarte Cosmetics based on the colours of the rainbow flag.

## MAKING A BRAND

The *micro-celebrity* is a person with an online presence in which they leverage their performance of authenticity and the attention from viewers and comments that it generates to connect advertisers to consumers. The tension between the projection of authenticity and the generation of income from the same activity, in this case vlogging about LGBT identity, arises because authenticity is partly signified by its distance from commercial circuits. Think, for example, of love as an authentic feeling. Love is enacted through various intimate communicative practices (hugging, talking, sex, etc.). While the exchange of gifts is often a part of displays of love and friendship, the closer gifting is to commerce, the less authentic it is felt to be. Similarly, intimate communicative practices are emptied of their signification as signs of deep or true feeling the more they are connected to commercial circuits. Although it is obvious to the viewer that the content they are watching has been monetarised, because of the adverts that appear before the video starts or because the vlogger promotes brands, promotions and adverts are not directly commented on by the vlogger. The influencer is more explicit in their promotion of particular brands or products, but in general, LGBT vloggers are not influencers in this direct sense. As Terri Senft says, the micro celebrity is adopting practices of people who historically have merged the self and their product (artists, entrepreneurs). She also points out that this practice and the relative ease with which it can be done through vlogging may be especially attractive to teens who are only able to 'count as people, rather than property' when they have managed to 'establish themselves as corporate entities: child celebrities, athletes, and so on' (2013:351).

Ryan's posts are edited within a standard format that opens with an edit of camera lenses that then fades, and with his name in capital letters within a rectangular frame centre image, and the tagline: 'transcend and trans4m'. A music clip accompanies the first five seconds. Music is played in the background on all of his posts. He also has a logo—the letters R and J in cursive in a small, peach-coloured circle that drops into the lower right-hand side of the screen and stays on screen throughout the post. The format of Ryan's channel has been consistent since he set it up when he was sixteen years old. There is nothing specifically queer about his branding, and the tagline 'transcend and trans4m', which could indicate that he is a trans man, could equally refer to a more general idea of overcoming and transforming.

After the introductory titles, the post begins with a black screen with white writing that says: 'I didn't transition because I hated myself. It was because I loved myself enough to believe I deserved to be happy in my lifetime'. The montage of the year taking T is all shot in his dormitory room at college. On the background is a calendar written onto a white board. The main colours are black and grey. He is wearing a grey shirt and a grey beanie, and his bed has black and grey bedding on it. The exception is a video of him in a car (not driving), one of him in the clinic looking nervous, perhaps waiting for the nurse, and then getting his shot from the nurse. In other clips, he injects himself with T. In one scene, he is with a girl and he says 'just got back in from the doctors'. They both smile. It then cuts to him improvising a song: 'I'm finally on testosterone' and then to him speaking to camera, 'one month on testosterone, you guessed it'. In this scene, he is wearing a red shirt. Visible on the wall is a dream catcher. Two months on T: visible on the wall are Harry Potter posters. Here he speaks about how sad he was two years ago when he first came out as trans. At the end of one year, after he says 'I did it', the background music shifts to upbeat tempo, fast-paced.

In another clip in the montage, he clicks his fingers and says 'testing 1, 2'—an action that he could have edited out but it is common in reality TV/webcam to draw attention to the videoing process. Similarly, about three-quarters through the video (5:39), he makes a mistake and says 'one month' instead of 'one year' on T. Again, he could have edited it out, so this should be read as a director/editorial decision to keep it in, and it adds to the sense of a lack of artifice, paradoxically, by drawing attention to the production process.

His second-most viewed video is about his new roommate's belief that he is a cis man and whether he is obligated to come out to her.[2] Given that he posts this on YouTube and also on Twitter, it seems that he is in some sense coming out to her, or at least there is a strong possibility that she will come across the video. In fact, the purpose of the video seems more to explain that he is now mostly living stealth, passes as a cis man '100 percent of the time' but is not ashamed of being trans, nor does he feel any obligation to come out as trans because 'it is my personal life and it doesn't really change anything', 'its very personal' (6:16/8:36).

In the video *Trans Masc Influencers Discuss Being the Representation* for The Advocate, an online LGBT-focused magazine, Ryan and another trans man, Mars Wright, talk about 'being the representation'. Ryan describes himself as having 'been a public figure since about 2015' when he started making videos on YouTube. He explains that the videos document his transition as something that he could look back on and 'that other people are also able to witness'. Mars Wright talks in an Instagram post about the importance of having trans masc content that does not presume a very narrow kind of masculinity that, as he says, means you drink beer and watch sports. Ryan talks about wanting to see more people of colour who are trans on television and film. The video is filmed head and shoulders to camera on a green background with animation and titles popping up on screen to illustrate some key messages. Both interviewees talk about the importance of being 'the representation', that is, of being visible to others who are like them (trans or trans men, a person of colour, a femme trans man). Ryan says he wants to 'see me on

screen', meaning other Latinx trans people. This idea of being the representation is a key break from earlier forms of representation of young
people in social-reform or social-problem films. While many of the films
analysed in the previous section were made by young black or queer
filmmakers, they were necessarily addressing a broader audience than
the people and communities depicted on screen. Some of their address
was to the audience as witnesses to what it is like to live in a violent
neighbourhood or to be forced to undergo conversion therapy, but these
witnesses were not necessarily also people who were, or would in the
future experience these forms of violence, racism and homophobia.

One of the key ways in which YouTube vlogging contrasts with films
is in relation to who is being interpellated by the video, who the video
assumes and constructs its audience to be. Even films that are made by
LGBT directors or adapted from LGBT writing and experience are implicitly or explicitly aimed, at least in part, at straight audiences. This is
almost inevitable, given the financial structuring of the film industry,
which requires several million dollars to be taken at the box office to
make a profit. Obviously, this is not the case for vloggers who simply
need the costs of a broadband connection and a camera.

The relatively low costs of vlogging, then, changes a key aspect of the
representation of LGBT+ teens on film: who they are addressed to. However, vloggers who are also mini-celebrities or influencers are monetarising their content or leveraging it in some way to secure financial outcomes. Despite the routine disavowals that they are seeking an audience
but, rather, are making content 'for me', vloggers need viewers if they are
to monetarise their accounts. Jessie Paege, for example, donated all the
advertising from her coming-out post to the Trevor Project but also secured a promotion with the makeup firm Tarte, who also donated to the
Trevor Project. In fact, the coming-out video was taken down from You-
Tube because of copyright issues over a song she sampled on the video[3]
but then edited and re-posted.

Tarte Cosmetics has annual revenue of about $35,000,000; as a point of
comparison, the Body Shop, who also market as a natural, cruelty-free
cosmetics brand, had annual revenue in 2018 of nearly $800,000,000. So
vloggers provide access for advertisers to a targeted market. However,
tie-in promotions are not limited to small firms. Jazz Jennings fronted
Johnson and Johnson's See the Real Me campaign for Clean & Clear in
2015. In addition to signing Jazz, the franchise launched an advertising
campaign in which a sixteen-year-old girl took over their social media
accounts. The director of the Clean & Clear franchise organization, Sa-
meer Agarwal, said, 'We were losing relevance with teen girls. As we
started to peel back the onion on why that had happened, it became clear
that we weren't putting out content in the places where they were watching content' (Smiley 2015).

It is surely uncontroversial to claim that advertising firms are recruiting LGBT youth to their campaigns in order to capture market share with teenagers and young adults. During London Pride this year (2019), I was struck by how many shops on the Pride parade route featured LGBT content. For many firms, this was no more than the use of slogans like 'Love is Love' or window displays of rainbow colours on flags or balloons. As I write this, I have a wristband I picked up at the march lying on my desk. It is in rainbow colours with 'Fujitsu'—the Japanese multinational IT firm—stamped on one side and '#BeCompletelyYou' on the other. These colours and slogans have the merit for advertisers that their poly-semiotic character means that they can be all things to all people. For LGBT marchers and their allies, it signals the firms' recognition of LGBT consumers and, even for some, will be taken as a genuine commitment by the firm to LGBT liberation. For people who are not familiar with LGBT discourse, the rainbow and the slogan can be taken as anodyne statements that signify something like 'motherhood and apple pie' or 'be happy'.

However, at least one store, Lululemon, the Canadian multinational athletic leisure-wear brand's flagship store in Regent Street, central London, unambiguously addressed their window display to the parade. The window display was painted with images of an ethnically diverse crowd of people holding banners with slogans on them including: 'Non Binary and Proud', 'Trans Rights Are Human Rights', 'Love Knows No Gender' and 'Gay and Proud'. The display was commissioned from British artist Jessica Sharville (http://www.jessicasharville.com/). All of the illustrated figures are wearing clothes from Lululemon's collection. Jessica was also in-store at Lululemon's Regent Street branch to do live illustration in the brand's windows. 'Completing the windows are a new collection of mannequins, standing side by side to give a sense of togetherness', says the puff piece on the display in *Retail Focus*. The promotion was commissioned from the advertising agency Lucky Fox, whose chief creative officer said, 'Shoppers are well versed in seeing the rainbow flag colours that are so synonymous with Pride, but we wanted to create something with more depth and sincerity' (Retail Focus 2019). What all of these slogans and the picture of diverse ethnicities and genders demonstrating signify is the core of what has become Rainbow capitalism's brand: you do you. This fits neatly with Lululemon's advertising strategy, which is based on salon-based retail, which has worked so well for Apple. In short, consumer capitalism through its appropriation of the LGBT struggle for equality is attempting to brand products—from IT tech to yoga pants, as a way to buy your most authentic self in order to live 'your best life', in another contemporary slogan that stitches social justice to consumer capitalism.

## CREATING PUBLIC SPACE IN PRIVATE SPACES

In chapter 6, on LGBT film, I noted the intense unhomeliness of the home for LGBT youth. It is perhaps unsurprising, given the low entry costs of these productions, that they are made at home, almost always in the producer's bedroom. However, given the presentation of the basic conflict LGBT+ youth are experiencing between them and their families, and specifically the withdrawal of unconditional love, it is surprising that LGBT teens are making coming-out videos in their bedrooms. In one remarkable statement, Ryan says that he is making his content while his parents are out because they don't know he is trans. This seems to support Boyd's (2014) contention that social media creates spaces for youth that escape the otherwise often intense surveillance of their parents.

Generally though, Ryan's story (of not being out to his parents) is an exception to vloggers' presentation of LGBT youth and their relationship to their families. Jazz Jennings, for example, has a television reality show that involves her entire family. She frequently refers to how supportive her family have been in enabling her to live as a girl and eventually to medically transition. Jessie Paege has a video where she comes out to her mother, who seems to already know or is certainly not surprised to find out that her daughter is bisexual. There are numerous videos on YouTube of young people coming out to their parents.

In contrast to the LGBT films analysed in chapter 6, which I noted were characterised by a lack of speech, here, somewhat paradoxically for a visual medium, the content is dominated by speech. Although the dominance of talk is noticeable in these productions, which almost entirely consist of talk to camera in closely framed shots made in the speaker's bedroom, the content of the talk is repetitive and simple in its messaging. The silence or taciturnity of the main protagonists in LGBT coming-out films conveys the deep internal conflict of the protagonists as they come to terms with the difficulty of being out in homophobic and transphobic environments, or even having the language to articulate their experiences. With very few exceptions, LGBTQ films do not depict public spaces in which queer youth can be freely and openly out. The most striking aspect of LGBTQ youth vlogs is not their often very low production values or the content but the creation of the private space of home (usually for teens, this is specifically their bedroom) as a public space, a meeting square for LGBTQ youth.

One of the ways that this public space is made is through directly addressing queer youth and offering advice and information. For example, Jazz Jennings begins her Q&A post *Jazz a Transgender Child Q&A* (730,693 views) by saying, 'Today I'm going to be making the Q&A video which was highly requested . . . here I am. I'm free and I'm really excited to just answer all your questions and help you face some of the problems you are going through' (0:24). As Jazz answers the questions, which she has presumably selected beforehand, her responses become less upbeat as she moves from questions about who she dates and what she likes about making mermaid outfits to how to respond to negative comments from peers and then how to deal with parents not accepting their trans child's gender identity. In response to this last question, she says, 'I feel awful. I can't imagine going through puberty of the opposite sex. I'm here for you. I'm fighting for you. That's what I do every day. . . . I hope you can feel the love of society' (4:30).

## THE CONFESSIONAL

If YouTube LGBT vloggers are more at home and more vociferous than those in teen film, they also have a completely different approach to narrative and to production values. Most vloggers deploy low production values and a DIY aesthetic. Most are filmed in the vlogger's bedroom. While the camera is generally tightly focused on the vlogger so that most videos are head-and-shoulder shots to camera, occasionally it pulls back to show more of the room. When it does so, it is mostly untidy, the bed may be unmade or stuff has been left on the bed. This messiness adds to the DIY aesthetic and conveys the idea that the talk is authentic or unscripted reality. The untidiness of the room seems to say: you (the viewer) have just dropped by, I wasn't expecting you, the place is a mess. Similarly, the speaker often moves towards the camera (and therefore the spectator) intensifying the sense of being personally spoken to. The monologue generally lasts somewhere between three and ten minutes and is usually simple and repetitive in its messaging.

While there is some attempt to convey a narrative arc and to build suspense around a 'reveal', this is done in the mode of textual rather than visual storytelling; over the course of viewing several videos from the same channel, it becomes clear that most videos simply repeat the same narrative dilemmas: I was assigned a gender at birth, I want to live as another gender, eventually (as a young adult) I will medically transition, in the meantime I dress, speak, act in ways that are consistent with my felt gender identity. Or, I realised that I was lesbian, or gay, or bisexual; eventually I had the courage to tell others that I am. Through doing this, I hope to give others the courage to do what I am doing and, through doing this, I create a space to be who I am. Some of this repetition is inevitable given that, for example, both Ryan and Jazz started vlogging as young teens, and therefore the scope for them to medically transition is limited (although Jazz does take puberty blockers). It is not until Ryan goes to college and Jazz turns eighteen, and they both have surgery and Ryan starts taking T, that new events shape their lives as transgender youth. Therefore in the early years of their vlogging, they have little content that they can use that is orientated to transitioning or coming out.

But more than this, these head-and-shoulders to camera vlogs seem to be borrowing from other genres than teen film, specifically reality television and news anchors or celebrity talk shows, on the one hand, and on the other, the confessional—the underlying mode that reality TV and talk shows both borrow from.

Teen vloggers are telling a personal story about their own life as a trans and/or LGB teen, but at the same time, they want to make themselves emblematic rather than idiosyncratic. This projection of their own, personal story as a universal (or, at least, an American story) is accomplished through the head-and-shoulders direct address to camera that indexes the anchor in the newsroom or the chat-show host. This dominating feature of LGBT vlogging is otherwise puzzling because it is visually uninteresting, but through this copying of the news anchor/chat-show host direct-to-camera address, the speakers both establish their lives as newsworthy, or at least engaging, and signify the veracity of their story. It also enables them to speak both ways: in a private address that mimics a one-to-one intimate encounter and a public address that creates a sense of public space and community.

The direct-to-camera address that is more or less closely framed around the head and shoulders conveys intimacy between the speaker and the listener. When the vlogger makes a post, they are interpellating their subscribers as particular kinds of people: their friends, their community, their supporters. But they also want to make each individual subscriber or random viewer feel that their post is a direct and personal communication to/with the spectator. The personal address on camera mimics or indexes a form of intimate communication, talking with friends, that serves to establish a connection between the vlogger and the viewer. This is accomplished visually, through sudden leaning into the camera, and verbally, through declarations of love and gratitude as well as through direct-address instructions like 'you can subscribe here'.

Reality television has reintroduced into television and film (and perhaps everyday life) a mode of speech borrowed from theatre in which a monologue reveals 'the inner life, secret thoughts and feelings of the characters' (Aslama and Pantti 2006:175). This is a mode that has largely been replaced in visual culture by dramatic conventions that emphasise the depiction of narrative events rather than the exposition of them (show, don't tell). While, as noted in chapter 5, the expository, narrative voiceover has persisted in black film, that may be because the voiceover is intended for the white spectator and serves the function that subtitles do in foreign-language films. It also connects an episodic mode of storytelling to make a more coherent or flowing narrative. In any case, it is not a common feature in other film modes. The monologue, in contrast to the narrative voiceover, is not so much expository as revelatory. It is the moment, as Aslama and Pantti point out, in which the emotional tone of the speech is intended to convey the authenticity of the speaker, the moment when their 'true self appears' (2006:175). They 'argue that the specific moments of talking alone are used on the whole as a truth-sign of direct access to the "real"' (2006:175). While a video diary, like a narrative voiceover, develops the story, the confessions of reality television monologues do not move the story on but rather 'feature emotional revelations, speculations and analyses' (2006:176). These televised confessions, especially when painful or highly emotional, convey an impression of both intimacy between the speaker and the viewer and the authenticity of their speaker's utterances (2006:179).

While Aslama and Pantti support the contention that the reality television monologue (or, I am suggesting, the vloggers coming-out story or narration of transition events) is in the mode of the confessional, they also contend that it necessarily fails to connect with the viewer because the viewer has no method to commit or participate. Therefore, it fails in their view to 'support the collective and shared but reflects and recreates a first-person, individualized society' (2006:180). This seems like rather an odd charge to level at reality television, which generally has no commitments to creating a collective but is in fact intended as a spectacle. The purpose of the intimate form of address and the attempt to convey the authentic or genuine feelings of the speaker is to secure the attention and investment of the reality television programme audience. This contrasts to the LGBT vloggers who want to also create a collective and shared experience and who are speaking primarily to others who are interpellated as part of the LGBT community.

Daniel Smith argues that the confessional soliloquy articulates a sense of the inexhaustible depth of the self. Discussing Augustine's *Confessions* as the origin text of the confessional soliloquy, he says: 'In the post-Romantic development of "inwardness" and self-reflexivity, this You is turned from a God (who in Augustine's theology curtails our creative imagination) to become our own inner-depths, an inwardness whose depths are inexhaustible. In this rendering, the central idea is "that each person *has his or her own original way of* being"' (Taylor 1989:184 cited in Smith 2017: 705, emphasis added), and our 'inescapable feeling of depth comes from the realization that whatever we bring up, there is always more down there. Depth lies in there being always, inescapably, something beyond our articulative power' (Taylor, 1989:390 cited in Smith 2017:705). LGBT vlogs, for example, the confessional vlogs of the 'It Gets Better' campaign Smith suggests are similar but different to the vlogs he analyses in which micro celebrities disavow their status, and express disquiet with their vlogging, which he sees as dramatizations of 'the politics of authenticity'. However, while the vlogs analysed in this chapter do not express disquiet with the practice of vlogging, and cannot exactly be described as confessional, they are very centrally concerned with displaying the work of becoming their authentic selves, which presupposes that this authentic self, the origin of the self, resides in an already in-place and deep interiority that pre-exists the socio-cultural formation of a sexual or gender identity. The project then is to align this deep interiority with an exterior expression, a project that can never be completed, not because the self is always contingent and plastic (as a post-structuralist account might claim) but because the interiority of the self is inexhaustible.

## AUTHENTICITY

For the connection between speaker and viewer to work effectively, the vlogger has to be able to convey a high level of authenticity. This is also accomplished in part by the close framing of head-and-shoulder shots. It is also done through the repetition of a narrative that says something like 'I have always been who I am now' of a deep interiority. The use of the surface to indicate the depth has a long history in visual culture, as discussed in chapters 2 and 10. The skill of the portrait artist, whether painter or photographer, is evidenced in the ability to visually capture the real character of the sitter. In vlogs in the United States, particular speech modes, direct address, close framing, and—perhaps above all—speech content convey this sense of the deep interiority of trans and LGB identities. A clear example of this is Jazz Jenning's *Story of Jazz: A Transgender Child*. It opens with Jazz standing in front of her bedroom wall, a mantelpiece behind her arranged with empty photo frames and mermaids (mermaids have become an icon of trans childhood). She introduces herself as 'a thirteen-year-old girl who just happens to be born in a boy's body and I'm trans gender'.[4] A collage of photos and home videos of her growing up follows with Jazz narrating their significance in a voiceover and occasional screen captions to underscore particularly pertinent points. A photo of her as a toddler wearing a baby jumpsuit and furry, plastic heels has a screen caption added: 'At 16 months I was wearing plastic dress up heels' (0:14). The camera zooms in on the shoes. 'Even before I was two I felt like a girl', says Jazz; 'as soon as I could crawl I would reach for girls' toys, as soon as I could speak I told my parents I was a girl'. In earlier videos, Jazz validates her gender identity primarily through her desire for 'girls' things', but as she gets older, this narrative changes slightly. So in this video, made in 2014 when she was fourteen years old, she says, 'I didn't just like girly things; I knew I was a girl trapped in a boy's body'. An inter-title says 'By Age 3, I was diagnosed with GID . . . GENDER IDENTITY DISORDER'. The collage continues: Jazz at a ballet class at four years old, clearly upset that she could not wear a tutu 'like the other girls'. Jazz at preschool with other four-year-old girls. The next inter-title says 'After my transition our family shared our story in the media and from then on I became a spokesperson and advocate for transyouth [sic]' (1:07). This is followed by several photographs of Jazz appearing in the media and a video of her speaking at the Trevor Project saying, 'I have a motto: everyone should be accepted for who they truly are' . . . just because someone's brain doesn't match to their body . . . means kids like us are unique and special' (1:34). Another video shows her at the GLAAD awards saying 'it's okay to step out of your shadow and just be who you are, just be true to yourself and express yourself because after all we are just kids and all kids deserve to be happy' (2:32). There is a photo of her on a magazine cover, named on *Fortune*'s 40 Under 40 List. Then there is the retelling of discrimination with home videos—not being allowed to use the girls' bathroom at age nine, banned from playing girls soccer at eight. There is an interview with Swedish journalist Renee Nyberg in which Nyberg asks what Jazz would wish for if she had a 'genie in a bottle'. She replies, 'I would not wish to not be transgender cos I like the way I am it's the person I am and I'm proud of myself and what I've accomplished. It's made me a braver person being transgender and it's just become a part of me'. A video of Jazz swimming in a mermaid costume and then lying on the beach ends the video as she says: 'I want to see every person have freedom to be who they are'.

## COMING-OUT VIDEOS

Most coming-out teen compilations on YouTube emphasise how accepting parents are towards their children, and the parent usually reassures the child by saying something like 'I already knew' and 'I will always love you, no matter what'. In *Seventeen*'s compilation,[5] for example, the only negative reaction is from Gianna Collier-Pitts's father, but this is because she did it by sharing a link to her Instagram account rather than speaking with him. *Teen Vogue*'s post of readers' coming-out stories is a compilation of videos intercut with one another. These play over a vaguely inspirational soundtrack. The videos are not professionally made, and although each is slightly different, they share the features of the YouTube vlogs discussed in detail in this chapter: close-up, neutral background, clearly spoken and conveying a simple message. The videos have been edited together to create an overall narrative arc. The first part of the narrative is each speaker identifying when they knew that they were gay, and are variations on the theme of 'I always knew'. The second is about coming out to parents and family and their responses: 'incredibly accepting', 'unconditional love and support', 'oh, Honey, I know'. These messages that coming out is you 'sharing who you are', which is therefore unlikely to attract hostility from anyone and especially not your parents, fits well with the overall celebratory message of rainbow capitalism: everything is already all right, you just need to accept it. However, the *Teen Vogue* coming-out stories do include accounts in which the family was not supportive: 'It was very hard for my Mom especially'; 'there was a bit of a learning curve'; 'I've felt really alone in my coming out process'; 'find out people who are similar . . . that's where you can flourish in your own being'; 'fake it til you make it, try to cultivate courage almost out of thin air . . . and you'll be surprised at how strong you are . . . stand by yourself'; 'I have never had to ask permission to be myself'; 'it gets better'; 'there's an entire community of people in the world who love you and accept you for who you really are'.

Jessie Paege was already an established YouTuber when she came out as bisexual in 2018. The original video she posted was taken down for copyright infringement, and she posted another in January 2019. The post recounting how the video was taken down is long (ten minutes) and takes a long time to say that it was taken down for copyright infringement and that she is doing it again and will post it. In fact, the 2018 video is still available on YouTube.[6] It begins with the inter-title 'Here is footage of my closeted struggles during the year'; 'coming out isn't sunshine and rainbows'; inter-title: 'and then I slowly started coming out to people'. In the first two minutes, she declares her fear, is crying, says she finds it hard to speak: 'Not going to lie, I feel defeated, scared, lonely'. The next scenes follow the inter-title 'and now I'm ready' and are several shots of her with rainbow flags, wearing rainbow t-shirts; the soundtrack plays 'just another day nothing in my way'. She is sitting in a field of flowers, even a baby with a rainbow rattle is included in the montage. From about three minutes into the collage, there are shots of her at Pride and with friends and influencers; she says later on in the same video that she was at Pride because she was invited to the kick-off party. Her manager spoke to her before the party and said, 'Make sure you describe yourself as an ally'. She did not want to come out because 'I was a closeted teenager'. At four minutes, it starts again: 'to an exciting future where I can finally be free'. Subscribe and follow me on Instagram; she says then, 'Just kidding [laughs] but if you want to'. 'I trust you all and I think its time you know . . . my first kiss was actually with a girl'. She then thanks people by first name who have helped her come out. She says 'she wrote notes [to speak to camera] but I'm just gonna, throw it away'. She recounts her school experiences of hearing *lesbian* as a term of abuse, and how she was upset about that and didn't know why, she felt uncomfortable about talking about relationships because she wanted to hide the fact 'that I was not only attracted to the other sex'. She says 'I genuinely know it will help other people' to come out. 'A lot of my tweets are addressed to myself, and also to help you guys out'. Her story is that she was involved in Pride and the LGBT community as an ally, but she was too anxious to come out and that this confused a lot of people. The video is in two parts, and the second part, which is also fifteen minutes long, explains how she got an audience of LGBT people through posting LGBT content but still had not come out and was 'your typical closeted teenager'. In another video she does come out to her mum in a two-part video. This begins with her saying that she has lost friends and followers after coming out and then cuts to her introducing her coming out and then coming out. Her mum says that she watches all her videos and thought that her daughter might be lesbian or bisexual ('I was like maybe she is') and felt fine to see her coming out on camera: 'It's a good thing'. Jessie asks, 'Was it surprising?' 'No'. So it seems clear that for her family there was no reason for her not to come out to them. 'We've always let you be you—right?' asks her mum. The video repeats this exchange for ten minutes. 'Everyone is getting more supportive but its still scary and it should still be celebrated'. 'Absolutely', replies her mum. 'If I didn't start YouTube and dye my hair pink I never would be talking about this right now; it would be something I hid my whole life'.

## OFF-LINE ACTIVISM

Ryan Flores, Jazz Jennings and Jessie Paege are all public figures with varying degrees of reach. Their activism is, if their vlogs are accurate reflections of their activism, almost entirely digital. It is not only their own YouTube channels but also other social media who have profiled them. Jazz has a larger number of followers and also has a TV show (*I Am Jazz*). She has received awards for her public profile and attended LGBT events. Online activists who use their online presence to do off-line organising seem to be less common. This contrasts to the digital political activism analysed in the next chapter, which shows a constant back and forth between digital and real-world organising. I think this is partly, perhaps entirely, an effect of being part of a spatially dispersed minority community. It may also be because YouTube vlogging is a less agile form than the kind of short messaging that is intended to bring people together in off-line events and organising. Lillian Lennon, for example, is a transgender activist in Alaska. She led a coalition to defeat Proposition 1, an anti–anti-discrimination bill in 2018. The campaign won. She did make short videos but posted them on Twitter. Her role as a field organiser in defeating Proposition 1 also led to LGBT digital spaces amplifying her work (for example, *New Now Next*[7]).

In her video on Twitter, Lillian Lennon says there's still more work to do because 'so many people don't understand the LGBTQ+ community. And it really has to do with not knowing us' whether because they are uninvolved or uneducated and that 'people need to get to know us before they judge us'.[8] In fact, she uses many of the same tropes that we have seen in other chapters are dominant in US political culture: that discrimination is a psychological error resulting from ignorance and therefore negative stereotyping of people who are perceived to be different, and that love overcomes hate. For example, when speaking about the campaign to the Advocate.com she says, 'I was able to explain that I'm a transgender woman myself. . . . I think it's hard to say to someone's face, "No, I don't agree that you should have equal rights."'[9] Clearly, the history of America shows that people find it very easy to say to someone's face that they do not deserve equal rights, yet this trope continues as a commonplace aspect of political discourse. Similarly, she says on her Twitter, 'We're coming, and we're coming with love and acceptance and diversity'. In chapter 5, I showed how the messages on the March on Washington for Jobs and Freedom used this same discourse, that love overcomes hate, that it dissolves the will to violence.

## CONCLUSION

LGBT vlogging creates a digital public space that enables a disparate, dispersed population to form a sense of community. It is in this sense that LGBT vloggers are 'the representation'. Speaking to an audience of other queer youth, they share their experiences and offer advice about how to be authentic. The modes of visual storytelling that they use to do this draw on other long-established genres and modes, including the confessional and reality television. For the most part, they do not draw on the same documentary, social-realist modes deployed in fiction film and in social-reform film discussed in sections one and two. The crossover between vlogging and other platforms is primarily between YouTubers and Instagrammers and mainstream media who use the stories, which they amplify to attract advertising revenue for a targeted, niche audience. This highlights two tendencies in all contemporary media: towards narrowcasting over broadcasting and the commercialisation of culture within advertising. Of course, within capitalist economies, culture is always also a commercial product. To draw the connections between the creation of LGBT digital communities and the ways in which these are leveraged and monetarised is not to dismiss the difference that it makes to young queers to have relatively extensive visual representation.

## NOTES

1. https://shortyawards.com/11th/jessiepaege.
2. https://www.youtube.com/watch?v=ZO7i-m_9RsI.
3. https://www.elitedaily.com/p/where-to-get-the-tarte-x-jessie-paege-pride-palette-for-positivity-rainbow-vibes-galore-17908165.
4. https://www.youtube.com/watch?v=Jbg-LdVdNk0.
5. https://www.youtube.com/watch?v=lhkuYGZyp_o.
6. https://www.youtube.com/watch?v=Ol6i1FC9qvA&list=PLqNiomsWd_HKeS-FkM9IluNxwidhsLopr&index=2.
7. https://www.facebook.com/watch/?v=233438140661960.
8. https://twitter.com/mslillianlennon/status/1013538950793842688?s=20.
9. https://www.advocate.com/pride/2019/5/28/meet-our-104-champions-pride-2019#media-gallery-media-3.

# NINE

## 'We the Wounded'

### Violence and Citizenship

In the previous chapter, I analysed the content of LGBT vloggers who are YouTube famous, micro-celebrities or influencers. Their onscreen presence and the celebrity status they have accrued within the frame of LGBT visibility has led, to some extent, to them aligning themselves with more than just their own liberation or authenticity, even while still largely using the narrative of being true to oneself. Jazz Jennings, who as a child, aligns herself with hegemonic narrative scripts about what femininity is, as a young adult, argues back against gender norms. She has engaged with LGBT event promotion and the public space of LGBT organising that is increasingly corporate. In those videos, one has a sense of youth vloggers engaging in the kind of self-brand building that Sarah Banet-Weiser (2012) discusses in *Authentic*. The brand originates from the person making the content, albeit within a visual culture familiar with the tropes of confessional reality TV, on the one hand, and factual news reporting, on the other, and is very alive to the possibility of the vloggers monetarising their presence on social media if they can build a large enough following.

In this chapter, I consider the process of becoming 'internet famous' from the opposite direction—starting with events that generated off-line movements connected with online digital networks. I begin with Black Lives Matter (BLM) because it has had a very visible influence on visual culture in its representation of contemporary young black life and politics; for example, in chapter 5, I analysed the film *The Hate U Give*, which derives its storyline and visual storytelling from police violence and Black Lives Matter's iconography. Black Lives Matter also opened up a space for new representations of black politics in film and television.

Some of these have then crossed over into organizing, for example, Yara Shahidi's (from the TV sitcom *black-ish*) voter-registration campaign (https://www.eighteenx18.com/). The success of Black Lives Matter in re-telling the story of police violence from the point of view of the injured and dead and their families and friends has also shaped the approach to social media of subsequent protest movements. The movement 'has become an archetypal example of modern protests and political engage-ment on social media' (https://www.pewinternet.org/2018/07/11/acti-vism-in-the-social-media-age/). BLM was not the first movement to mob-ilise social media to amplify the threat that the state posed to its citizens: both the Zapatistas (1994) and the Arab Spring (2011) have been analysed as movements that leveraged the networking affordances of social media. For Black Lives Matter, whose initial focus was (and to a large degree, remains) police violence against black people, the easy visualisation of the problem in photography and film (Freelon et al. 2016:82) and the history of state violence against black people in the United States lent themselves very effectively to dissemination on social media. However, despite an iconography of protest and a visibility in popular culture that makes BLM appear to be a youth movement, it seems that deeper en-gagement with the politics of BLM is being done by older (thirty- to fifty-year-old) activists and creatives.

## BLACK TWITTER AND YOUNG BLACK TWITTER

Social media 'virality' has come to be associated with the take-up of hashtags that circulate outside of and generate action in the off-line world. The success of social media in providing a space for self-expres-sion, commentary and citizen journalism for groups whose narrative framings and actual news stories are largely absent from mainstream media is indicated by the high take-up of Twitter by black people. Black and Hispanic social media users are more likely (about half of all black and Hispanic social media users) than whites (one-third of white social media users) to say that these platforms are important 'for expressing their political views or for getting involved with issues that are important to them' (Lenhart et al. 2010). This resonates with other research that suggests that black people account for a 'disproportionately large share of users' on Twitter (2010:8). However, whether Black Twitter is also Young Black Twitter is less certain. In their analysis of Twitter users and open websites engaging with Black Lives Matter in the year between George Zimmerman's acquittal for the murder of unarmed teenager Trayvon Martin in July 2013 and the death of Freddie Gray in May 2015, Freelon et al. (2016) found that young people, aged eighteen to twenty-four are underrepresented in their activity on most of the BLM 'network'.

In their study, Freelon et al. grouped the tweets shared on hashtags related to police violence against black people and black lives matter into 'communities' based on re-tweets, likes and comments. In what they call 'phase one' of the movement, they show that 'Young Black Twitter' can be conceptualised as a number of communities of different sizes that communicate and re-tweet one another but are connected by very thin lines to the larger hub of New York City media, government and left wing activists (2016:38). Young Black Twitter communities in phase one mostly re-tweeted a single tweet repeated verbatim by multiple high-user accounts. It described Eric Garner's death and was illustrated by a dip-tych of an image of his smiling face and another of him being choked to death and the hashtag 'retweet'. It was shared thirty-six thousand times. The authors note the 'radical departure of subject matter it represents for the accounts that shared it'. The accounts sharing the tweet rarely en-gaged with public affairs or 'hard news'. They focused on music, sport and relationships 'rarely venturing into the realm of public affairs or 'hard news'. Circulating a single verbatim message about Garner, rather than commenting, reproduces the 'one-to-many communication flow [that] is similar to that of traditional mass media and is not present to nearly the same extent in the political neighbourhood [of Twitter users]' (2016:40). While on the one hand suggesting that Young Black Twitter serves as young black people's CNN (as Public Enemy's Chuck D once said of hip-hop), on the other hand, it is largely separate from BLM acti-vism and much less political overall (2016:76).

## POLICE VIOLENCE ON CAMERA

Black Lives Matter mobilised with the tagline 'a movement, not a mo-ment', and it successfully mobilised federal and state attention to the issue of police violence. Indeed, not unlike the representation of the civil rights movement in the 1960s, the images of police officers murdering black citizens and the army and police response to the subsequent citizen protests in US towns and cities circulated globally. Visual evidence was central to the ability of BLM to get police violence and state injustice against black citizens into the international and national press.

The youthfulness of many of the victims was also a central part of the narrative of #BlackLivesMatter because it established the lack of culpabil-ity of the victims or, more accurately, made the youthfulness of the tar-gets of police and 'law and order' violence an argument for their inno-cence. (It is also worth noting how the fact of innocence becomes the ground of the debate, as if proof of guilt would justify being executed by the police.) That the Black Lives Matter hashtag began with a Facebook post following the acquittal of George Zimmerman for the murder of then–seventeen-year-old Trayvon Martin indicates the importance of childhood, an imagined and now impossible future, and why the slogan caught the attention of national and international media and Black Twitter. Trayvon Martin was not killed by the police; he was killed by a citizen who successfully used stand-your-ground laws in his defence for the murder of an unarmed child. Although the jury acquitted him, there was widespread protest over the injustice of the verdict.

The murder of eighteen-year-old Michael Brown by the police in 2014 added power to the narrative that 'they are killing our children', as did the murder of twelve-year-old Tamir Rice. The ghost of Emmett Till haunted these images, and his murder was often indexed in images and reports on what some referred to as the 'new Jim Crow'. Shaun King, for example, journalist at the *New York Daily News* and prominent Black Lives Matter advocate (https://twitter.com/NYDailyNews/status/682046719467585537), in December 2015 reported: 'No justice for Tamir Rice makes him our modern day Emmett Till'.

Although the failure to deliver justice for Trayvon Martin led to the coining of the phrase and the BLM hashtag, it was the murder by police of Mike Brown in Ferguson, Missouri, and the failure to indict the police officer for murder that led to huge street protests and rapid spikes in the use of the BLM hashtag. It spiked again when the Minnesota police officer who shot and killed Philando Castile was acquitted, but the largest spike was in 2016 when five police officers were killed by a sniper following protests in Dallas in July 2016. Whereas Ferguson saw tweets hovering around 200,000 for several months in November 2014, the Dallas shootings saw posts of around 1.3 million with the single highest tweet volume on November 24, 2014, the day that Michael Brown's killer was not indicted (Freelon et al. 2016). There was another, smaller spike, on the day that Eric Garner's killer was not indicted (December 3, 2014), and after that, the daily tweet count never again crossed one million (2016:22).

The most-shared Twitter images in this period were: a photomontage of two images of a line of police officers facing a line of black protesters (shared 46,506 times). They are remarkably similar. In both, the police hold batons in their hands. The only discernible difference (other than that the left-hand picture is in black and white and the right-hand in colour) is that the police have faceguards on their helmets and riot shields. The left-hand image is from the 1960s, the right-hand one from Ferguson in 2014: an image of Michael Brown lying in the road with two police officers, one of whom is Darren Wilson, looking over his dead body (shared 41,618 times). The original image was taken by Ferguson rapper, Thee Pharaoh. Other most-shared images are: Eric Garner with his family (three children) shared 29,743 times, and Garner graduating (shared 28,073 times); three stills of Eric Garner being choked to death by the police, from a screenshot from the video posted by the *New York Daily News* (shared 27,647 times, also shared 80,000 times on Facebook); and an image of a white man and a black man, each asking how much the other's life is worth (shared 24,322 times) (Freelon et al. 2016).

## YOUTUBE AND INSTAGRAM: ACCIDENTAL 'ACTIVISTS'

While I am suggesting that the LGBT vloggers discussed in the previous chapter differ from other political activists in the ways that they use social media, the connections between social media and mainstream media are very similar. Mainstream-media journalists mine social media to find stories with enough traffic or visibility to suggest that they might hold the attention of mainstream-media readers/audiences and perhaps even bring in new readers. One example of this is black Baltimore photographer Devin Allen. Allen took the photograph of a protestor running towards the camera as a line of police officers run towards him, which was picked up by *Time* magazine for their cover of May 11, 2015, with '1960' crossed out and replaced with '2015' and the text 'What Has Changed and What Hasn't.' Allen was twenty-six years old, a year older than Freddie Gray, whose murder sparked the protests in West Baltimore in 2015.

*Time* has a circulation of two million and an estimated readership of twenty million. Devin Allen's photograph was identified by *Time* from his Instagram account of images of the Baltimore protests, images which were subsequently published in his book *A Beautiful Ghetto* (2017) (https:/ /garage.vice.com/en_us/article/qv33vb/devin-allen-street-photography). He has said, 'I used Instagram, Twitter to get my photos out. Social media is a game changer for journalism. It gives people that can't be heard a voice' (https://abcnews.go.com/US/photos/black-lives-matter-movement-photos-44402442/image-45637195). 'The photos he posted during the 2015 Baltimore uprising became viral hits, shared again and again by influencers like the singer Rihanna' (https://ivoh.org/story/how-photographer-devin-allen-helps-baltimore-youth-reclaim-their-narra-tives/).

Devin Allen also produced the 2018 lookbook for sports brand Under Armour (https://about.underarmour.com/news/2018/08/ua-forge-96-bal-timore-lookbook-devin-allen). It was the fee for that work which made it possible for him to continue as an independent photographer (https:// ivoh.org/story/how-photographer-devin-allen-helps-baltimore-youth-re-claim-their-narratives/). He and a friend, another Baltimore resident, also did a photography workshop sponsored by Red Bull, again pointing to the very material commercial circuits within which social media activism and its visual culture operate.

Devin Allen's photography, or at least the way that it has been taken up in the mainstream media and established him as a professional photographer, is unusual for Black Lives Matter's visual activism. What

the image that got him on the front page of *Time* speaks to is the continuing power of iconic images that compel the spectator to look, partly because of their chain of inter-textuality: a chain that is literally written into
*Time*'s caption '2015/1960'.

The most striking and frequent aspect of BLM's visual imagery are
videos of black people dying on camera. These videos of black people
killed by the police, often at point-blank range, are shocking but also
semiotically ambivalent in the long history of the visual culture of black
people's deaths in the United States; it is far from assured that the fact of
death, of murder, is sufficient to garner public sympathy and that white
supremacists do not derive pleasure from their circulation as they have
done in the past, when photographs of the murders of black people by
lynching were circulated as tourist souvenirs among white populations
in the United States.

The images of police brutality towards black people, often taken by
young adults on their phones, are made as evidence, not as spectacle.
They may be compared to the photographs of the early reform photographers who saw the camera as a technology for capturing evidence. They
remind us that the division of the visual portrait into the mug shot and
the photo album continues in the age of social media. This evidential
quality of the camera is what led President Obama's administration to
recommend the use of police body cameras, and grants were made available to provide them. A report in 2017 of a random-controlled trial of
body-cam use and its impact on police behaviour in Washington, DC,
showed that body cams did not change police behaviour (http://
bwc.thelab.dc.gov/The-
LabDC_MPD_BWC_Working_Paper_10.20.17.pdf). From a different perspective, Copwatch has also said that police body cams are unlikely to
lead to police being held to account because of the difficulty of getting
footage released into the public domain. However, in at least one case,
the murder of Laquan McDonald in October 2014 by police officer Jason
Van Dyke, it was the footage which led to Van Dyke's indictment for
murder (www.youtube.com/watch?v=xaXuT9sxCnI; en.wikipedia.org/
wiki/Murder_of_Laquan_McDonald). Laquan was seventeen years old
when he was shot. The police officer who killed him used sixteen bullets.
His murder was not covered by the national press. The police claimed it
was justifiable homicide because of the threatening way that Laquan was
acting. Subsequently, a citizen filed a Freedom of Information Act request
for the body-cam footage; the clear visual contradiction between his actual behaviour and the written testimony of the officer who shot him led to
a number of demonstrations, but none were well attended or got national
coverage. The trial found the shooter guilty of second-degree murder.
The other officers involved were acquitted.

These videos enter the public domain because someone with a mobile
phone camera was at the event and filmed it and then uploaded it to

social media. Ramsey Orta was twenty-two years old when he filmed his friend Eric Garner being choked to death by New York police on Staten Island. It was the first 'in a wave of recordings of African-Americans in violent confrontations with white police officers to command national attention' (Josh Sanburn, *Time*). In fact, the video's release did not generate much attention. It was not until Michael Brown's death less than a month later that social media traffic increased for Mike Brown and Eric Garner. Tweets on the video jumped to 12,589,097, with 1,734,541 unique users. Nor was it Michael Brown's death that sparked the outburst of social media activity, but the protests in Ferguson. 'Three individuals played an outsized role in spreading the word about Brown's death far beyond the St. Louis area that evening: St. Louis-based rapper Tef Poe (@tefpoe); Michael Skolnik (@michaelskolnik), a New York City–based entrepreneur and activist; and Shaun King (@shaunking), an Atlanta-based activist and writer for the *New York Daily News*. At 6:42 p.m. CST, Poe posted a chilling photo of Brown's dead body lying in the street' (Freelon at al. 2016:31). The brutality of the police response attracted international condemnation; for example, Amnesty New Zealand tweeted that 'the situation in Ferguson has prompted us to send human rights teams. First time we've deployed inside the United States.' This quote tweeted a Buzzfeed.com article with a photo taken by Lucas Jackson of Reuters of a crowd of young black men holding up their hands in the 'don't shoot' gesture that became associated with the movement (https://www.buzzfeednews.com/article/chrisgeidner/amnesty-international-takes-unprecedented-us-action-in-fergu#4gkzun0).

The murder of twelve-year-old Tamir Rice was captured on police body cams. The murder of twenty-five-year-old Freddie Gray in Baltimore was recorded by his friend Kevin Moore and uploaded to YouTube. Kevin Moore is now an activist with Copwatch. He was not featured in *Time*'s article on the Baltimore protests which used Devin's photograph as a front cover. Feiden Santana filmed Walter Scott's 2015 murder in North Charleston, South Carolina. He was initially reluctant to release the video because of fear of police retaliation. Santana says that he shared stills from the video on Facebook when police officer Michael Slager's testimony contradicted what Santana had seen. The distribution of the video led to Slager being fired and indicted for murder.

Police killings are not enough to spark national, let alone international attention. Activists have to work to disseminate narratives and share information. In 2015 and 2016, the *Guardian* counted police killings and showed low numbers of people under eighteen shot by police (https://www.theguardian.com/us-news/ng-interactive/2015/jun/01/the-counted-police-killings-us-database), but who were disproportionately black (c5/20). In total, around five hundred people in the United States are killed by the police annually. Copwatch, established in 1990 in Berkeley, encourages people to film instances of police violence, on the assumption that this kind of 'reverse surveillance' will force the police to be less violent or be held to account when they are. What Black Lives Matter succeeded in doing, through encouraging the circulation of these images on Twitter and other social media with #BlackLivesMatter, was to gather together stories of police violence from multiple sites and make them into a single story—police murder black people.

In his paper on digital counterpublics and BLM, Marc Lamont Hill notes that video footage has (probably) led to different outcomes to incidents of police brutality against black youth than the police involved likely expected. He uses the term *new surveillances* to indicate that the same surveillance technologies used to 'criminalize Blackness are being repurposed by Black citizens, particularly Black youth, to resist the criminalizing techniques of State power. Specifically, smartphone technology has enabled Black youth to digitally capture (through photography, video, and livestreaming) everyday interactions with law enforcement without the support of mainstream corporate media outlets or state-owned surveillance technologies like street light cameras or surveillance drones' (2018:290); for example, in June 2015, video of Corporal David Eric Casebolt violently throwing a black girl to the ground at a pool party and drawing his gun on two black boys was recorded on smartphones and uploaded to YouTube and then distributed widely on Black Twitter (2018:291). He was fired. Similarly, video in October 2015 of a school resource officer, Deputy Ben Fields, assaulting a student and dragging her out of her classroom was uploaded to YouTube and distributed on Twitter. Under public pressure, Fields resigned.

Although circulation of images on Twitter has certainly changed the terms of police surveillance and led to police being indicted for murder, the justice system continues to fail black Americans. The video of Eric Garner is still available on YouTube. This video was taken by his friend, who is now in prison for unrelated offences and has been repeatedly harassed by the police since he posted the video. An officer was investigated for Eric Garner's murder, but as I am writing in this chapter in July 2019, the decision was released by the US attorney Richard Donoghue to not charge any of the officers involved. According to Justice Department sources, this decision was made by the US attorney general William Barr (Laughland 2019).

Black Lives Matter's rejection of respectability politics was also important in enabling them to take control of the narrative. Whereas previous campaigns to push back against state and public racism, for example, by the NAACP, had focused on the blamelessness of the victim and their respectability, BLM was deeply sceptical about respectability politics; the fact that BLM was started by three black women activists, Alicia Garza, Patrisse Cullors and Opal Tometi, one of whom (Alicia Garza) is also queer, probably had something to do with that. After the grand jury refused to indict the officer who killed Michael Brown and protests erupted in Ferguson, President Obama said that the young protesters do not 'look like . . . traditional civil rights demonstrator[s]' and that progress will not be accomplished 'by throwing bottles [or] smashing car windows. That won't be done by using this as an excuse to vandalize property. And it certainly won't be done by hurting anybody' (Gross 2017:422). The Garner family have now been campaigning for five years to see the justice that was denied Eric Garner.

## MARCH FOR OUR LIVES

The visual culture of Black Lives Matter resonates with the visual cultures of black film, discussed in chapter 5, and of abolitionism and the post–Black Reconstruction debates around the routes to black political power. Themes of economic independence versus political representation (or, more precisely, which comes first); the representation of the evidential archive versus the representation of the sentimental family album; and Afro-pessimism versus Afro-optimism move in and out of view in the imagery of Black Lives Matter (the hashtag online and the protests off-line). The child as innocent and the youth as a figure of incipient futurity, so prominent in the representation of white Anglo and white immigrant lives, are not as visible in Black Lives Matter. Indeed, and ironically, the visuality of Black Lives Matter predominately is in images of death and near death: images captured out of necessity, to record and provide evidence of injustice. The prominent exception is Devin Allen. As he points out, the idea of the camera as a tool for representation (of portraiture and beauty) was not part of his neighbourhood culture. He was seen as peculiar, even laughable. In response, he has started an initiative to get cameras into the hands of black children and train them how to take photographs. So far, he has distributed 150 cameras. In short, even on social media—lauded for its ability to change the story, to get the narratives and perspectives of marginalised groups heard and amplified—the visual means of production remain largely out of reach of working-class African Americans. While camera-phone saturation has been reached, the quality of images still matters in determining what gets circulated and taken up; but most importantly, without significant political power that is determined to hold the state to account in its treatment of citizens, viral images do not lead to justice.

The question of who really gets to change the story and how much that ability is over-determined by class and race came to the fore in the apparent success of another movement, March for Our Lives (M4OL). This movement was formed after a shooting by a former student at Marjory Stoneman Douglas (MSD) High School in Florida, in which seventeen students and one teacher were murdered. The students themselves quickly articulated their anger at the gun laws that enabled the shooter to kill their fellow students and their determination to make this a #Never-Again moment. They attracted significant celebrity endorsement and high-profile media coverage. The slogan itself, March for Our Lives, where 'our' is left unspoken and is therefore universal, contrasts to the slogan 'Black Lives Matter', which, in the need for its articulation, recognises that black life, for the state and much of the mainstream media, does not matter.

Mass shootings in the United States are not a rare occurrence. Five months earlier, twenty-seven people had been killed in a shooting by a white gunman at a predominately white Baptist church in Texas. The shooter was interrupted by a local man who had a collection of guns and ammunition and who, on hearing the shooting, took an AK47 from his stock and went to the church. For the NRA's 'good man with a gun' slogan, this was a positive news story. It seems likely that March for Our Lives was able to leverage wealthy, liberal benefactors who wanted a campaign that could dent support for the NRA, and wanted to support a well-organised group with good optics who had a clear demand and were within months of being voters themselves. On February 20, 2018, Oprah Winfrey tweeted in response to George Clooney and Amal Clooney's donation to the march: 'George and Amal, I couldn't agree with you more. I am joining forces with you and will match your $500,000 donation to "March For Our Lives." These inspiring young people remind me of the Freedom Riders of the 1960s who also said we've had ENOUGH and our voices will be heard'.

While, with the notable exception of the school's student magazine, most of the optics made in the early days of organising for the march were not produced by the students, their performances demonstrate a familiarity with media message framing and the optics of video production. Take, for example, the speech that Emma Gonzalez, one of the MSD students, made at the Washington rally. In front of a crowd of over two hundred thousand people, she opened her speech by reading out the names and hobbies of the teenagers who were killed in the school shooting. She then stood in silence on the podium for six minutes and twenty seconds—the same length of time that the gunman continued to shoot. The camera switches between Gonzalez's impassive face and the watching crowds, homing in on the faces of young people. She ends with 'fight for your lives before its someone else's job'. The speech was recorded by CBS News and posted on YouTube[1] where it currently (June 2019) has over 250,000 views. The prolonged silence in a speech could have failed badly. Indeed, as the camera pans the crowd, it seems clear that some people are not sure how to react. At six minutes, fifteen seconds, someone comes onto the stage and whispers in her ear. She continues to stand in silence. Exhibiting quite astonishing poise, discipline and confidence. An earlier speech, made while she was holding notes, a long speech with a lot of detail in it, was less successful in holding the audience's attention or in their subsequently recalling what she said. Except for her repeated use of the line 'we call BS', which she says she coined as a snappy phrase, not wanting to say the word *bullshit* because there was no need to be offensive.

March for Our Lives is very active on social media. Their Instagram account has 359,000 followers, their Twitter account has 453,000 followers, their YouTube channel has 8,168 subscribers, and their Facebook page has 288,000 likes. It is likely that many people follow or like all three sites, meaning that the total network membership is in the range of 296,000 to 1.2 million. In addition, people can share posts without following the account; for example, their Generation Lockdown video on their YouTube channel had 137,569 views, although they only had around eight thousand subscribers. So while the reach of social media may seem relatively small, the circulation of images is large. For comparison, the *New York Times* has three million paid digital subscribers and the *Washington Post* has a daily digital circulation of one million. March for Our Lives mobilised somewhere between 200,000 and 800,000 people for the march on Washington in March 2018.

Its Instagram account (www.instagram.com/marchforourlives/) is reminiscent of the lantern slide shows of the nineteenth century. Still images and short clips of video are organised into themes that can be swiped through and that deliver an impression of the problem, the mobilisation and the solution (in this case, gun-law reform). The archive of M4OL Instagram includes, for example, a montage of the photographic portraits of the seventeen teenagers who were killed in the Parkland shooting (https://www.instagram.com/p/Bt1e4fLHJ60/) and reminds me of the montage of the youth who were mutilated by guards of King Leopold II's regime in the Congo and whose photographic portraits were used as evidence of the regime's violence.

In this post (https://www.instagram.com/p/BqK_p1BHIoi/), a montage of news clips and stills opens with the famous lines of Martin Luther King Jr's 'I Have a Dream' speech spoken over the lunch-counter protests to desegregate public space and then cuts to the Vietnam war protests; defending the sacred from the Dakota Access Pipeline; Black Lives Matter; and then M4OL. The central message is that 'young people lead the fight for justice'[2] and 'young people throughout history have been change makers for justice'. On their YouTube account they have the video (2:11) *Generation Lockdown*. It opens with a circle of adults, presumably teachers, being told that they are going to learn from an expert how to conduct a lockdown. The expert is then introduced. She is an eleven-year-old girl, Kayleigh. She explains to them what happens in a lockdown. Her speech is punctuated with still photographs of children and young adults in a school shooting and others practicing or actually in a lockdown. It ends with Kayleigh singing a song that her teacher made up to sing along to with his students. The screen is black for a few seconds, and text appears on the screen that explains that 95 per cent of children in public schools in the US practice lockdown drills. The lyrics are: 'Lock down, lock down, lets all hide / lock the doors and stay inside / crouch on down / don't make a sound / and don't cry or you'll be found'. Sung in a high pitch with a jaunty tune, not unlike a nursery rhyme, the contrast between the meaning of the words and the style of delivery produces the uncanny effect of horror.

On March 23, 2018, only five weeks after the shooting, *Teen Vogue* ran a piece on 'why we choose to march' in which Emma Gonzalez (who is also credited with making the film) says 'why we choose to march', and she and three others—two students from MSD and African American teen Nza-Ari Kheppa, who started an organisation called 'project orange tree' in 2013 after her friend Hadiya was shot near her school (Hadiya had performed at Obama's inaugural the previous week and, probably for that reason, this murder caught some press attention). The campaign has a Facebook page (last posted on June 2018) and got the colour orange adopted as the colour of the anti-gun-violence movement. The video 'Why we Choose to March' has had nearly three hundred thousand views on *Teen Vogue*'s YouTube channel, Teen Vogue Take, which is 'a weekly multi-platform digital show that explores the intersection of pop culture and social justice'. Emma Gonzalez's text for the article ends with this:

> The media afforded a group of high school students the opportunity to wedge our foot in the door, but we aren't going through this alone. As a group, and as a movement, it's vital that we acknowledge and utilize our privilege, use our platforms to spread the names of the dead and the injured, promote ideas that can help spread kindness rather than hostility, support those who aren't being heard, take our voices and use them together with the megaphones provided.
>
> We the Wounded of the United States, in Order to form a more perfect Future, establish Justice, ensure domestic Tranquility, provide for the common People, promote the general Welfare, and secure the Blessings of Liberty to ourselves and our Generations to Come, do ordain and establish this March for the United States of America.

The *Teen Vogue* cover has an image of five teenagers (2 black boys, a black girl, an Asian girl and a white girl) raising their hands in the 'don't shoot' pose that went viral after Michael Brown was killed. The *Teen Vogue* mast is above their heads and the caption at the bottom of the image is: 'You're killing us'. The slogans March for Our Lives, 'You're killing us' and 'hands up, don't shoot' rhetorically connect Black Lives Matter to gun regulation. The black girl who appears on the *Teen Vogue* video is the only one of the five girls on the video who is not an MSD school student. The intention is presumably to address some of the criticisms of the MSD campaign by engaging with black youth who live in high-gun-crime areas but whose random murder generally does not get national press attention.

It is worth mentioning here that *Teen Vogue*'s marketing strategy is to engage with user-generated content and mine potential readers to establish the content of the magazine (https://www.mediapost.com/publications/article/296209/what-every-marketer-can-learn-from-the-winning-str.html). Condé Nast, *Teen Vogue*'s owners, has moved into events and in 2018, organised two *Teen Vogue* summits (in New York City and LA) with a programme squarely aimed at bringing in social justice Gen Z audiences. In 2018, *Teen Vogue* went entirely digital. Although the gun issue generated higher reader numbers, the magazine still saw a fall in circulation the following week.

In a video for the *New York Times* on the new student activism, journalist Neeti Upadhye (www.nytimes.com/video/us/100000005761059/student-protests-neveragain-parkland.html) says, 'These survivors are presenting their personal stories of loss as part of their fight converting grief into power by getting into the face of adults'. She connects March for Our Lives to the Dreamers and Black Lives Matter, who have all involved, she says, college-educated Millennials. While this is true, these movements also involved many more people who were not college educated, but the assumption that effective political movements require college education and to be young is an enduring one in US political culture. A particularly poignant moment in the video is a clip from Obama's speech announcing DACA (Deferred Action for Childhood Arrivals) addressing undocumented Dreamers and saying, 'You can come out of the shadows'. President Trump has tried to reverse DACA, and in June 2018, an appeal against the reversal was in the US Supreme Court. Another video, by two *New York Times* journalists, Sameen Amin and Yousur Al-Hlou, reports on Southside Chicago students who were preparing to go on the March on Washington against gun violence. Several of the young black people in the video have lost friends and relatives caught in the crossfire of gang shootouts. They had met the Florida teenagers in Florida and in Chicago and discussed the differences between the on-going insecurity and violence they face, and the lack of attention it gets, and the one-off violence the Florida MSD students faced.

In contrast to the lack of interest in the insecurity that black teenagers face on a daily basis on Chicago's South Side, the MSD students made not only the *New York Times* but also the *Washington Post* (www.youtube.com/watch?v=1s5J1L3fucI). Their own school magazine (www.eagleeye.news/news/msd-mourns-the-loss-of-students-and-teachers-at-candlelight-vigil/) was entered for a Pulitzer Press and got a special mention (www.nytimes.com/2019/04/16/us/pulitzer-parkland-stoneman-douglas-eagle-eye.html). That the students at MSD made the pages of the *New York Times* and the *Washington Post* partly speaks to the power of an effective media campaign but also to the lack of national debate on the gun violence affecting African American communities.

## SOUTH DAKOTA PIPELINE

Jasilyn Charger was one of the first people to set up camp at the Standing Rock Reservation in April 2016. Reveal News made a video hosted on YouTube about her life and her involvement in the protest. The film is just over five minutes long. It opens with a figure walking across a snow-covered field towards a line of houses and away from the camera. The soundtrack was made by APM Music and is a generic Native American–style music. It accompanies the entire film in the background as Jasilyn narrates her story of becoming an activist and her perspective on how the protests unfolded and what she will do now that the pipeline has been approved. The music is lilting, peaceful, and meditative. It establishes and maintains the narrative of a non-conflictual intervention, one that is underscored by Jasilyn's narrative, which emphasises the protests as a personal journey that is about protecting the land and does not need to involve conflict with the police. She emphasises, for example, the role of the youth in de-escalating violence that she implies came from the protestors rather than the police. The only diegetic music in the film is from a middle-aged man sitting down and playing a small flute pipe. In contrast, ABC News film on the protests opens with diegetic drumming and singing—giving both voice and action to the protestors (https://www.revealnews.org/article/one-year-at-standing-rock/). However, like Jasilyn, another member of the youth council on the ABC film, Daniel Grassrope—twenty-five years old—also emphasises that the point of the protest is spiritual: 'we're here to pray'; 'we're not here to antagonise the police'. After this introduction, the title of the film is shown: 'The Seventh Generation: Youth at the Heart of the Standing Rock Protests'. People from the Indigenous Youth Council speak to the camera, explaining their hopes for the success of the opposition, the run to Washington from South Dakota. They mention Jasilyn as one of the founder members. Other than a couple of sentences in which 'our friend Jasilyn' is mentioned, Jasilyn does not appear in the ABC film.

The ABC News feature program 'The Seventh Generation: Youth at the Heart of the Standing Rock Protests' (https://www.youtube.com/watch?v=1Rz_TkpysKk) centres several members of the international Indigenous Youth Council and their self-identification as the 'seventh generation' and their commitment, along with other indigenous activists at the Dakota Access Pipeline camps as 'protectors' of the land rather than protestors and as peaceful and prayerful. They insist that this is how they will win, not through violence. They try to engage the police in prayer, and they do so by asking for forgiveness as well as offering forgiveness.

The film ends shortly after President Donald Trump signs an order instructing the army to expedite the pipeline and the campers were evicted.

While 'the seventh generation' echoes many of the themes talked about by Jasilyn in the Reveal film, its narrative arc constructs of a different relationship of the indigenous youth protectors to the land, to their identity as indigenous peoples, and to one another from *One Year at Standing Rock. One Year* was released in April 2017. In March 2018, Jasilyn was part of Levi's and Girlgaze's launch #IShapeMyWorld Film Series for Women's History Month (https://www.teenvogue.com/story/levis-girl-gaze-ishapemyworld-film-series-womens-history-month). Girlgaze was founded by Amanda de Cadenet (b. 1972), a former model and sometime actor and a part of a British aristocratic family. Girlgaze is an example of how the language of social justice ('representation matters') is appropriated by business to increase market share among young women. Despite its hashtag, it is predominately run by women, not girls (the CEO is forty-six years old).

The film Levis and Girlgaze made is a short (3:44) called *Jasilyn: Activist of the Land* (http://www.levistrauss.com/2018/03/19/levis-girlgaze-team-tell-stories-inspiring-women/). In it, the collectivity of the activists who call themselves 'the seventh generation' is elided in favour of a story of individual recovery and the connection of that recovery with the Levi's tag 'live in Levis'. The construction of Jasilyn as an individual whose activism is her recovery fits well with the branding that Levi and #girlgaze promotes of exceptional individuals, an exceptionalism that is in opposition to the collective character and co-creation of movements that resist the profit logics of capital. Not only does brand activism serve to drive consumers to a specific brand in a crowded market, but it also reshapes the significance of the activism that it appropriates. In this instance, the irony of the capitalist appropriation of an anti-capitalist movement is further underscored by the identification of the brand Levi with the masculine individualism of the white pioneer/cowboy (Salazar 2010) and the history of the foundation of America in the appropriation and theft of American Indian land.

## CONCLUSION

Black Lives Matter has provided a model for other forms of activism that use the reach of social media to mobilise across the United States and internationally. It succeeded in building a platform that collected together hundreds of stories of police violence into a single message. Although the issue that got most traction in social media was the murder of young people and children by the police, it seems that it was not predominately a youth movement and has not succeeded in building a mass movement of young people. March for Our Lives took many of the tactics of Black

Lives Matter to build its campaign and did succeed in getting hundreds of thousands of young people on the March on Washington. The simplicity of their message—increase gun control—and the means to accomplish it through voter registration campaigns echoed other campaigns in the history of social reform, which ultimately depend on the idea that US democracy fails particular groups of citizens because particular groups of citizens have failed US democracy by not voting or have been prevented from voting. It is also evident in M4OL that, in contrast to BLM, the media saw the financialisation possibilities of connecting with these young 'change-makers' who were affluent, and about to enter college. No Dakota Access Pipe Line (No DAPL) has also been successful in using visual media to reach national and international audiences and mainstream media and advertisers have leveraged and monetarised this visual content.

Something interesting is happening in visual representation of children and youth on social media. Black Lives Matter and No DAPL contest the very basis of racial capitalism in the colonialism and racism that founded the United States. Furthermore, their visual representation is developed from face-to-face struggle and protest. In contrast to earlier visualisation of social reform and protest movements, the purpose of these representations is not to educate spectators but to build a movement both on- and off-line. When M4OL interpellates US youth as 'we the wounded', they also extend Black Lives Matter's implicit argument that injury and violence are the basis for making legitimate, even irrefutable political claims. That it is children who are suffering through being subjected to harm adds to the weight of those claims.

## NOTES

1. https://www.youtube.com/watch?v=Dz6YarZ5upE.
2. https://www.youtube.com/watch?v=0IM4p62p3M0&time_continue=117& app=deskt.

# TEN

# Theorising Childhood, Visual Culture and Technology

Conventions within visual culture about how to represent the child or what the child represents shift with broader cultural shifts; but the child and the youth always have a distinct iconography situated within a distinct semiotics. This chapter traces how the iconography and semiotics of childhood were shaped by the technologies of visualisation that have developed since the invention of photography.

By the middle of the eighteenth century, if not earlier, the child in European visual culture was a symbol of innocence and lack of guile. The emergence of the representation of modern childhood in Western art is now acknowledged (in contrast to Ariès) to begin in the mid-eighteenth to mid-nineteenth centuries. In her reappraisal of Ariès, Kate Retford cites James Steward, who in his essay for a 1995 exhibition held at Berkeley, entitled 'The New Child: British Art and the Origins of Modern Childhood 1730–1830' wrote that in this period, 'The child now dominates the canvas and the natural setting. No longer vulnerable, the child is a symbol of confidence for the future' (cited in Retford 2016:402). In her discussion of what she terms the 'infant academy' (after the title of one of Joshua Reynold's paintings), or humorous paintings of children engaged in artistic pursuits, Rosenthal (2004) notes that for Reynolds 'and many of his contemporaries, childhood was also associated with a state of innocence that guaranteed a seemingly truthful recognition of nature' (Rosenthal 2004:615). Similarly, Anne Higonet, in her *Pictures of Innocence* (1998), dates the representation of childhood innocence from late eighteenth-century British portraiture. Emma Barker also comments in her discussion of Greuze's *Girl with a Dog* that the second part of the eighteenth century 'is commonly said to have witnessed the emergence of a distinctively modern conception of childhood as an age of innocence, which found visual expression first and foremost in portraits of children by British artists (2009:426). Johnson (1990) points out that French childhood and family cultures in the eighteenth century were divided between an emergent sentimentality about children's capacities and characters, which is later reflected in and developed by Rousseau, and the persistence of a Puritan ethic, elaborated in medical discourse of constraint, including the swaddling and binding of children's bodies.

In the early eighteenth century, Chardin painted many depictions of children that traced, Johnson argues, this new sentimentality and appreciation of children's peculiar characters and childhood as a stage of development. In her analysis of Chardin's *Soap Bubble*, for example, she reads the figure to the left of the youth as a young child engaged in a process of learning. For the spectator, the bubbles, in the tradition of Dutch emblematic painting that audiences would have been familiar with, may have signified the ephemerality of life but, since such an interpretation would escape the figure (the young child) depicted in the painting, she suggests that the spectator is being educated to attend to new ideas about the specific modes of learning that children are engaged in. For her, 'Chardin's images of the child will consistently perform this dual function of representing education and of educating the spectator' (1990:59). Here then, a second symbolic function of the image of the child can be discerned: of the child as, paradoxically, educating the adult. This is a reversal that we have seen repeatedly in the previous chapters in this book, especially since the 1960s when the 'kids took it over', but it is surprising to see it emerge so early in visual culture.

In another analysis of the same painting, Herbert (2001) suggests that this genre painting is a representation of the *bildung* that will determine the fate of the youth, and that the soap bubble he blows over the ledge and into the future signals the indeterminancy of the future, while the toddler or smaller child who struggles to reach the eye level of the soap bowl symbolises the passage of time through childhood. These themes of innocence, the future, and the child as the source of truth continue to inflect Western visual culture as it develops in photography and moving image. Retford also crucially points to 'the new emotional and aesthetic response to the child that emerged in this period, which has led us to identify it as witnessing the emergence of "modern" childhood' (Retford 2016:410).

Innocence is also bound up with vulnerability. Emma Barker comments on how Sebastian Mitchell in his analysis of Reynold's *The Age of Innocence* finds the girl's vulnerability carries both 'an injunction to the protect the child' and 'conveys the uncomfortable sense that she may need to be protected from you' (Mitchell 2001:126 cited in Barker 2009:436). This seems like a particularly heterosexual man's point of view on vulnerable young femininity, but Barker's point that innocence is constituted in relation to the 'experience that undermines it' points to an interpretation of *innocent* as meaning *sexually inexperienced* rather than *lacking culpability*. This threat that the spectator poses to the innocence of childhood is, says Barker, 'even truer of Greuze's painting, given the way that it positions the spectator as an intruder' (Barker 2009:436). It is also worth noting the melodramatic tone of Barker's comment: 'For male spectators of the period, Greuze's painting thus offered an identification either as the father figure who can preserve her from this fate or as the predator who will one day take advantage of her' (2009:436). If she is correct in her interpretation, it also pushes back the emergence not only of childhood innocence but of the melodramatic imagination on which so much visual culture of childhood depends for its legibility.

The other convention that can be traced to this period is the portrait of the lone child, again emerging much earlier than one might imagine from the extant photographic record. While some suggest that this enables the child to play symbolic functions all the more effectively, others suggest that it signifies a new interest in the child's individuality.

Visual representation is also connected to and derives its iconography from religious cultures. In Western visual cultures, dominated by Christian mythology, the Christ child and the New Testament repositioning of original sin elevates the child as a figure of innocence while the humanisation of the relationship between the divine and the world is evident in the representation of the Madonna and child from the twelfth century. In their refutation of Simon Shama's thesis in his *Embarrassment of Riches* that Protestant Calvinist culture was responsible for a new attitude of love for children and affectionate marriage, Dekker and Groenendijk push back to a much earlier period the appearance in visual culture of a loving relationship between parent and child. They contend that in visual culture, the loving mother of the Christ child is depicted in Florence Renaissance art as early as the twelfth century. They cite Southern's assessment, about the *Madonna of Dom Rupert* in twelfth-century Liege, that 'The Mother has lost her remoteness; the [Christ] Child has laid [put] down the symbols of his wisdom and authority. Only the inscription from Ezekiel round the border discloses the hidden divinity; all else is humanity, frailty and love' (Southern 1973:229 cited in Dekker and Groenendijk 1991:n.p.), and in a similar vein, they point to the work of Giotto, and Luca della Robbia, 'culminating in the very, very human "Madonna della Sedia" of Sanzi Raphael' (1991:n.p.).

## PHOTOGRAPHY AND FILM ENTERS INTO A VISUAL CULTURE THAT ALREADY KNOWS HOW TO READ THE IMAGE OF THE CHILD

Greuze's *The Little Orphans* shows the continuity between the forms of representation in art and those in the emergent photography of social

**Figure 10.1.  Jean-Baptiste Greuze, The Little Orphans/Two children with a dog, ca. 1785.**

reform. These forms of representation are also connected with cultures of feeling. The figure of the child as it becomes visible outside of religious iconography interpellates the spectator as a feeling subject, who reacts with appropriate sentimentality to the appealing gaze of the semi-naked, chubby, infant. In the eighteenth century, sentimentality emerges into the public sphere for the first time. While sentimental feeling had long been gendered as characteristic of women, the eighteenth century in Europe saw the emergence of the 'man of feeling', and this figure signifies the entry of sentiment into the art of government. The representation of the child as a vulnerable subject, appealing to the sympathy and sentiment of the spectator and the spectator's ability to respond appropriately to that image, comes to signify the moral certitude of the spectator. The place of the child in this visual culture of sentiment is part of that broader shift in political cultures, itself produced in response to the emergence of the stranger as a distinctive characteristic of urbanisation. The child was central to what Gerard (2002) calls 'pathetic sentiment'; an exchange between 'a suffering being . . . and a sympathetic listener or viewer' (2002:554). Gerard goes on to describe what sounds like a description of the melodramatic mode: a connection between two characters established through the telling of a tale of 'undeserved woe' (2002:554).

Hence, when the photograph enters into visual culture from the mid-nineteenth century, the viewer (and, indeed, the photographer) already has a well-defined set of tropes about how to visually stimulate sentimental affect in the spectator and the place of children (and women) in this, frequently melodramatic, mode. The photographic representation of the child, often with another older child or youth or their mother is quickly established as a trope of social-reform photography, directly referencing the emergence of both the sentimental spectator and the individual child as a fit subject for representation in the preceding two centuries.

## THE ARCHIVE AND THE ALBUM

However, the new technology of the camera, the mechanical reproduction of the image, also stimulates, perhaps even demands, new practices of representation and spectatorship in which the child also has a significant place. As the images proliferate, the child's image is subject to the same division between the mug shot and the portrait, the archive and the family album, that Alan Sekula theorises in 'The Body and the Archive' (1986). While Walter Benjamin famously wants to argue for the revolutionary potential of the photographic image, as many theorists have shown, photography was also both implicated in and enabled the circulation and development of racist discourse. Shawn Michelle Smith, for example, shows in her 'Baby's Picture Is Always Treasured' (1998), how the practice of photographing babies and young children for inclusion in family albums articulated, or at least converged, with the desires of eugenicists to get white families to document their genealogy and the birth and development of their child using the developing conventions of scientific recording. So that, at the same time that the image of the child proliferates in visual culture as a sentimental touchstone, it also emerges as a scientific object, akin to the mug shot of the criminal in the archive in its scientific pretensions. However, unlike the portrait versus the mug shot, in the sentimental child versus the developing child, the images converge and supplement one another. It is not a binary, nor even a double facing but rather an interlacing of these ways of viewing the child. The photographer of the lone, dirty, bedraggled and half-dressed orphan crouched in the doorway of a New York tenement wants to interpellate the sentimental spectator partly by invoking what the child is not but should be: clean, well dressed, in the heart of the family.

This deployment of a scientific mode, or what Sekula is calling the 'mug shot', to represent children is also evident in other photographs of children that were widely popular in the late nineteenth century, for example Charles Darwin's *The Expression of the Emotions in Man and Animals* (1872) and Oscar Rejlander's *Ginx's Baby* (1871), which went on to sell three hundred thousand copies (Lebeau 2008:9).

## The Democratisation of Visual Culture

Towards the end of the nineteenth century (1888), George Eastman, the founder of Eastman Kodak, marketed a twenty-five-dollar camera, pre-loaded with film, with the slogan 'You press the button, we do the rest.' This was followed in 1900 with the one-dollar Brownie camera. Within five years, about ten million people in the United States owned cameras, an expansion of the market that effectively democratised visual culture. The Brownie was advertised in magazines for women and for children. It was intended as something more than a toy but less than a 'real' camera. Mark Oliver (2007) points out that its marketing to children, its very affordable price, and its take-up by women has led to it being more or less ignored in most accounts of the development of the Kodak.

The significance of the Brownie, in Mark Oliver's account, is that its conjoining of 'human time' and 'fairy time' (the Brownie was named after a mythical sprite) and the incorporation of the camera into the Brownie's mythic-fictional world 'both indicates and spreads a growing anxiety about the undocumented life. Sprites once content with a quiet and invisible domesticity learn to seek photographic proof of their expeditions. Similarly, potential consumers, especially women and children, learn that their own previously invisible lives need mediatized expression' (2007:11).

To consolidate the place of the camera in and for childhood, the firm created its Brownie Camera Club of America. To be a member, a child had to be under sixteen years of age, live in North America, and own a Brownie camera. The club had its own 'literature, photo competitions and exhibitions and advertisements in children's magazines' intended to generate a sense of belonging that, notwithstanding their construction as consumers, also formed children as members of an imagined community. One of the company's advertising slogans was 'Let the Children Kodak!'.

In chapter 3, the father of Denise McNair, one of the girls murdered by a white supremacist in Birmingham, Alabama, in 1963, recalls that in Spike Lee's documentary 4 *Little Girls*, Denise asked him to 'take a picture of me Daddy' with her Brownie camera. Of course, as Oliver points out, this attempt to frame photography storytelling as an expression of children's creativity, almost as their right to expression, is 'not to say that corporate interests do not invade the life of the camera's user (which, Eastman hopes, will be revisited as a series of "Kodak moments"), but certain narrative decisions rest in the hands that press the buttons. In other words, the Brownie enthusiast is promised authorial status, however mediated the production of his or her story' (Oliver 2007:16). Changes in the technology of photography expanded the possibility for children to have some control over their visual storytelling. Photography began that shift of children's visual representation from object to subject that this book is interested in. The shift from production *about* to production *by* the young subjects depicted, and the impact of this on political visual culture that I discuss in this book primarily in relation to Web 2.0, also has this much earlier genealogy.

## THE INVENTION OF THE FILM ALSO STARTS WITH THE CHILD AS ITS SUBJECT

The shift backwards and forwards between the scientific and the sentimental, the portrait and the mug shot, the family album and the archive, continued to inflect the depiction of children in documentary photography and in forms of documentary film throughout the twentieth century. From its inception, the legibility of generation (both childhood and old age), of gender and of race were both taken up by and re-inscribed through film and photography. Silent film and popular, melodramatic theatre depended on the easy recognition of often exaggerated visual tropes. Film depended more than theatre on the pleasure of looking. These combined in early film to depict particular figures, especially the young child and the feminine woman, as stimulating the visual pleasure of the audience. Vicky Lebeau's *Childhood and Cinema* opens with a still taken from an 1897 film in which C. Francis Jenkins is coaxing a reluctant and naked young child to stand before the camera. This image, she suggests, indicates the 'level of connivance between (early) cinema and the spectacle of the child'. 'Child Life', she notes, was one of the 'most popular genres of Victorian film' (2008:7).

The important place of melodrama in early film also strengthens the role not only of women, as has been widely recognised, but also of children in visual culture. For example, as Charlie Chaplin's films move from comedy and slapstick towards melodrama and social commentary, the figure of the child becomes more important, most obviously in *The Kid*, in which Chaplin takes over the role of mother to Jackie. In this role, Charlie feeds, changes and bathes the infant, educates the boy 'in street smarts and etiquette' and worries about him when he gets sick (Woal and Woal 1994:7). His despair when his ability to look after the child is questioned (a questioning prompted by both his class and his gender) 'finds its reflection in classic maternal melodramas' (ibid.).

In a discussion of the development of silent film and visual culture and its connection to tropes of race, gender and generation, it is necessary to address the significance for political visual culture of the racialization of American narrative cinema and its origins in the repeatedly cited D. W. Griffiths racist film *Birth of a Nation* (1915). Oscar Micheaux, an African American writer and director, directed *Within Our Gates* in 1919; his film is often seen 'as a direct response to *Birth of a Nation*' (Haenni 2015). Whether or not it was, and Micheaux himself denied a direct relationship between the two films, Micheaux's work to make films that spoke to black audiences' experiences also points to the importance of attending to film and visual culture of childhood as shaped by the wider social and political forces that they wanted to depict. In so-called mainstream film, the continuation of the dominance of not only white characters but of life told from the perspective of whites continues to determine Hollywood output. Black life continues to be seen as marginal to the interests of audiences, and crossover from black audiences (who continue to have a larger share of cinema audiences than whites) to white-focused films (or those with one or two black characters) has shaped Hollywood production. Consequently, it is only in moments when the film industry is in crisis that Hollywood makes room for more innovative films and tries to capitalise on specific cultural trends among minority audiences to re-populate the market for film. The incorporation of social issues and contemporary youth political culture into mainstream film and, especially, television helps to explain why Hollywood is a contradictory space and to explain the role of marketing in enabling Hollywood and television to be at one and the same time producing films and programmes that re-inscribe and producing others that contest and unsettle contemporary racist and sexist ideologies. Arguably, this proliferation is enabled by developments in film and broadcast technology that enable the splitting of the market into relatively fine slices so that, via social media and search algorithm prompts, audiences can curate their own entertainment without having to engage with other productions, by the same companies, that they are not interested in, whether from a political or aesthetic point of view.

Developments in film technology and of professional training for filmmakers in the late twentieth century opened up space for young filmmakers. The highly influential LA School and the directors associated with 'New Jack cinema' were in their early twenties, and even late teens when they had their directorial debuts. Hollywood's restless search for new markets, intensified at a time of financial crisis in the industry, opened up space for young black filmmakers because of the success of the music industry in capturing youth markets, partly through producing content made by young performers and artists. This also expanded the connections between visual and aural cultures and markets, as well as other 'tie-ins' between film, music, clothes and other commodities.

## YOUTH AS MAKERS OF CONTENT FOR SMALL AND MOBILE MEDIA

Young directors and screenwriters to some extent closed the gap between lives depicted on screen and the producers of those images, but it is the emergence of user-generated content or participatory media that has changed the landscape of political visual culture not only on social media platforms but more broadly. The relatively low barriers to amateurs creating and disseminating short films that directly address issues of social justice where the producer and the audience converge has profound implications for the public visual culture of youth and social reform.

In chapters 8 and 9, I showed how young activists have succeeded in using social media platforms and videos with low-production values (and therefore low cost barriers) to amplify their messages and capture the attention of national and even international political discourse, including about police violence against black people and communities, ownership of Indian land and natural resources, and gun violence. I also showed how LGBT youth have created virtual public spheres and communities for geographically dispersed queer children and youth.

However, these processes are not without their contradictions. Felix Stalder agrees that the front end of social media of Web 2.0 may 'advance semiotic democracy' but also argues that the back end of Web 2.0 is creating 'new forms of control and manipulation, masked by a mere simulation of involvement and participation' (2012:242). One of the critiques of these new forms of control and manipulation is that the creation of data about consumers that is then translated by algorithms into prompts to buy targeted goods is enabled through activity on social media that not only tells advertisers who we are but enables advertisers to manipulate our desires to literally make us new kinds of persons. A related critique is that users of social media are engaged in immaterial and unremunerated labour that capital benefits from.

However, the conceptualization of the work of users as 'immaterial labour' (Barnet-Weiser 2012) ignores the fundamentally material base of user-generated content. Profiles of users are economic assets that platforms sell to advertisers who can then both craft advertisements for and base their advert placement on these profiles. It is advertising and the

courting of future high earners as they enter into adulthood that is driving the relationship between corporate media (for example, *Teen Vogue*)
and social media users on platforms like Instagram, Facebook and You-
Tube. As Wilkie correctly argues, code theory—drawing on a non-materi-
alist deployment of Foucauldian bio-politics and Deleuze and Guattari's
(1983) concept of the 'decoding' economy—claims that 'capitalism is depicted around an endless cycle of releasing and recapturing excessive
creative energies generated by social practices, not just those traditionally
considered "work"' (2017:165). In this conceptualization of the relationship between digital technology and capitalism that follows Deleuze and
Guattari's (1983) concept of the 'decoding' economy, the use of social
media disrupts 'the boundaries between work time and spare time, labour and play' (Fuchs 2014:126 cited in Wilkie 2017:15). However, as
Wilkie argues, '[w]hile much of the internet economy does rely on mone-
tized information—for example in the form of targeted advertising—
their massive capital reserves primarily represent the accumulation of
surplus value produced elsewhere' (2017:173).

In arguing that surveillance capitalism is not qualitatively different to
liberal capitalism, and is in fact just another manifestation of it, I am not
suggesting that there are not troubling questions to be answered about
the relationship between commerce and (political visual) culture. Social
media is demonstrably producing larger audiences and platforms than
face-to-face political culture produced for a loosely defined social justice
politics that is primarily being generated by young people and is for and
about young people and their relationship to politics. Young people in
the United States, many of whom are Generation Z digital natives, have
shown that they can produce very effective visual content. However, that
content is both being directly monetarised (mostly in the kind of community building that LGBT youth have engaged in) and linked to advertising strategies directly, as seen in Levi's #girlgaze campaign in chapter 9.
So the questions that remain (and really the answers will depend on the
political commitments of the reader) are: Can social justice be accomplished within capitalism, and is the revolution being broadcast on social
media?

## TELEVISION, VISUAL PUBLIC CULTURE AND NARROWCASTING

In tracing the ways that youth and children have been depicted in and
worked with political visual culture, I have only touched on television in
passing. This is not because television is not an important medium for
understanding this relationship. Indeed, the move towards narrowcasting that television began has arguably been more influential on internet
visual culture than either film or photography and, as I discussed in
chapter 8, modes derived from television, especially reality television and

news broadcasting, have clearly influenced the mode of social media visual production by young digital activists.

There is a copious academic literature on children's television, most of which focuses on the impacts of television on socialisation of children. Logically, children's television might have been a good place to start to understand the nexus of political visual culture and childhood. However, what I am more interested in is how television is shaping the move towards narrowcasting and small productions. Television is transforming the relationship between viewer and content in ways that seem to borrow, on the one hand, from film and documentary and, on the other, from social media (YouTube, Instagram). This has been made possible by developments in technology that have dramatically reduced the entry costs to video production and dissemination. At the same time, audiences, especially young audiences, are increasingly looking for content that speaks directly to their experiences and interests. The boundaries between 'previously discrete forms (text, film, broadcasting, video, and sound recordings) are increasingly blurred, challenging established practices and paradigms' (Kompare 2005:198 cited in Jenner 2014:258). Kompare's view that centralized, one-way content will become less and less common echoes advertisers claims that advertising can no longer disseminate messages but must make content that is dialogic with consumers. As I discussed in chapter 8, this convergence and dissolving of 'discrete boundaries' is both giving larger platforms to minority voices and commercialising them to strip them of any fundamentally transformative content in relation to consumer capitalism.

As with film, changes in technology and changes in regulation have both contributed to the refashioning of what television can be. In the first period, from the invention of television to the early 1980s, there were few channels, and broadcasters were speaking to mass audiences. In the 1970s and 1980s, the deregulation of the industry and the emergence of cable channels led to new branding strategies, including developing 'quality' programmes of long-form narrative television. The proliferation of networks also meant that content had to be focused on smaller and more homogenous or niche audiences who paid for content through subscription or advertising.

In what Amanda Lotz characterises as the 'post-network era', we are seeing increased audience fragmentation and viewers curating content from multiple platforms including Netflix, Amazon, Now TV, and so forth. In the 1990s, several companies, including AOL, Time Warner, Microsoft, Apple, and WebTV, were developing 'interactive televisions' (iTVs). The Hollywood writers' strike of 2007 and 2008 was about, among other issues, what this proliferation of viewing platforms and commodification of their 'diegetic universes' (e.g., video or online game tie-ins) meant for their share of profits, and this prompted what Curtin calls a rethinking of 'the spatial logic of electronic media' (Jenner 2014:260) that he terms 'matrix media' and Jenner calls 'TV IV'. Netflix is exemplary of this new 'matrix media'. It moved from video-on-demand services, mostly of content previously screened on other platforms (e.g., cinema, DVD), to producing its own content of original dramas. This shift was an intensification or expansion of smaller shifts in distribution and innovative forms of advertising (e.g., webisodes for TV drama) that was appearing elsewhere, but this intensification also signaled a qualitative shift in the relationship between production and consumption. It leveraged a market for quality TV drama that HBO had already established, and it 'builds on models of individualised viewing practices and self-scheduling of TV' (Jenner 2014:268).

These processes are highly relevant to the concern of this book with understanding how visual culture interacts with processes of social reform and the ways in which postmodern capitalism intensifies and diversifies its capacity to absorb criticism and even leverage it to produce new sites of capital formation. Television programmes that represent social justice discourses are proliferating, and it is important to make sense of their significance for mobilising for social change. As Nealon says, 'There are myriad social and political dangers latent in the neoliberal truisms of finance capital, but the rigid normalization of cultural options isn't paramount among them (2012:21 cited in Jenner 2014:268).

Central to the debate about how television interacts with social-reform agendas in relation to both the representation of youth and, increasingly, an address to youth are the issues of narrowcasting, micro-casting and, central to the capacity of both, algorithms that direct the viewers attention, often across multiple social media platforms, to content that is like the content they have just consumed/watched. As Jonathon Cohn notes in his article on TiVo algorithms, 'My TiVo Thinks I'm Gay', some of this commentary overstates the deterministic capacity of algorithms as well as bracketing out the work that is done (he says by humans, but presumably a lot of this is also done by AI) to update algorithms: 'These technologies may affect certain cultures, but they are also—simultaneously and irrevocably—transformed by such cultures as well' (2016:678). He goes on: 'With a few notable exceptions, just as algorithmic culture scholarship tends to present algorithms as opaque, static, and despotic, it also presents users as incapable of critical reflection, transgressive actions, or the simple act of decoding that has been a central facet of Cultural Studies since its beginning' (2016:678).

Whether viewers are 'cultural dopes' or critical decoders of content, the shift from broadcasting to narrowcasting has clearly shaped both production and viewing practices. Television as the 'electronic hearth' transmitting to a 'mass and heterogeneous audience' (Lotz 2007:5) is no longer with us. Increasingly, television is adopting the strategy used much earlier by the magazine industry to target narrow audiences. Joseph Turrow has argued that advertisers have demanded this shift towards narrowly targeted audiences. While the benefits for advertisers are clear, he cautions against the dangers for public culture of the development of 'gated informational communities' that it produces (cited in Lotz 2016:36). That said, the idea that television was a national conversation or electronic public sphere (Lotz 2007:42) glosses over the extent to which that conversation was directed in the United States to white audiences and excluded the experiences of black audiences (indeed, as I discussed in chapter 3, programmes of social events, for example, the March on Washington, that represented black experience continued to do so for a presumptive white audience). In any case, television increasingly operates as a 'subcultural form' that 'reproduces a similar experience as the electronic public sphere, but among more narrow groups that share particular cultural affinities or tastes' (Lotz 2007:43) or, I would add, political commitments.

## CONCLUSION

This book has attempted to understand how changes in visual technology have shaped the relationship between spectators and subjects from the invention of photography to Web 2.0. It has done so by focusing on US visual political culture and its representation of children and youth in projects of social reform, broadly conceived. Three broad approaches to this visual representation were explored: the child as the object in the image; the child as the subject of the image; and the child as the producer, subject and audience for the image. Connecting these three approaches is a shared visual political culture, which did not spring fully formed into existence with the development of mechanical reproduction of the image, but borrowed from other art forms, painting, literature and theatre to develop a mode for representing the suffering child. This shared political culture that connected suffering to citizenship and political rights, continues to inflect visual culture but it has to also be recognised that the political economy of racism shaped socio-cultural fields, complicating the relationship between suffering innocence and social reform. In the period when social-reform photography was focusing on child labour, child poverty and child homelessness, it invariably turned the camera on the white child, whereas black activists often wanted to disrupt the representation of black children (and adults) as suffering subjects. Not until Black Lives Matter, I want to suggest, did the figure of the wounded black child become an image that black activists consistently mobilised to demand recognition; the fact that the movement pointed back to the open casket of Emmett Till as its reference point shows how hidden the injury to black youth and children has been in the visual representation of social reform.

Social media and digital television have changed the visual public sphere. While, as I argued above, mass television never broadcast to the whole nation, and the electronic public sphere has always been as partial as the real-world public sphere, increasingly images, whether photography or film, and their interpretation circulate within and proliferate subcultures. There are very positive aspects to this. LGBTQI youth who are always geographically dispersed now have access to a virtual community that affirms and creates their identities. I showed how social media is able to amplify messages and bring young people together in real time and space to mobilise for social change. There is unprecedented representation of progressive political messages on television. One of the potentially negative aspects of this is that digital communities amplify their own messages but do not connect with others. When digital communities organise in real-world spaces across their related but sectional interests, this can mobilise many different demographics, as I showed in the previous chapter.

Suffering and the tragedy of early loss is one of the ways that the figure of the child is mobilised in political visual culture; the other is in the promise of futurity, the idea of the next generation as the engines of change. This trope is very evident in social media where the promise of youth as not only literally being the next generation and the future but, as activists for progressive social change, is repeatedly indexed. In the end, it seems that technology has not substantially changed the modes of representation of children and youth in the ways that I expected when I started the research for this book. Indeed, the extent to which social justice messages are being emptied of meaningful content by their take-up as advertising messages to sell commodities checks any fantasy that visual technology made by young people can see the change you want to be.

# Bibliography

Aitken, Ian. 1990. *Film and Reform: John Grierson and the Documentary Film Movement.* Cinema and Society. London: Routledge.

Alexander, Jonathan, and Elizabeth Losh. 2009. "'A YouTube of One's Own?' 'Coming Out' Videos as Rhetorical Action." In *LGBT Identity and Online New Media*, edited by Christopher Pullen and Margaret Copper, 37–50. New York: Routledge.

Allen, Kim, and Heather Mendick. 2013. "Keeping It Real? Social Class, Young People and 'Authenticity' in Reality TV." *Sociology* 47 (3): 460–76. https://doi.org/10.1177/0038038512448563.

Allen, Robert Clyde, and Annette Hill, eds. 2004. "Prime-Time TV in the Gay Nineties: Network Television, Quality Audiences, and Gay Politics." In *The Television Studies Reader*, by Ron Becker. London: Routledge.

Anker, Elisabeth. 2005. "Villains, Victims and Heroes: Melodrama, Media, and September 11." *Journal of Communication* 55 (1): 22–37.

Antony, Mary Grace, and Ryan J. Thomas. 2010. "'This Is Citizen Journalism at Its Finest': YouTube and the Public Sphere in the Oscar Grant Shooting Incident." *New Media & Society* 12 (8): 1280–96. https://doi.org/10.1177/1461444810362492.

Arendt, Hannah. 2006. *On Revolution.* New York: Penguin Books.

Aslama, Minna, and Mervi Pantti. 2006. "Talking Alone: Reality TV, Emotions and Authenticity." *European Journal of Cultural Studies* 9 (2): 167–84. https://doi.org/10.1177/1367549406063162.

Astrom, B. 2015. "The Symbolic Annihilation of Mothers in Popular Culture: Single Father and the Death of the Mother." *Feminist Media Studies* 15 (4): 593–607.

Banet-Weiser, Sarah. 2012. *Authentic TM: Politics and Ambivalence in a Brand Culture.* Critical Cultural Communication. New York: New York University Press.

Barker, Emma. 2009. "Imaging Childhood in Eighteenth-Century France: Greuze's Little Girl with a Dog." *The Art Bulletin* 91 (4): 426–45. https://doi.org/10.1080/00043079.2009.10786146.

Beirne, Rebecca. 2012. "Teen Lesbian Desires and Identities in International Cinema: 1931–2007." *Journal of Lesbian Studies* 16 (3): 258–72. https://doi.org/10.1080/10894160.2012.673925.

Besley, Tina. 2010. "Digitized Youth: Constructing Identities in the Creative Knowledge Economy." *Review of Contemporary Philosophy* 9 (2010): 11–39.

Bignell, Jonathan. 2005. *Big Brother.* London: Palgrave Macmillan UK. https://doi.org/10.1057/9780230508361.

Black Media Collective. 2016. "American Honey Review." *Black Media Review Collective* (blog). October 11, 2016. https://blackmediareviewcollective.blogspot.com/search?q=+american+honey.

Bleach Anthony C. 2010. "Postfeminist Cliques?: Class, Postfeminism, and the Molly Ringwald–John Hughes Films." *Cinema Journal* 49 (3): 24–44. https://doi.org/10.1353/cj.0.0209.

Boltanski, Luc. 1999. *Distant Suffering Morality, Media, and Politics.* Cambridge: Cambridge University Press.

Bonilla, Yarimar, and Jonathan Rosa. 2015. "#Ferguson: Digital Protest, Hashtag Ethnography, and the Racial Politics of Social Media in the United States: #Ferguson." *American Ethnologist* 42 (1): 4–17. https://doi.org/10.1111/amet.12112.

Bottomore, Stephen. 2014. "The Lantern and Cinematograph for Political Persuasion before WW1: Towards and Introduction and Typology." In *Screen Culture and the*

*Social Question, 1880–1914*, edited by Ludwig Vogl-Bienek and Richard Crangle, 21–34. KINtop Studies in Early Cinema 3. Bloomington: Indiana University Press.

Boxer, Sarah. 2014. "Why Are All the Cartoon Mothers Dead?" *The Atlantic* 314 (1).

"Boy Kumasenu." 1957. *Monthly Film Bulletin*, March 1957. http://www.colonialfilm.org.uk/node/332.

Boyd, Danah. 2014. *It's Complicated: The Social Lives of Networked Teens*. New Haven, CT: Yale University Press.

Boyd, Todd. 1997. *Am I Black Enough for You? Popular Culture from the 'Hood and Beyond*. Bloomington: Indiana University Press.

Bradbury-Rance, Clara. 2016. "Desire, Outcast: Locating Queer Adolescence." In *International Cinema and the Girl: Local Issues, Transnational Contexts*, edited by Fiona Handyside and Kate Taylor-Jones, 85–95. New York: Palgrave Macmillan US. https://doi.org/10.1057/9781137388926_7.

Bradley, Regina N. 2017. "Introduction: Hip-Hop Cinema as a Lens of Contemporary Black Realities." *Black Camera* 8 (2): 141. https://doi.org/10.2979/blackcamera.8.2.08.

Brewster, Ben. 1997. *Theatre to Cinema: Stage Pictorialism and the Early Feature Film*, edited by Lea Jacobs. Oxford: Oxford University Press.

Brigard, Emilie de. 2003. "The History of Ethnographic Film." In *Principles of Visual Anthropology*, edited by Paul Hockings, 3rd edition, 13–44. Berlin: Mouton de Gruyter.

Brody, Richard. 2016. "American Honey's Silent Youth." *New Yorker*, October 5.

———. 2018. "'The Hate U Give,' Reviewed: An Empathetic, Nuanced Portrait of a Teen's Political Awakening." *New Yorker*, October 19. https://www.newyorker.com/culture/the-front-row/the-hate-u-give-reviewed-an-empathetic-nuanced-portrait-of-a-teens-political-awakening.

Brooks, Peter. 1995. *The Melodramatic Imagination: Balzac, Henry James, Melodrama, and the Mode of Excess: With a New Preface*. New Haven, CT: Yale University Press.

Brownlow, Kevin. 1990. *Behind the Mask of Innocence*. London: Cape.

Bruzzi, Stella. 2000. *New Documentary: A Critical Introduction*. London: Routledge.

Buckley, Matthew S. 2009. "Refugee Theatre: Melodrama and Modernity's Loss." *Theatre Journal* 61 (2): 175–90.

Burman, Erica. 1999. "Appealing and Appalling Children." *Psychoanalytic Studies* 1 (3): 285.

Caron, Caroline, Rebecca Raby, Claudia Mitchell, Sophie Théwissen-LeBlanc, and Jessica Prioletta. 2017. "From Concept to Data: Sleuthing Social Change-Oriented Youth Voices on YouTube." *Journal of Youth Studies* 20 (1): 47–62. https://doi.org/10.1080/13676261.2016.1184242.

Chouliaraki, Lilie. 2006. *The Spectatorship of Suffering*. London: SAGE Publications.

Clark, Elizabeth B. 1995. "'The Sacred Rights of the Weak': Pain, Sympathy, and the Culture of Individual Rights in Antebellum America." *Journal of American History* 82 (2): 463–93. https://doi.org/10.2307/2082183.

Cohn, Jonathan. 2016. "My TiVo Thinks I'm Gay: Algorithmic Culture and Its Discontents." *Television & New Media* 17 (8): 675–90. https://doi.org/10.1177/1527476416644978.

Collins, Janelle. n.d. "Easing a Country's Conscience: Little Rock's Central High School in Film." *Southern Quarterly* 46 (1): 78–90.

Cosgrove, Denis E. 1998. *Social Formation and Symbolic Landscape*. Madison: University of Wisconsin Press.

Crangle, Richard, and Ludwig Vogl-Bienek. 2016. *Screen Culture and the Social Question, 1880–1914*. Bloomington: Indiana University Press. http://www.jstor.org/stable/10.2307/j.ctt1bmzn5t.

Cripps, Thomas. 1993. *Slow Fade to Black: The Negro in American Film, 1900–1942*. Oxford: Oxford University Press.

Cunningham, Daniel Mudie. 2011. "New Queer White Trash Cinema." In *Queer Popular Culture: Literature, Media, Film, and Television*, edited by Thomas Peele, 169–82. New York: Palgrave Macmillan US. https://doi.org/10.1007/978-1-349-29011-6_12.

Dawson, Leanne. 2015. "Passing and Policing: Controlling Compassion, Bodies and Boundaries in *Boys Don't Cry* and *Unveiled/Fremde Haut*." *Studies in European Cinema* 12 (3): 205–28. https://doi.org/10.1080/17411548.2015.1094258.

Dekker, Jeroen J. H., and Leendert L. Groenendijk. 1991. "The Republic of God or the Republic of Children? Childhood and Child-Rearing after the Reformation: An Appraisal of Simon Schama's Thesis about the Uniqueness of the Dutch Case." *Oxford Review of Education* 17 (3): 317–35. https://doi.org/10.1080/0305498910170306.

De Ridder, Sander, and Sofie Van Bauwel. 2015. "The Discursive Construction of Gay Teenagers in Times of Mediatization: Youth's Reflections on Intimate Storytelling, Queer Shame and Realness in Popular Social Media Places." *Journal of Youth Studies* 18 (6): 777–93. https://doi.org/10.1080/13676261.2014.992306.

Diawara, Manthia, ed. 1993. *Black American Cinema*. AFI Film Readers. New York: Routledge.

———. 2017. "Noir by Noirs: Towards a New Realism in Black Cinema." *African American Review* 50 (4): 899–911. https://doi.org/10.1353/afa.2017.0145.

Doherty, Thomas Patrick. 2002. *Teenagers and Teenpics: The Juvenilization of American Movies in the 1950s*. Rev. and Expanded ed. Philadelphia: Temple University Press.

Driscoll, Catherine. 2011. *Teen Film: A Critical Introduction*. English ed. Film Genres. Oxford: Berg.

Driver, Susan. 2007. *Queer Girls and Popular Culture: Reading, Resisting, and Creating Media*. Mediated Youth, vol. 1. New York: Peter Lang.

Ebert, Roger. 2009. "Precious: Based on the Novel Push by Sapphire." Rogerebert.com. November 4. https://www.rogerebert.com/reviews/precious-based-on-the-novel-push-by-sapphire-2009.

Elsaesser, Thomas. 1987. "Tales of Sound and Fury: Obsevations on the Family Melodrama." In *Home Is Where the Heart Is: Studies in Melodrama and the Woman's Film*, edited by Christine Gledhill. London: BFI Publishing.

Field, Allyson Nadia. 2015. *Uplift Cinema: The Emergence of African American Film and the Possibility of Black Modernity*. Durham, NC: Duke University Press.

Field, Allyson Nadia, Jan-Christopher Horak, and Jacqueline Najuma Stewart, eds. 2015. *L.A. Rebellion: Creating a New Black Cinema*. Oakland: University of California Press.

Fischer, Lucy. 1996. *Cinematernity: Film, Motherhood, Genre*. Princeton, NJ: Princeton University Press.

Fisher, Rebecka Rutledge. 2005. "Cultural Artifacts and the Narrative of History: W. E. B. Du Bois and the Exhibiting of Culture at the 1900 Paris Exposition Universelle." *MFS Modern Fiction Studies* 51 (4): 741–74. https://doi.org/10.1353/mfs.2006.0009.

Fox-Amato, Matthew. 2019. *Exposing Slavery: Photography, Human Bondage, and the Birth of Modern Visual Politics in America*. New York: Oxford University Press.

Francis, Terri. 2007. "Cinema on the Lower Frequencies: Black Independent Filmmaking." *Black Camera* 22 (1): 19–21.

Freelon, Deen, Charlton D. McIlwain, and Meredith D. Clark. 2016. "Beyond the Hashtags: #Ferguson, #Blacklivesmatter, and the Online Struggle for Offline Justice." The Center for Media and Social Impact. http://archive.cmsimpact.org/sites/default/files/beyond_the_hashtags_2016.pdf.

French, Philip. 2010. "Precious." *The Observer*, January 31, 2010. https://www.theguardian.com/film/2010/jan/31/precious-review-philip-french.

Gaines, Jane. 1987. "'The Scar of Shame': Skin Color and Caste in Black Silent Melodrama." *Cinema Journal* 26 (4): 3. https://doi.org/10.2307/1225187.

Gates, Henry Louis Jr. 2016. "Frederick Douglass's Camera Obscura." *Aperture* 223 (Vision and Justice): 26–29.

Genova, James Eskridge. 2013. *Cinema and Development in West Africa*. Bloomington: Indiana University Press.

Gerard, W. B. 2002. "Benevolent Vision: The Ideology of Sentimentality in Contemporary Illustrations of a Sentimental Journey and the Man of Feeling." *Eighteenth-Century Fiction* 14 (3): 533–74.

Gledhill, Christine. 1987. "The Melodramatic Field: An Investigation." In *Home Is Where the Heart Is: Studies in Melodrama and the Woman's Film*, edited by Christine Gledhill. London : BFI Publishing.

———. 2000. "Rethinking Genre." In *Reinventing Film Studies*, edited by Linda Williams and Christine Gledhill. London: Arnold; Co-published in the United States of America by Oxford University Press.

González, Jesús Ángel. 2015. "New Frontiers for Post-Western Cinema: Frozen River, Sin Nombre, Winter's Bone." *Western American Literature* 50 (1): 51–76. https://doi.org/10.1353/wal.2015.0025.

Gordon, Marsha, and Allyson Nadia Field. 2016. "The Other Side of the Tracks: Nontheatrical Film History, Pre-Rebellion Watts, and Felicia." *Cinema Journal* 55 (2): 1–24. https://doi.org/10.1353/cj.2016.0016.

Grierson, John. 1933. "The Documentary Producer." *Cinema Quarterly* 2 (1): 7–9.

Guerrero, Ed. 1993. *Framing Blackness: The African American Image in Film*. Culture and the Moving Image. Philadelphia: Temple University Press.

Gurevitch, Leon. 2010. "The Cinemas of Transactions: The Exchangeable Currency of the Digital Attraction." *Television & New Media* 11 (5): 367–85. https://doi.org/10.1177/1527476410361726.

Haenni, Sabine. 2015. "Birth of a Nation." In *The Routledge Encyclopedia of Films*, edited by Sarah Barrow, Sabine Haenni, and John White, 87–91.

Hagelin, Sarah. 2013. *Reel Vulnerability: Power, Pain, and Gender in Contemporary American Film and Television*. New Brunswick, NJ: Rutgers University Press.

Halberstam, J. 2001. "The Transgender Gaze in Boys Don't Cry." *Screen* 42 (3): 294–98. https://doi.org/10.1093/screen/42.3.294.

Haralovich. 1990. "All That Heavan Allows: Color, Narrative, Space and Melodrama." In *Close Viewings an Anthology of New Film Criticism*, edited by Peter Lehman. Tallahassee: Florida State University Press.

Havlin, Natalie, and Celiany Rivera-Velázquez. 2015. "Against Conformity: Families, Respectability, and the Representation of Gender-Nonconforming Youth of Color in Gun Hill Road and Pariah." In *Feminist Erasures: Challenging Backlash Culture*, edited by Kumarini Silva and Kaitlynn Mendes, 106–28. London: Palgrave Macmillan UK. https://doi.org/10.1057/9781137454928_7.

Herbert, James D. 2001. 'A Picture of Chardin's Making.' *Eighteenth-Century Studies* 34 (2): 251–74. JSTOR, www.jstor.org/stable/30053968.

Higonnet, Anne. 1998. *Pictures of Innocence: The History and Crisis of Ideal Childhood*. London: Thames and Hudson.

Hill, Marc Lamont. 2018. "'Thank You, Black Twitter': State Violence, Digital Counterpublics, and Pedagogies of Resistance." *Urban Education* 53 (2): 286–302. https://doi.org/10.1177/0042085917747124.

Hine, Lewis. 1909. "Social Photography: How the Camera May Help in the Social Uplift," Proceedings of the National Conference of Charities and Correction, June 9–16, Buffalo, NY. Edited by Alexander Johnson (Fort Wayne, IN: Press of Fort Wayne, 1909): 355–59.

Hird, Myra. 2001. "Appropriating Identity: Viewing Boys Don't Cry." *International Feminist Journal of Politics* 3 (3): 435–42. https://doi.org/10.1080/14616740110078211.

Hoggart, Richard. 1971. *The Uses of Literacy. Aspects of Workingclass Life, with Special References to Publications and Entertainments*. Reprinted. London: Chatto, Windus.

Holmes, Martha Stoddard. 2001. "Performing Affliction: Physical Disabilities in Victorian Melodrama." *Contemporary Theatre Review* 11 (3/4): 5.

Horak, L. 2014. "Trans on YouTube: Intimacy, Visibility, Temporality." *TSQ: Transgender Studies Quarterly* 1 (4): 572–85. https://doi.org/10.1215/23289252-2815255.

Jackson, Gregory S. 2003. "Cultivating Spiritual Sight: Jacob Riis's Virtual-Tour Narrative and the Visual Modernization of Protestant Homiletics." *Representations* 83 (1): 126–66. https://doi.org/10.1525/rep.2003.83.1.126.

Jackson, Lynne. 1987. "The Production of George Stoney's Film 'All My Babies: A Midwife's Own Story' (1952)." *Film History* 1 (4): 367–92.

Jackson, Sarah J., and Brooke Foucault Welles. 2016. "#Ferguson Is Everywhere: Initiators in Emerging Counterpublic Networks." *Information, Communication & Society* 19 (3): 397–418. https://doi.org/10.1080/1369118X.2015.1106571.

Jenner, Mareike. 2014. "Is This TVIV? On Netflix, TVIII and Binge-Watching." *New Media & Society* 18 (2): 257–73. https://doi.org/10.1177/1461444814541523.

Johnson, Dorothy. 1990. "Picturing Pedagogy: Education and the Child in the Paintings of Chardin." *Eighteenth-Century Studies* 24 (1): 47–68. https://doi.org/10.2307/2738986.

Kakoudaki, Despina. 2002. "Spectacles of History: Race Relations, Melodrama, and the Science Fiction/Disaster Film." *Camera Obscura* 17 (50): 109.

Kang, Nancy. 2016. "Audre's Daughter: Black Lesbian Steganography in Dee Rees' *Pariah* and Audre Lorde's *Zami: A New Spelling of My Name*." *Journal of Lesbian Studies* 20 (2): 266–97. https://doi.org/10.1080/10894160.2015.1062972.

Kaveney, Roz. 2006. *Teen Dreams: Reading Teen Film from Heathers to Veronica Mars*. London: I. B. Tauris.

Keeling, Kara. 2003. "'Ghetto Heaven': *Set It Off* and the Valorization of Black Lesbian Butch-Femme Sociality." *The Black Scholar* 33 (1): 33–46. https://doi.org/10.1080/00064246.2003.11413202.

Keller, Jessalynn Marie. 2012. "Virtual Feminisms: Girls' Blogging Communities, Feminist Activism, and Participatory Politics." *Information, Communication & Society* 15 (3): 429–47. https://doi.org/10.1080/1369118X.2011.642890.

Kelly, Erin. 2000. "Habermas on Moral Justification." *Social Theory & Practice* 26 (2): 223–49.

Kompare, Derek. 2005. *Rerun Nation: How Repeats Invented American Television*. New York: Routledge.

Koven, Seth. 1997. "Dr. Barnardo's 'Artistic Fictions': Photography, Sexuality, and the Ragged Child in Victorian London." *Radical History Review* 69 (Fall): 6–45. https://doi.org/Article.

Kress, G., and T. Van Leeuwen. 2002. "Colour as a Semiotic Mode: Notes for a Grammar of Colour." *Visual Communication* 1 (3): 343–68. https://doi.org/10.1177/147035720200100306.

Lamunière, Michelle. 2012. "Sentiment as Moral Motivator: From Jacob Riis's Lantern Slide Presentations to Harvard University's Social Museum." *History of Photography* 36 (2): 137–55. https://doi.org/10.1080/03087298.2012.658694.

Laughland, Oliver. 2019. "Eric Garner: No Charges against White Police Officer over Chokehold Death." *The Guardian*, July 16.

Lebeau, Vicky. 2008. *Childhood and Cinema*. Locations. London: Reaktion Books.

Lenhart, Amanda, Kristen Purcell, Aaron Smith, and Kathryn Zickhur. 2010. "Social Media & Mobile Internet Use among Teens and Young Adults." Pew Research Center. https://www.pewinternet.org/2010/02/03/social-media-and-young-adults/.

Lewis, Jon. 1992. *The Road to Romance & Ruin: Teen Films and Youth Culture*. New York: Routledge.

Linscott, Charles (Chip). 2017. "All Lives (Don't) Matter: The Internet Meets Afro-Pessimism and Black Optimism." *Black Camera* 8 (2): 104–19.

Loiperdinger, Martin. 2014. "The Social Impact of Screen Culture 1880–1914." In *Screen Culture and the Social Question, 1880–1914*, edited by Ludwig Vogl-Bienek and Richard Crangle, 9–20. KINtop Studies in Early Cinema 3. Bloomington: Indiana University Press.

Looft, Ruxandra. 2017. "#girlgaze: Photography, Fourth Wave Feminism, and Social Media Advocacy." *Continuum* 31 (6): 892–902. https://doi.org/10.1080/10304312.2017.1370539.

Lotz, Amanda D. 2007. *The Television Will Be Revolutionized*. New York: New York University Press.

Lu, Jessica H., and Catherine Knight Steele. 2019. "'Joy Is Resistance': Cross-Platform Resilience and (Re)Invention of Black Oral Culture Online." *Information, Communication & Society* 22 (6): 823–37. https://doi.org/10.1080/1369118X.2019.1575449.

Lubiano, Wahneema. 1991. "But Compared to What?: Reading Realism, Representation, and Essentialism in School Daze, Do the Right Thing, and the Spike Lee Discourse." *Black American Literature Forum* 25 (2): 253–82. https://doi.org/10.2307/3041686.

Massood, Paula J. 1996. "Mapping the Hood: The Genealogy of City Space in 'Boyz N the Hood' and 'Menace II Society.'" *Cinema Journal* 35 (2): 85–98.

———. 2003. *Black City Cinema: African American Urban Experiences in Film.* Culture and the Moving Image. Philadelphia: Temple University Press.

McCracken, Allison. 2017. "Tumblr Youth Subcultures and Media Engagement." *Cinema Journal* 57 (1): 151–61. https://doi.org/10.1353/cj.2017.0061.

Mercer, John, and Martin Shingler. 2004. *Melodrama: Genre, Style, Sensibility.* London: Wallflower.

Miller, Brandon. 2017. "YouTube as Educator: A Content Analysis of Issues, Themes, and the Educational Value of Transgender-Created Online Videos." *Social Media + Society* 3 (2). https://doi.org/10.1177/2056305117716271.

Mills, Brandale. 2018. *Black Women Filmmakers and Black Love on Screen.* Transformations in Race and Media. London: Routledge.

Miramura, Glen Masato. 1996. "On Fathers and Sons, Sex and Death: John Singleton's Boyz N the Hood." *Velvet Light Trap* 14.

Moeschen, Sheila C. 2006. "Suffering Silences, Woeful Afflictions: Physical Disabiity, Melodrama, and the American Charity Movement." *Comparative Drama* 40 (4): 433–54.

Monaghan, Whitney. 2016. *Queer Girls, Temporality and Screen Media: Not "Just a Phase."* London: Palgrave Macmillan.

Moon, Michael, and Colin Talley. 2010. "Life in a Shatter Zone: Debra Granik's Film Winter's Bone." *Southern Spaces*, June. https://southernspaces.org/2010/life-shatter-zone-debra-graniks-film-winters-bone.

Morgan, David. 2009. "The Look of Sympathy: Religion, Visual Culture, and the Social Life of Feeling." *Material Religion* 5 (2): 132–54. https://doi.org/10.2752/174322009X12448040551567.

Muigai, Wangui. 2019. "'Something Wasn't Clean': Black Midwifery, Birth, and Postwar Medical Education in All My Babies." *Bulletin of the History of Medicine* 93 (1): 82–113. https://doi.org/10.1353/bhm.2019.0003.

Newey, Katherine. 2000. "Climbing Boys and Factory Girls: Popular Melodramas of Working Life." *Journal of Victorian Culture (Edinburgh University Press)* 5 (1): 28.

Noble, Safiya Umoja. 2014. "Teaching Trayvon: Race, Media, and the Politics of Spectacle." *The Black Scholar* 44 (1): 12–29. https://doi.org/10.1080/00064246.2014.11641209.

Olivier, Marc. 2007. "George Eastman's Modern Stone-Age Family: Snapshot Photography and the Brownie." *Technology and Culture* 48 (1): 1–19.

Ortner, Sherry B. 2017. "Social Impact without Social Justice: Film and Politics in the Neoliberal Landscape: Film and Politics." *American Ethnologist* 44 (3): 528–39. https://doi.org/10.1111/amet.12527.

Padva, Gilad. 2004. "Edge of Seventeen: Melodramatic Coming-Out in New Queer Adolescence Films." *Communication and Critical/Cultural Studies* 1 (4): 355–72. https://doi.org/10.1080/1479142042000244961.

Pritchard, Eric Darnell. 2017. "Black Girls Queer (Re)Dress: Fashion as Literacy Performance in Pariah." *QED: A Journal in GLBTQ Worldmaking* 4 (3): 127. https://doi.org/10.14321/qed.4.3.0127.

Raun, Tobias. 2018. "Capitalizing Intimacy: New Subcultural Forms of Micro-Celebrity Strategies and Affective Labour on YouTube." *Convergence: The International Journal of Research into New Media Technologies* 24 (1): 99–113. https://doi.org/10.1177/1354856517736983.

Reid, Mark. 1993. *Redefining Black Film.* Berkeley: University of California Press.

Retail Focus. 2019. "Lululemon X Jessica Sharville X Lucky-Fox-Pride." Retail Focus. July 5. https://www.retail-focus.co.uk/lululemon-x-jessica-sharville-x-lucky-fox-pride/.

Retford, Kate. 2006. *The Art of Domestic Life: Family Portraiture in Eighteenth-Century England*. New Haven, CT: Yale University Press.

———. 2016. "Philippe Ariès's 'Discovery of Childhood': Imagery and Historical Evidence." *Continuity and Change* 31 (3): 391–418. https://doi.org/10.1017/S0268416016000254.

Reynolds, Glenn. 2015. *Colonial Cinema in Africa: Origins, Images, Audiences*. Jefferson, NC: McFarland & Company.

Rice, Tom. 2010. "Colonial Film Unit." Colonial Film: Moving Images of the British Empire. August 2010. http://www.colonialfilm.org.uk/production-company/colonial-film-unit.

Rigney, Melissa. 2003. "Hollywood: Boys Don't Cry and the Transgender Body Film." *Film Criticism* 28 (2): 4–23.

Roffman, Peter, and Jim Purdy. 1981. *The Hollywood Social Problem Film: Madness, Despair, and Politics from the Depression to the Fifties*. Bloomington: Indiana University Press.

Rony, Fatima Tobing. 1996. *The Birth of Whiteness: Race and the Emergence of U.S. Cinema*, edited by Daniel Bernardi. New Brunswick, NJ: Rutgers University Press.

Rosenthal, Angela. 2004. "Infant Academies and the Childhood of Art: Elisabeth Vigee-Lebrun's Julie with a Mirror." *Eighteenth-Century Studies* 37 (4): 605–28. https://doi.org/10.1353/ecs.2004.0048.

Ross, Sharon Marie, and Louisa Ellen Stein, eds. 2008. *Teen Television: Essays on Programming and Fandom*. Jefferson, NC: McFarland.

Ross, Steven J. 1998. *Working-Class Hollywood: Silent Film and the Shaping of Class in America*. Princeton, NJ: Princeton University Press.

Salazar, James B. 2010. "Fashioning the Historical Body: The Political Economy of Denim." *Social Semiotics* 20 (3): 293–308. https://doi.org/10.1080/10350331003722851.

Schewe, Elizabeth. 2014. "Highway and Home: Mapping Feminist-Transgender Coalition in Boys Don't Cry." *Feminist Studies* 40 (1): 39–64.

Schwenk, Melinda M. 1999. "Reforming the Negative through History: The U.S. Information Agency and the 1957 Little Rock Integration Crisis." *Journal of Communication Inquiry* 23 (3): 288–306. https://doi.org/10.1177/0196859999023003006.

Sekula, Allan. 1986. "The Body and the Archive." *October* 39: 3–64.

Senft, Theresa. 2013. "A Companion to New Media Dynamics." In *A Companion to New Media Dynamics*, edited by John Hartley, Jean Burgess, and Axel Bruns, 346–54. Chichester: John Wiley & Sons.

Sexton, Jared. 2009. "The Ruse of Engagement: Black Masculinity and the Cinema of Policing." *American Quarterly* 61 (1): 39–63.

———. 2017. *Black Masculinity and the Cinema of Policing*. Cham: Palgrave Macmillan.

Shachar, Hila. 2018. "'He Said We Can Choose Our Lives': Freedom, Intimacy, and Identity in *Blue Is the Warmest Colour* (2013)." *Studies in European Cinema* (January): 1–16. https://doi.org/10.1080/17411548.2018.1432121.

Shary, Timothy. 2012. "Teen Films: The Cinematic Image of Youth." In *Film Genre Reader IV*, edited by Barry Keith Grant. Austin: University of Texas Press.

Singer, Ben. 2001. *Melodrama and Modernity: Early Sensational Cinema and Its Contexts*. New York: Columbia University Press.

Siomopoulos, Anna. 2006. "Political Theory and Melodrama Studies." *Camera Obscura: Feminism, Culture and Media Studies* 21 (2): 179–83.

———. 2012. *Hollywood Melodrama and the New Deal: Public Daydreams*. New York: Routledge.

Sloan, Kay. 1988. *The Loud Silents: Origins of the Social Problem Film*. Urbana: University of Illinois Press.

Smiley, Minda. 2015. "Google Debuts 'Behind the Scenes' Video Series on YouTube Featuring 'Clean & Clear.'" March 16. https://www.thedrum.com/news/2015/03/16/google-debuts-behind-scenes-video-series-youtube-featuring-clean-clear.

Smith, Daniel R. 2017. "The Tragedy of Self in Digitised Popular Culture: The Existential Consequences of Digital Fame on YouTube." *Qualitative Research* 17 (6): 699–714. https://doi.org/10.1177/1468794117700709.

Smith, Lindsay. 1998. *The Politics of Focus: Women, Children, and Nineteenth-Century Photography*. The Critical Image. Manchester: Manchester University Press.

Smith, Shawn Michelle. 1998. "'Baby's Picture Is Always Treasured': Eugenics and the Reproduction of Whiteness in the Family Photograph Album." *Yale Journal of Criticism* 11 (1): 197.

———. 1999. *American Archives: Gender, Race, and Class in Visual Culture*. Princeton, NJ: Princeton University Press.

———. 2000. "'Looking at One's Self Through the Eyes of Others': W. E. B. Du Bois's Photographs for the 1900 Paris Exposition." *African American Review* 34 (4): 581–99.

Smith, Victoria L. 2015. "Highways of Desolation: The Road and Trash in Boys Don't Cry and Monster." *South Central Review* 32 (2): 131–50. https://doi.org/10.1353/scr.2015.0017.

Smyth, Rosaleen. 2013. "Grierson, the British Documentary Movement, and Colonial Cinema in British Colonial Africa." *Film History* 25 (4): 82–113. https://doi.org/10.2979/filmhistory.25.4.82.

Soukup, P. A. n.d. "Looking at, with, and through YouTube [TM]." 2014. *Communication Research Trends. Centre for the Study of Communication and Culture* 33 (3).

Southern, Richard W. 1973. *The Making of the Middle Ages*. Reprinted. Hutchinson University Library. London: Hutchinson.

Spivak, G. 1988. "Can the Subaltern Speak?" In *Marxism and the Interpretation of Culture*, edited by Cary Nelson and Lawrence Grossberg. Basingstoke: Macmillan Education.

Stalder, Felix. 2012. "Between Democracy and Spectacle: The Front-End and the Back-End of the Social Web." In *The Social Media Reader*, edited by Michael Mandiberg, 242–56. New York: New York University Press.

Stead, Peter. 1991. *Film and the Working Class: The Feature Film in British and American Society*. Cinema and Society. London: Routledge.

Stein, Arlene. 2016. "Transitioning Out Loud and Online." *Contexts* 15 (2): 40–45. https://doi.org/10.1177/1536504216648150.

Steward, J. C. 1995. *The New Child: British Art and the Origins of Modern Childhood 1730–1830*. Berkeley: University Art Museum and Pacific Film Archive.

Sundell, Michael. 1986. "Golden Immigrants at the Gold Door: Lewis Hine's Photographs of Ellis Island." *Social Text* 16, 168. https://doi.org/10.2307/466291.

Szasz, F. M., and R. H. Bogardus. 1974. "The Camera and the American Social Conscience: The Documentary Photography of Jacob A. Riis." *New York History* 55 (4): 409–36.

Taylor, Clyde R. 2008. "Black Cinema and Aesthetics." In *A Companion to African-American Philosophy*, edited by Tommy Lee Lott and John P Pittman. Hoboken, NJ: John Wiley.

Terri, Francis. 2014. "Whose 'Black Film' Is This? The Pragmatics and Pathos of Black Film Scholarship." *Cinema Journal* 53 (4): 146–50.

Thanhouser, Ned. 2011. "Reconstructing Thanhouser: *The Twenty-Five-Year Journey of a Citizen Archivist*." *The Moving Image* 11 (2): 90–99. https://doi.org/10.1353/mov.2011.0035.

Van Leeuwen, Theo. 2008. "New Forms of Writing, New Visual Competencies." *Visual Studies* 23 (2): 130–35.

Victor, Daniel. 2017. "Pepsi Pulls Ad Accused of Trivializing Black Lives Matter." *New York Times*, April 5, 2017, sec. B.

Vogl-Bienek, Ludwig, and Richard Crangle, eds. 2014. *Screen Culture and the Social Question, 1880–1914.* KINtop Studies in Early Cinema 3. Bloomington: Indiana University Press.

Wall, David C., and Michael T. Martin, eds. 2015. *The Politics & Poetics of Black Film: Nothing But a Man.* Studies in the Cinema of the Black Diaspora. Bloomington: Indiana University Press.

Watkins, S. Craig. 1998. *Representing: Hip Hop Culture and the Production of Black Cinema.* Chicago: University of Chicago Press.

Wells, Karen. 2012. "The Gaze of Development after the Cultural Turn." In *Social Research after the Cultural Turn,* edited by Sasha Roseneil and Stephen Frosh. New York: Palgrave Macmillan.

Welsh, Jean. 2015. "Saturday Night and Sunday Morning (1960)." In *The Routledge Encyclopedia of Films,* edited by Sarah Barrow, Sabine Haenni, and John White, 473–75. London: Routledge.

Wexler, Laura. 1988. "Black and White and Color: American Photographs at the Turn of the Century." *Prospects* 13 (October): 341–90. https://doi.org/10.1017/S0361233300006785.

Wilderson, Frank B. 2010. *Red, White & Black: Cinema and the Structure of U.S. Antagonisms.* Durham, NC: Duke University Press.

———. 2015. "Social Death and Narrative Aporia in *12 Years a Slave.*" *Black Camera* 7 (1): 134–49. https://doi.org/10.2979/blackcamera.7.1.134.

Wilkie, Rob. 2017. "When Left Theory 'Leaves Behind the Dream of a Revolution': Class and the Software Economy." In *Media and Class: TV, Film, and Digital Culture,* edited by June Deery and Andrea Lee Press, 163–75. New York: Routledge, Taylor & Francis Group.

Williams, Linda. 2001. *Playing the Race Card: Melodramas of Black and White from Uncle Tom to O.J. Simpson.* Princeton, NJ: Princeton University Press.

———. 2017. "*Blue Is the Warmest Color*: Or the After-Life of 'Visual Pleasure and Narrative Cinema.'" *New Review of Film and Television Studies* 15 (4): 465–70. https://doi.org/10.1080/17400309.2017.1376889.

Willis, Jessica L. 2008. "Sexual Subjectivity: A Semiotic Analysis of Girlhood, Sex, and Sexuality in the Film *Juno.*" *Sexuality & Culture* 12 (4): 240–56. https://doi.org/10.1007/s12119-008-9035-9.

Woal, Michael, and Linda Kowall Woal. 1994. "Chaplin and the Comedy of Melodrama." *Journal of Film and Video* 46 (3): 3–15.

Woods, Clyde Adrian. 1998. *Development Arrested: The Blues and Plantation Power in the Mississippi Delta.* The Haymarket Series. London: Verso.

Yochelson, Bonnie. 2014. "The Jacob A. Riis Collection: Photographs for Books and Lantern Lectures." In *Screen Culture and the Social Question, 1880–1914,* edited by Ludwig Vogl-Bienek and Richard Crangle, 83–96. KINtop Studies in Early Cinema 3. Bloomington: Indiana University Press.

Young, Iris Marion. 1990. *Justice and the Politics of Difference.* Princeton, NJ: Princeton University Press.

Zwarg, C. 2011. "Easy A, or Who's Your Daddy?: The Scarlet Letter Once More." *Adaptation* 4 (2): 219–25. https://doi.org/10.1093/adaptation/apr006.

## FILMOGRAPHY

Akhavan, Desiree. 2018. *The Miseducation of Cameron Post.*

Aldrich, Robert. 1968. *The Killing of Sister George.* Palomar Pictures. Dist.: Cinerama.

Arnold, Andrea. 2016. *American Honey.* Maven Pictures. Dist.: Protagonist Pictures.

Blue, James. 1964. *The March.* USIA.

Burnett, Charles. 1978. *Killer of Sheep.* oscilloscope.

Coogler, Ryan. 2013. *Fruitvale Station.* Forest Whitaker's Significant Productions OG Project.

Coogler, Ryan. 2018. *Black Panther*.

Daniels, Lee. 2009. *Precious*. Lee Daniels Entertainment. Dist: Lionsgate.

Deutch, Howard. 1986. *Pretty in Pink*. Paramount (Prod. and Dist.).

Dickson, Bob, Alan Gorg, and Trevor Greenwood. 1965. *Felicia*.

Flaherty, Robert. 1948. *Lousiana Story*. Robert Flaherty Productions (Dist. Lopert Films).

Gerwig, Greta. 2017. *Lady Bird*. A24 Films (Prod. and Dist.).

Graham, Sean. 1952. *Boy Kumasenu*. http://www.colonialfilm.org.uk/node/332.

Granik, Debra. 2010. *Winter's Bone*. Anonymous Content. Dist.: Fortissimo Films.

Gray, F. Gary. 2015. *Straight Outta Compton*. Universal. Dist.: Universal.

Green, David Gordon. 2000. *George Washington*. Free Country U.S.A. Dist.: Janus Films.

Guggenheim, Charles. 1956. *A City Decides*. Charles Guggenheim Assoc. Dist.: Universal.

———. 1964. *Nine from Little Rock*. Guggenheim Productions (also distributed).

Haigh, Andrew. 2017. *Lean on Pete*. The Bureau. Dist.: Celluloid Dreams.

Harris, Mark Jonathan. 2000. *Into the Arms of Strangers: Stories of the Kindertransport*. Sabine Films. Dist.: Warner Bros.

Jackson, Peter. 1994. *Heavenly Creatures*. Wingnut Films. Dist.: Miramax.

James, Steve. 1994. *Hoop Dreams*. KTCA Minneapolis. Dist.: Fine Line.

Jenkins, Barry. n.d. *Moonlight*. A24 Films (Prod. and Dist.).

Kazan, Elia. 1955. *East of Eden*. Warner Bros (Prod. and Dist.).

Kechiche, Abdellatif. 2013. *Blue Is the Warmest Color*.

Klein, Jim, and Julia Reichert. 1971. *Growing Up Female*. New Day Films.

Lee, Spike. 1988. *School Daze*. Columbia Pictures (Prod. and Dist.).

———. 1989. *Do The Right Thing*. 40 Acres & a Mule. Dist.: Universal Pictures.

———. 1994. *Crooklyn*. Universal. Dist.: Universal.

———. 1997. *4 Little Girls*. 40 Acres & a Mule. Dist.: Direct Cinema Ltd.

Livingston, Jennie. 1990. *Paris Is Burning*. Art Matters Inc. Dist.: Jane Balfour Films.

Loach, Ken. 1969. *Kes*. Kestrel Films. Dist.: United Artists.

Nichols, George O. 1912. *The Cry of the Children*.

Parks, Gordon. 1971. *Shaft*.

Parks, Gordon Jr. 1972. *Superfly*. Superfly. Dist.: Warner Bros.

Peirce, Kimberley. 1999. *Boys Don't Cry*. Fox Searchlight (Prod. and Dist.).

Ray, Nicholas. 1955. *Rebel Without a Cause*.

Rees, Dee. 2011. *Pariah*.

Reisz, Karel. 1960. *Saturday Night and Sunday Morning*. Woodfall Film Productions.

Reitman, Jason. 2007. *Juno*. Fox Searchlight. Dist.: Twentieth Century Fox.

Renaud, Brent. 2007. *Little Rock Central: 50 Years Later*.

Richardson, Tony. 1959. *Look Back in Anger*. Woodfall Film Productions. Dist.: Warner Bros.

———. 1961. *A Taste of Honey*. Woodfall Film Productions (Continental Distributing).

Sagan, Leontine. 1931. *Mädchen in Uniform*. Deutsche Film-Gemeinschaft. Dist.: Sceencraft Pictures.

Shuker, Gregory. 1963. *Crisis: Behind a Presidential Commitment*. ABC News. Dist.: Direct Cinema, Ltd.

Singer, Aubre. 1947. *Basuto Boy*. BFI. http://www.colonialfilm.org.uk/node/64.

Singleton, John. 1991. *Boyz n the Hood: Increase the Peace*. Hood. Columbia Pictures.

Stevens, George. 1956. *Giant*. George Stevens Productions. Dist.: Warner Bros.

Stoney, George. 1953. *All My Babies: A Midwife's Own Story*. Georgia Department of Public Health.

Swackhammer, James. 1946. *From Fear to Faith*. BFI. http://www.colonialfilm.org.uk/node/212.

Tarantino, Quentin. 2012. *Django Unchained*. The Weinstein Company. Dist.: Lantern Entertainment.

Tillman, George Jr. 2009. *Notorious*. Fox Searchlight (Prod. and Dist.).

————. 2013. *The Inevitable Defeat of Mister & Pete*. iDeal Partners Film Fund. Dist.: 13 Films.

————. 2018. *The Hate U Give*. Fox 2000 (Dist.: Twentieth Century Fox).

Van Peeples, Melvin. 1971. *Sweet Sweetback's Baadasssss Song*. Yeah. Dist.: Cinemation Industries.

Wiseman, Fred. 1968. *High School*. Osti Productions. Dist.: Zipporah Films.

Wyler, William. 1961. *The Children's Hour*.

# Index

# About the Author

**Karen Wells** is Professor of Human Geography in the Department of Geography, Birkbeck, University of London, where she researches childhood, visual culture and international development. She is the author of *Childhood in a Global Perspective* and *Childhood Studies: Making Young Subjects*.

www.ingramcontent.com/pod-product-compliance
Lightning Source LLC
Chambersburg PA
CBHW030650270326
41929CB00007B/302